August 2017

HAPPY ANNIVERSARY!

Perhaps Paris in 2018?

Love, Cynthia + Kurt

W9-ASV-990

CURIOSITIES OF PARIS

CURIOSITIES OF PARIS

An idiosyncratic guide to overlooked delights . . . hidden in plain sight

Dominique Lesbros

Translated by Simon Beaver

THE LITTLE BOOKROOM
NEW YORK

METROPOLITAIN
ACHAT DE CHEVAUX
Tabio
Je t'aime...
82
佛光普照

Contents

The ICON ▶ denotes a chapter presented in the form of a walking tour.

My thanks to Adjudant-Chef Philippe Lafargue, Monsieur Ara, Major Patrice Havard, Gilles Thomas and Christian Colas, all experts who very kindly provided me with invaluable information. My thanks also go to Jean-Claude Fornerod, who shared some particularly fascinating finds with me.

Foreword

What catches our eye when we walk down the street? "Stores," eagerly suggests a teenage girl; "Monuments," a tourist enthuses; "Pretty girls," leers a Don Juan; "What I might step in," a jaded Parisian mutters.

But what wonders could they see if they just adopted a different point of view and let their curiosity roam free, focusing on those odd little details that lurk at sidewalk level or up near the roofs of buildings? We are surrounded by thousands of tiny oddities that we do not understand and so ignore: a scrap of rusty iron driven into a wall, a flaking plaque, a crooked slab...

This Rosetta Stone of the obscure invites you to hunt down those abstruse quirks, put a name and a story to them, and learn why they exist. It supplies valuable hints that readers may then use in their own way to interpret future discoveries. Its catalog of peculiarities forms a rich mine of opportunities for exploration: once you catch the bug, you will find new subjects of interest every day. Even the most familiar walks can yield previously unnoticed surprises. Simply cross to the other side of the street and find out. The aim of this art (known technically as *interstitial tourism*) is to explore the nooks and crannies of the urban landscape, rather than its more aristocratic facets. There is no better way to come to know your city and feel its heartbeat.

Like a colossal cabinet of curiosities gleaned from all over Paris, this book catalogues a miscellany of offbeat details, views, and facades, grouping them by theme. Most are easily visible to anyone paying attention. They include various objects and structures that once served a useful everyday purpose: wells, pumps, corner guards, oratories, scrapers, sandboxes... Sadly, this modest legacy is undervalued in the modern urban fabric and is tending to disappear, scorned by the Monuments Historiques authority, which prizes pedigree rather than mongrel landmarks.

In these pages, you will encounter many relics. The turn of phrase is not simply a verbal flourish: we are dealing with tangible, very visible traces of the past that have survived the ravages of time, vandalism, and renovation.

During my investigations in the field, passers-by have occasionally stopped, followed my gaze and asked me what I am looking at. I tell them. Believe me, my greatest reward is when they answer: "Amazing! I come this way every day and I'd never noticed that!"

This book does not claim to be exhaustive. It is eager to expand, taking in other finds. I would be very grateful if you would share with me any you may discover at this address: dominique.lesbros@free.fr.

35, rue de l'Annonciation, 16th
(see p. 24)

1 Paris, equine capital

Not so long ago (in 1900), 80,000 members of the horse family—including donkeys and mules—labored in a city adapted to their needs. Paris was even more densely populated with horses than the Meuse, a *département* popularly considered to be the most equine in France.

The animals were harnessed to pull buses, carriages, and carts carrying domestic waste, construction materials, and so on. Almost every tradesperson used them for transport: farmers, firefighters, deliverymen, undertakers, and others. Some workers earned their living directly from the animals, including grooms, coachmen, blacksmiths, farriers, saddlers, harness makers, horse traders, and renderers.

Thousands of draft horses were imported to Paris from the Perche, Boulonnais, Nivernais, and Picardie regions of France. The Percheron breed, a champion at hauling loads while at a trot, pulled buses and especially milk carts, which were horse-drawn as recently as the 1930s. The sturdier Boulonnais was better suited to hauling heavy goods at a walking pace along the quays of the Seine or down the boulevards that led to Les Halles, the wholesale food market. British and Anglo-Norman thoroughbreds had the honor of treading the cobbles of more elegant districts, pulling private or official carriages. On Sunday, these noble beasts paraded at their leisure down the allées of the bois de Boulogne and cours La Reine, where the aristocracy went to see and be seen. Town houses were equipped to receive horses and carriages, and the great department stores had stables close at hand (in the rue du Bac for Le Bon Marché or the île de la Cité for Le Bazar de l'Hôtel-de-Ville). Later, though, horses were replaced by automobiles and gradually disappeared from the urban landscape. They were much mourned by the collectors of fresh manure, the fertilizer of choice for potted plants. So what evidence remains of this former equine ubiquity? A great deal: carriage entrances, corner guards, sculptures, street names, and more.

In the days of the équipage

Hôtel de Sully. 62, rue Saint-Antoine, 4th

97, rue de Lille, 7th

On the right in the yard

Most town houses had stables, which were generally located in their right wing behind archways high enough for horse-drawn vehicles to pass and be parked. Today, when you enter the inner courtyards of these houses, you can immediately recognize the former stables from their entrances, which are larger than other doorways. The Marais is especially well equipped in this respect. In fact, stables were not limited to town houses; they were also to be found in the yards of more modest tenement buildings.

79, rue Réaumur, 2nd

Hôtel d'Albret. 31, rue des Francs-Bourgeois, 4th

Carriage hire

People who could not afford a carriage and team were able to hire one when needed. At the entrance to 101, rue du Bac (on the left-hand pillar), a worn inscription announces: *Loueur de voitures de service* (Renter of Service Carriages). If you enter the yard, you can see the former stables (now parking garages for automobiles) on the left behind high wooden doors.

101, rue du Bac, 7th

The Hermès fireworks expert

Famous all over the world for its luxury products, Hermès was originally (in 1837) a manufacturer that produced harnesses and various other items for horses. When it moved to the rue du Faubourg-Saint-Honoré in the second half of the 19th century, it widened its range of products and began to supply riding articles, horse blankets, and silks for jockeys, as well as leather bags for saddles and riding boots. When automobiles began to replace horses, Hermès focused its skills on "saddle-stitched" bags and luggage. To celebrate the brand's 150th anniversary in 1987, a white horse was hoisted onto the roof of each of the four Hermès stores around the world and a military pyrotechnic expert was brought in for the occasion to put on a fireworks display, offering a reminder of past glories and symbolizing the company's dynamic modern nature.

The cour des Petites-Écuries stands on the site of the Petites Écuries royales (Small Royal Stables), active in the middle of the 18th century.

Corner of rue du Faubourg-Saint-Honoré and rue Boissy-d'Anglas, 8th

Stagecoaches

Until 1873, horses were used to transport mail. Along the routes, they stopped at a series of coaching inns that supplied fresh horses, enabling the stage-coach to continue to the next stop. The inns where the animals ate and rested were equipped with stables, a farrier's shop, and a hostelry serving "stirrup cups." Regulations stated that coach drivers had to cover a post (a distance of about 9 kilometers) in no more than one hour. Later, the spread of rail transport ended the age of the mail coach in 1873. There was a coaching inn in a courtyard in the avenue de Flandre in the 17th century. Stagecoach drivers met there when they stopped on their way to Paris or Flanders. The first building on the left with its triangular pediment is original, while the others (roughcast in pink and white) were constructed later according to the same model.

52, avenue de Flandre, 19th

The imperial stables of the Louvre

In 1860, Napoleon III had stables built in the palais du Louvre that could accommodate up to 150 horses and carriages. The stables came with fodder sheds and rooms for coachmen and staff, as well as the premises of the Premier Écuyer (First Equerry). Only used for 10 years, the stables surrounded today's cour Visconti and cour Lefuel. From the windows of the sculpture room of the Denon wing, the horseshoe-shaped ramp (based on the one in Fontainebleau) that took the horses up to the training ring can still be seen. On the tympanum of the arena door, there is a sculpture of three galloping horses created by Pierre-Louis Rouillard. The balcony of the apartments of the Premier Écuyer, who was responsible for the imperial stables, is decorated with a horse's head.

Musée du Louvre, 1st (Denon wing)

Luxury stagecoaches

The 9th arrondissement was home to the greatest number of horses (as many as 6,500). In the rue Pigalle was the headquarters of a large transport company that provided mail, passenger, and moving services from the 16th century until 1873. It was recognized for its well-suspended, rainproof, double-glazed coaches, which could be hired for 20 *centimes* per horse per kilometer (the stagecoaches not only carried mail, but passengers, too). In the courtyard, parking garages have now replaced the sheds and stables, which were demolished in 1969 (although the drinking trough has survived). The stone horse's head that originally decorated the yard has been moved into the building's lobby to protect it from the elements, but you can see it on display from the street. The one above the drinking trough is a copy.

69, rue Pigalle, 9th

From stalls to studios

Not far from the Observatoire de Paris is the Barrière d'Enfer (Hell's Fence). It was a major staging post in the 17th century (the first on the Orléans road). In the early 20th century, its stables were converted into artists' studios. The sculptor Paul Belmondo worked in one of them. The roofs and facades are magnificently well preserved and the entire building was recently assigned to the campus of the Observatoire de Paris; a few artists still remain, but most of the stalls are now used as research labs by scientists.

77, avenue Denfert-Rochereau, 14th

7, rue de Provence, 9th

27, rue de Grenelle, 6th

For a ration of hay...

Why can metal bars (with or without hooks) still be seen on a few carriage entrances? They actually held fodder for horses. Hay was packed in the space between the bar and the door, and the animals could feed from this manger without having to stoop too much.

The coachman's nightmare at the corner of rue du Sabot

The rue du Sabot takes its name from a sign that was there in 1523. Nobody knows whether it was in the form of a clog or a horse's hoof —*sabot* means both— but one thing is certain: the exit leading from this street to the rue Bernard-Palissy was so narrow and difficult to negotiate that in around 1900, it became part of the road test for drivers of four-horse coaches.

Instructions for coachmen

On the left-hand wall of the entrance to the reception building of the hôpital de la Salpêtrière, you can just make out a notice dating back to the 19th century. It tells coachmen to take their horses into the hospital. Then, at the entrance of the former municipal funeral parlor, you can see a notice instructing hearse drivers to *Entrer au pas* (Enter at a walk).

47, boulevard de l'Hôpital, 13th
108, rue d'Aubervilliers, 19th

Corner of rue du Sabot and rue Bernard-Palissy, 6th

A well-deserved break at the water trough

The end of the rue de l'Abreuvoir seems to nestle in a hollow... for a very good reason: the paved basin below the balustrade was a water trough, where animals (horses, donkeys, cows, sheep, etc.) were brought in the evening to drink and soak their hooves after toiling in quarries or fields, or on the highways, or after a long day's grazing. Their antics in the pool shaded by lime trees provided a free show that always attracted curious onlookers: urchins, washerwomen, chatting nursemaids, the middle classes out for a stroll, and artists in search of inspiration.

15, rue de l'Abreuvoir, 18th

Heave-ho!

How did you climb onto your mount (donkey or horse) when your joints were stiff with rheumatism or your movements hampered by a dress or even a cassock? That was the problem facing old men, women, and the clergy. Fortunately, help was at hand in the form of mounting blocks or *pas-de-mule*, located here and there around the city. The one in the second cour de Rohan (a private location) is the last one remaining in Paris.

Cour de Rohan, 6th

5 and 11-13, rue Geoffroy-Saint-Hilaire, 5th

The horse-traders' haunt

Paris's horse market changed location more than once over the centuries. In 1687, it was moved from the city center to the faubourg Saint-Victor (between the rue Duméril and the boulevard de l'Hôpital), where there was already a pig market. It occupied a long, rectangular area 250 meters long by 50 meters wide, with a main alley and two side alleys shaded by four lines of trees. The animals were tethered to posts hammered into the ground. In 1760, a building was constructed (it can still be seen at 5, rue Geoffroy-Saint-Hilaire) to provide offices and accommodations for the market inspectors. There was an inspection every Wednesday and Saturday (in the morning for the pigs and in the afternoon for the horses, mules, and donkeys), and on Sunday for carriages and dogs. The sign on the building at 11, rue Geoffroy-Saint-Hilaire offers a reminder of the market.

Memento of the horse market on the dead-end street bearing its name

Horse trials

The rue de l'Essai, which ran between the rue Poliveau and the horse market, was called rue Maquignonne (Horse Trader Street) in the 17th century. There, potential buyers would test-ride horses for sale and that led to the name change (*essai* means "trial" or "test"). The street was cut off by the boulevard Saint-Marcel when that thoroughfare was opened on the market site in 1857.

Rue Brancion and rue des Morillons, 15th

Rue de l'Essai, 5th. The horsepower is now under the hood.

Les halles de Vaugirard

In 1907, the horse market moved again, this time to the rue Brancion, by the Vaugirard horsemeat abattoirs. A branch railroad track connecting to the Petite Ceinture belt line was used to transport the animals. The market closed in 1976, along with the Vaugirard slaughterhouses, and the site was turned into a park. Three traces of its past remain: the belfry, which once stood at the center of the auction market; the two horse markets by the rue Brancion (now home to an antique book market); and, finally, a horse's head displayed on a raised gate at the corner of rue Brancion and rue des Morillons.

Rue Jacques-Baudry, 15th
A fresco painted by Filip Mirazovic in 2007 sums up the past of the Vaugirard district, which centered on its abattoirs in the first half of the 20th century.

The site of today's place Édouard-VII (9th) was once a depot of the Compagnie générale des petites voitures, which housed 500 horses and 200 carriages there.

The world's greatest cavalry division

Every day, thousands of passengers were carried by the Compagnie générale des omnibus, whose vehicles were pulled by horses whose numbers reached 16,500 in 1875-1895. The CGO used Ardennais and Percheron horses with dark coats, thought to be more becoming to the buses. Each animal had an identification number above its feeding rack. They worked three to four hours a day, covering 18 kilometers (the maximum allowed). From time to time, they were sent to the countryside to rest: vacations were very necessary because of the grueling nature of their work. Housing all these horses was a heavy responsibility for the CGO, which even built stables on the boulevard Saint-Martin that included a floor entered via an outside mezzanine.

A manure-extraction tunnel

In 1889, the Compagnie générale des omnibus had 48 depots for some 40 bus routes. The most heavily used line was Madeleine-Bastille, which carried 30,000 passengers a day. Its depot on the boulevard Bourdon was one of the company's biggest, holding more than a thousand horses. It was sensibly located next to the port de l'Arsenal, which handled its supply needs: grain sacks arrived by boat and were taken up to the quay by freight elevator. They were then transferred onto small carts that carried them through a tunnel to the depot's basement. Manure, which was sold as a fertilizer, was brought out on the return trip. The tunnel entrance can still be seen in a wall of the port de l'Arsenal.

Port de l'Arsenal, next to boulevard Bourdon, 4th

© ARCHIVES RATP

The CGO tram: a heavy car equipped with stairs leading up to the top deck.

The crowd admires the last trip of the horse-drawn omnibus, 11 January 1913.

©ALBERT HARLINGUE/ROGER-VIOLLET

The joyous sendoff of Saint-Sulpice-La Villette

On the January 11, 1913, the horse-drawn bus service between Saint-Sulpice and La Villette made its last journey. To general indifference? On the contrary, it was a celebratory rather than a solemn occasion according to reports in the press of the day. The public naturally regretted the unavoidable disappearance of certain specialized trades (coachman, groom) but such progress was met with a wave of enthusiasm that swallowed up the occasional tear of woe.

The Champs-Élysées: from horses to automobiles

Why are there so many automobile dealers on the avenue des Champs-Élysées? Simply because they were the natural successors of horse dealers and carriage makers. Since the avenue was on the way to the bois de Boulogne, where many people went to see and be seen, farriers, coachbuilders, saddlers, and harness and leather-goods makers astutely set up shop on the thoroughfare from 1822 on, and built an international reputation. In the 1880s, the coachbuilders of the Champs-Élysées outclassed their British rivals, winning the race for comfort and elegance hands down.

In those days, the famous Le Fouquet's café-restaurant was just a horse-and-carriage bistro. Then, when horses were supplanted by the horsepower of the internal-combustion engine, the artisans made way for the car dealers. *(See also Sandboxes, p. 219).*

This painting in the galerie des Arcades reflects the special relationship between horses and the avenue des Champs-Élysées.

Corner guards

These fenders were designed to protect the corner of a building from the wheels and axles of carriages, fiacres, and coaches. Carriage entrances used by coach drivers were equipped with guards, as were buildings on street corners. Corner guards were very important because the carriages of the past were much longer and harder to steer than the automobiles of today. Some of the surviving guards are conical stones without or without metal hoops, while other, cast-iron models come in the form of bows, spirals (known as "Haussmannian models"), balls, cones, or original, decorative designs. You simply have to cast your eyes down to see hundreds of pairs of them at ground level.

1

Iron bollards

1 87, rue Vieille-du-Temple, 4th
2 82, boulevard Haussmann, 9th
3 48, rue de Vaugirard, 6th

1

2

Metal spirals

1 11, boulevard du Temple, 3rd
2 3, rue Washington, 8th
3 15, rue des Filles-du-Calvaire, 3rd

3

1

Two guards are better than one

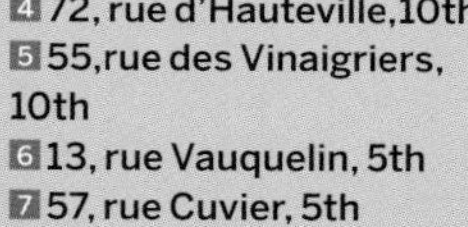

4 72, rue d'Hauteville,10th
5 55,rue des Vinaigriers, 10th
6 13, rue Vauquelin, 5th
7 57, rue Cuvier, 5th

1 Cour d'Angoulême, Hôtel des Invalides, 7th
2 58, rue du Faubourg-Poissonnière, 10th
3 106, rue Vieille-du-Temple, 4th
4 15, place des Vosges, 4th
5 16, rue du Parc-Royal, 4th
6 110, rue Vieille-du-Temple, 4th

A history of horsemeat

89, rue Cambronne, 15th

Eating horsemeat was once taboo, totally unthinkable, and actually forbidden by law and the church. Then, in the middle of the 19th century, mentalities changed. In 1825, a member of the health and hygiene commission of the Paris Prefecture of Police announced that he had come round to the argument that horsemeat could usefully feed "convicts and indigent populations." In 1847, the zoologist Isidore Geoffroy-Saint-Hilaire, the son of the great naturalist, and the Napoleonic army surgeon Dominique Jean Larrey went even further, demonstrating the value of horsemeat for human consumption. They were backed by various horsemeat advocates who organized banquets to win over gourmets and change people's way of thinking. Their mission was accomplished in 1866 with the publication of a decree that authorized horsemeat for human consumption and strictly regulated its sale, imposing veterinary inspections, clear identification of horse-butcher's stores, etc. The Société Protectrice des Animaux had joined the campaign and was pleased with the decision. It felt that slaughter in an abbatoir governed by rules based on animal welfare was better than a horrifying end in the rendering pit—until then the fate of every horse.

1 bis, rue Cadet, 9th

Unequivocally equine signs

A month after the official authorization in 1866, the first horse-meat butcher shop opened. Many others were to follow. The famine caused by the Prussian siege of Paris in 1870-1871 finally convinced even the most dubious. Hailed for its fortifying properties and sold at half the price of beef, horsemeat proved to be the people's dish par excellence. By 1905, Paris was home to 311 horse-butcher's stores and there were 200 stalls selling horsemeat in the city's markets. By law, such points of sale had to be distinguished from traditional butcher's stores, so they had large, clearly visible signs, such as the mosaic in the Marais (which has been there since 1949) or a horse's head above their storefronts.

7, rue Fizeau, 15th

3, rue Poncelet, 17th

Corner of rue du Roi-de-Sicile and rue Vieille-du-Temple, 4th

9, rue des Petits-Carreaux, 1st

The champion of horsemeat

Near the old horse market stands a monument to the men of the horsemeat industry who died during the First World War. On the other side is a bust of Émile Decroix (1821- 1901), a military veterinarian known as the champion of horsemeat.

Rue Brancion, 15th

Manes of bronze

Horses stand in the center of many Paris squares. They are the trusty steeds of proud royal and military riders. The posture of these equestrian statues follows a code: a horse rearing on its hind legs signifies that its rider died in combat, a single raised foreleg means that the rider was assassinated or died of wounds received in battle, and, finally, when all four hooves are on the ground, the dignitary died in their bed.

The custom (which also applies to paintings) is not a strict rule, though, as is shown by the statue of Louis XIV in the place des Victoires: the horse is rearing even though the king died of gangrene in his bed. However, a *passant* horse (i.e. one that seems to be moving at a walk) is a symbol of peace or mercy, while a rearing or galloping horse suggests victory.

2, place des Victoires, 1st
Above the Hartford store, an image of the equestrian statue of Louis XIV that stands in the center of the circular place des Victoires.

The horse with the cheval-de-frise

This cast-iron, formerly gilded horse sculpted by Pierre-Louis Rouillart first reared in the gardens of the old Trocadéro palace for the Universal Exhibition of 1878. It was accompanied by a rhinoceros by Alfred Jacquemart and an elephant by Emmanuel Frémiet. The menagerie was moved to the musée d'Orsay for the 1937 Universal Exposition.

Parvis du musée d'Orsay, 7th

The legend of Bayard

A bronze sculpture displayed on the facade of the CARAN (French National Archive Reception and Research Center) at the end of the rue Charlot catches the eye of passers-by: it shows two persons in the round and two others in bas-relief below a ludicrously tiny horse. The work by Yvan Theimer alludes to the medieval legend that gave the street its name: the story of the four sons of Aymon and their magical horse, Bayard.

7, rue des Quatre-Fils, 3rd

In front of the Hôtel-de-Ville, along the Seine, the statue of Étienne Marcel, killed by an assassin, his horse with a raised foreleg.

The Marly Horses

These chargers rear at the foot of the Champs-Élysées. They are known as the "Marly Horses" because Louis XV commissioned Guillaume Coustou to sculpt them for the drinking trough at the château de Marly. They were moved during the Revolution. These are actually concrete copies. The Carrara marble originals are in the cour Marly of the musée du Louvre, protected from the vibrations caused by passing armored vehicles that apparently weakened them every July 14 during the national military parade.

Corner of Champs Élysées and place de la Concorde, 8th

The Horses of the Sun

On the pediment of the hôtel de Rohan-Strasbourg (which holds some of France's National Archives) are four horses emerging from fleecy clouds. These Horses of the Sun are being watered by the servants of Apollo, who are using a large seashell for the purpose. The bas-relief, made by Le Lorrain in the 18th century, is displayed above the door of the town house's former stables.

87, rue Vieille-du-Temple, 3rd

Top to bottom
28, rue Boissy-d'Anglas, 8th
97, rue de Lille, 7th
35, rue de l'Annonciation, 16th

Heads not tails

The sign of a horse's head marks the locations of former stables. They can be on facades visible from the street, or in courtyards, up at the second floor, or at head height. The lower versions are often equipped with a ring to which halters could be tied. Another clue to the former presence of stables is large doors on the right of the yard *(see p. 9)*.

Lalanne's donkey

Real or not? It is hard to tell from a distance. Close up, though, it becomes apparent that the donkey is cast in bronze. Without this work by François-Xavier Lalanne, there might be no statue of a donkey in Paris.

Parc Georges-Brassens, 15th

Forbidden to under-21s

When the first wooden-horse carousels appeared at the start of the 19th century, they were for adults rather than children to enjoy. In fact, they remained an adults-only attraction until the 1920s. Since they were awkward to transport, they were always set up near stations, giving country people who had come to work in town an opportunity for a little fun. Horses were chosen to equip these carousels since they ennoble the rider's posture and because it was more usual to ride horses than any other beasts. Now found on the grand esplanades and in the public gardens of Paris, these rides delight both children and their elders.

Square Louise-Michel, 18th

Today's horses

Who says there are no more horses on the streets of Paris? Horses are very much a feature of the city. They provide an escort for the head of state, patrol tourist locations, and clear the undergrowth in woods.

An old-fashioned sign for modern horses in the alleys of the bois de Vincennes.

© GARDE REPUBLICAINE

The Republican Guard Cavalry

A telling scent floats in the air on the boulevard Henri-IV near the quartier des Célestins, where much of the Republican Guard Cavalry Regiment is quartered. The last mounted regiment of the French army carries out state-protocol and public-safety missions on horseback, patrols tourist locations, and stands ready near stadiums when major sports events are held. The excellent riding skills of its soldiers are proverbial. The quartier des Célestins is home to 180 horses, a veterinary service, a farrier's shop, an arena, and a riding track.

Caserne des Célestins. 18, boulevard Henri-IV, 4th

© GARDE REPUBLICAINE

Centre équestre de la Cartoucherie. Bois de Vincennes, 12th

In the saddle

A number of schools offer riding lessons on the outskirts of the capital. The Société d'équitation de Paris has two hectares in the heart of the bois de Boulogne on a historically protected site dating back to the Second Empire. The centre équestre de La Villette has a stable of 70 ponies and horses. Apart from offering standard training, the centre équestre de la Cartoucherie, near the bois de Vincennes, also teaches stunt riding.

Société d'équitation de Paris. Route de La Muette, 16th
Centre équestre de La Villette. 9, boulevard Macdonald, 19th

In need of boots or bridle?

Where can you buy saddles, stirrup leathers, saddle pads, boots, riding hats, and bridles? Easy: in those specialized Parisian stores that supply riders with the equipment they and their mounts need. Padd Étoile and Guibert Paris are entirely devoted to horse-riding, elegant riding wear, and the welfare of mounts. To find out all about the equine world, head for the specialty bookstore Cavalivres.

Padd Étoile. 177, boulevard Haussmann, 8th
Guibert Paris. 22, avenue Victor-Hugo, 16th
Cavalivres. 21, rue du Sentier, 2nd

Trotting and galloping

Vincennes is the world's leading racetrack in its number of meetings (a meeting being a program of races held on the same day). It hosts more than 170 a year. Most prestigious international races organized in France are held there. Auteuil is the temple of steeplechase and Longchamp the cathedral of level racing, but the characteristic genre at Vincennes is trot: saddle-trot (where the jockey is on horseback) and trot with a sulky (where the jockey rides on a small, two-wheeled chariot pulled by the horse). Many different kinds of experts are needed to tend to the occupants of the 142 individual stalls: breeders, trainers, jockeys, stable girls and boys, vets, horse dentists, saddlers, and farriers all lavish great care on the trotters.

2, route de la Ferme, 12th

Many bars make much of their income from the the Pari mutuel urbain. Betting on horse races was legalized in 1881

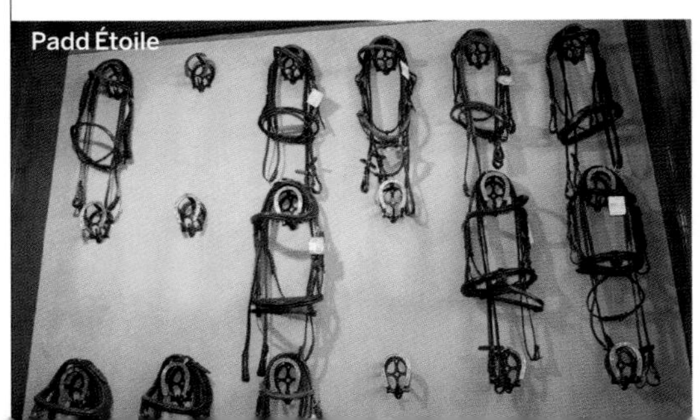

Padd Étoile

© CHRISTOPHE NOËL

Ardennes horse in the bois de Vincennes

Draft horses

Three Ardennes horses have been carrying out maintenance work in the bois de Vincennes since 1998. They cost less than a tractor and are far more eco-friendly. Their tasks vary according to the season. In winter, they haul logs from different forestry sites and carry firewood. In the warmer months, they help to transport green waste (leaves, chips, offcuts, branches, etc.), spread ground material in tree-irrigation basins, harrow bridle paths, water trees and shrubberies, and more. In the evening, they enjoy a well-earned meal at the Pesage farm. The Jardin des plantes botanical garden has also taken on a Poitou donkey, which is a great help to the gardeners.

© PARIS CALÈCHES

Carriage rides

Encouraged by efforts to make traffic greener, carriages are making a comeback. Paris Calèches, a horse-drawn carriage tour service company, offers four different itineraries leaving from the Eiffel Tower in either an ordinary trap or an opulent Cinderella-style coach.

www.pariscaleches.com

Le Cirque d'hiver (11th) stages many equestrian shows.

2 The City of Light

In the Middle Ages, each day when the sun went down the city of Paris was plunged into an impenetrable darkness much appreciated by criminals. In 1318, the city had only three official public streetlamps. It was not until 1524 that a parliamentary decree enjoined the city's bourgeoisie to install and light a lamp at the window of their houses at their own expense. The initiative was not very successful.

Place de l'Hôtel-de-Ville, 4th *(see p. 35)*

Then, in the 17th century, Police Lieutenant La Reynie introduced an extensive lighting system, intended to maintain law and order. However, the candles provided only a pale, hesitant light—when they were not snuffed out by the wind or rain. In 1782, there was significant progress with the installation of 1,200 streetlamps fueled by tripe oil manufactured on the île aux Cygnes. Their light was bright and steady.

Gaslights took over in the mid-19th century. Then, when the Universal Exposition was held in 1878, 32 lampposts equipped with electric street lighting were installed to illuminate the avenue de l'Opéra. At the start of the 20th century, both lighting systems coexisted. The last gas lamps were converted to electricity in 1962.

Today, 110,000 streetlights line the thoroughfares of Paris, spaced 25 to 30 meters apart. The City of Light is proud of its soubriquet and its distinctive street lighting. There is a clear Parisian style whose main characteristics are the standardized height of lamps (9 meters on automobile traffic streets and 4 meters in pedestrian precincts) that produces a double awning of light over the city; lighting fixed to facades on brackets wherever possible to avoid obstructing sidewalks (this is the case for half of all streetlights); lampposts crowned with a swan's-neck bracket holding a light source in a sphere; fluorescent globes or metal-iodide lamps providing white light in pedestrian precincts; and high-pressure sodium lamps emitting an orange-yellow light along streets carrying traffic.

Vestiges of oil lighting

Left to right
14, rue des Trois-Portes, 5th
Between 8 and 10 rue des Grands-Augustins, 6th

A niche in a wall

This characteristic hollow (carved from the stone with a groove running from it) is a relic of oil-fueled street lighting. The cast-iron housing it once contained had a locking hatch, turning it into a small, secure case. Lamplighters of the time did their rounds twice a day: in the early afternoon to carry out maintenance work and then at nightfall to light the lamps, which went out on their own when all their fuel was burned. The lamplighter would open the hatch with his key, fit his crank to the square shaft of the capstan, and lower the lamp to a comfortable working height. Once he had carried out his daily maintenance (changing wicks and replacing glass when necessary; filling the tank and cleaning the glass and silvered-copper reflector), he would winch the lamp back up and lock the hatch before moving on to perform the same tasks on the next lamp a few dozen meters away. Few of these niches remain. Almost all have been filled during renovation work on facades. As far as we know, only two remain: rue des Grands-Augustins (intact) and rue des Trois-Portes (groove cemented).

8-10, rue des Grands-Augustins, 6th (intact)
14, rue des Trois-Portes, 5th (channel filled in with cement)

The oil-lamplighter. He is working on a lantern on a rope attached to a post. The system was the same for wall-bracket lights. (Engraving by Carle Vernet, private collection)

Vestiges of gas lighting

The arcades in the galeries de l'Odéon (below, 6th) were the beneficiaries of the first gas lighting (in 1815), followed by passage des Panoramas (1817).

Through the window of a philately store at 11, passage des Panoramas (at right, 2nd), there is still a gas burner attached to the wall.

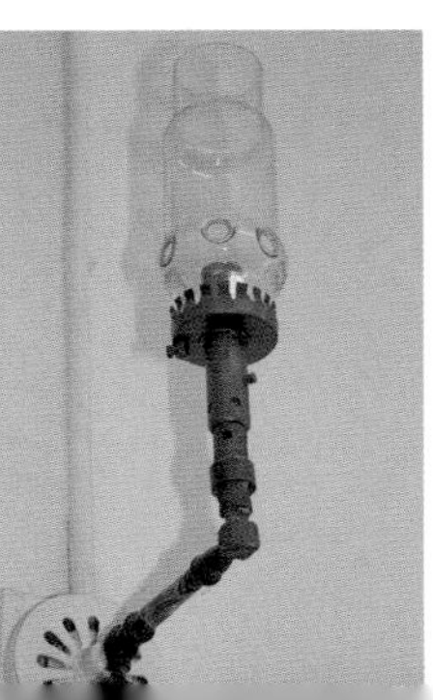

Butterfly burners

Why were these stems set along the pediment of the former école Laillier, now the Laillier building of the hôpital Saint-Louis (door 42)? To the uninitiated, they appear to be pigeon spikes, but they are actually an antique gas-light manifold with rows of hundreds of burners. The flames were not sheltered in any way and so were vulnerable to the slightest breeze or drop of rain. Despite their exposed position, they have survived to this day (although they are obviously no longer in use). Coincidentally, Louis XVIII had one of the very first Parisian gasworks constructed in the hôpital Saint-Louis in 1824.

Facing 65, rue Bichat, 10th

The one and only Léon

Léon is the only gas streetlamp still working in Paris. In 1975, when gas fixtures were converted from "town gas" to "natural gas," all the remaining fixtures of the public gaslight network in the Paris suburbs were converted to electricity—except for two in Malakoff (one on the sentier du Tir, the other on the impasse Ponscarme). They owed their miraculous survival to a handful of local inhabitants who refused to see them electrified. The one on the impasse Ponscarme was restored many years ago and a copy was added on either side. All three were equipped with modern mantle-type burners, but were subsequently electrified at the start of the 2000s. However, the lamp on the sentier du Tir remains intact. Its Auer burner is still in operation and it shines continuously day and night (to protect the hundred-year-old incandescent mantle which would be damaged by contraction or expansion each time it were lit or turned off). Maintained by an association called Les Amis de Léon (The Friends of Léon), it is very different than its neighbors in the same small street with its clear panes and golden light—almost as bright as the glow supplied by its electric cousins.

In the courtyard of the Commerce-Saint-André (6th), there are lanterns containing butterfly burners that have been adapted to hold electric light bulbs.

©LUMIARA

4-6, sentier du Tir, 92240 Malakoff. This pedestrian street has two sections. Léon is in the wider one.

Wall boxes

These elegant cast-iron plaques fitted to the base of each of the lamps on the Pont-Neuf are not simply ornamental. They cover a niche that held the valve used to turn off the gas supply for repair or maintenance. The date inscribed on these plaques, 1854, was the year when renovation work was done, including the installation of the current lampposts. In the galleries of the hôtel des Invalides, you can see rusty cases that served the same purpose connected to overhanging lamps.

Pont-Neuf, 1st

Hôtel des Invalides, 7th

Top to bottom
Place du Palais-Royal, 1st
Rue de Castiglione, 1st

ID tags

On various small arcades bordering a street or garden, you may notice little, old-fashioned metal plates. They are ID tags to identify the lamps above, so people could let the authorities know when a lamp was not working. They were marked with a P for Paris, the number of the arrondissement, the serial number, and the crown of the city. They may be found in the jardin du Palais-Royal, rue de Rivoli, and place des Pyramides (1st).

Lamplighters' rails

In each neighborhood in the 19th century, a man in overalls would be seen at nightfall and dawn carrying a ladder and long pole and stopping every 25 meters. His job was to light and extinguish the gas burners. Some lampposts are still equipped with the metal bar on which the lamplighter would rest his ladder if maintenance work was necessary (the ladder was not needed to light or turn off the burner; the pole was used). Barely 20 lampposts still have a bar rail. The last lamplighters were laid off in the 1950s and turned

Pont Marie, 4th

their hand to the installation and maintenance of electrical cabinets.

3 and 7, quai de l'Horloge, 1st
Pont Marie, 4th
Square Auguste-Cavaillé-Coll, 10th

Morris columns: temples of gas culture

The appearance of Morris columns, used to display municipal and then theatrical announcements, coincided with the generalization of gas lighting around 1850. Their hollow pillars were used as closets by lamplighters, who kept their equipment in them: poles, fuel (oil and alcohol), overalls, incandescent mantles, gas-burner lamp glass, etc. It was there that the workmen's supervisors gave them their instructions before they went on their rounds. When gas lighting was phased out, the spaces in the columns were used to store street-cleaning supplies or to house lavatories or public telephones.

Above
Facing 148, boulevard de Grenelle, 15th. Painted silver, the column blends into the pillars that support the overhead Métro viaduct. This may be the last first-generation Morris column used by lamplighters.

A well-preserved building

Not far from parc Monceau, there is a luxury building that still has many devices formerly fueled by gas. Their workings are visible: two burner stands under the porch, lights in the courtyard, and two sets of monumental chandeliers in the stairways. The chandeliers are strung down all the floors like beads on a wire and are operated by both electrical circuits and small gas burners.

4, avenue Hoche, 8th

Projecting numbers

These triangular numbers above entrances were once all lit by gas (and eventually electricity). At the end of the Second Empire, it was compulsory to install them on the buildings owned by the City of Paris, as well as those built on land formerly belonging to the City (sold to individuals or developers with that proviso). Behind the blue glass, a flame was lit at nightfall using a valve just below the lantern. There are still many lamps of this kind, but sadly none of them works anymore. At 70, rue de Rivoli, there is an example of this kind of lit number that is apparently unique, but in shape only. The little valve lever is clearly visible below it.

Left to right

172, boulevard Saint-Germain, 6th
42, boulevard Saint-Marcel, 5th
70, rue de Rivoli, 1st

Allegories at the Opéra

In the golden age of gas, the Opéra-Garnier, which naturally had to be a showcase for technology, cast floods of light all around. Lighting also played a very symbolic role at the Opéra. Today, in the Grand Lobby on the first floor, visitors can admire (immediately as they arrive) four busts of women set on columns. A few details show them to be allegories for candle, oil, gas, and electric lighting. Around the neck of the "gas muse" is a delightful gas-pipe necklace decorated with valves, and her headgear is a charming gas tank. There is also a winged gas allegory near the ceiling in the ante-lobby, close to the Soleil rotunda.

Opéra-Garnier, 9th

No smoke without fire

Some fire stations still have their distinctive signs: lanterns with the word "Pompiers" in white on their panes of red glass. They bear a certain resemblance to the city's last traditional tobacconist's signs: in the form of a conical lantern with red glass. It can be seen in the place du Costa-Rica, which was once also equipped with gas burners.

26, rue Blanche, 9th
50, rue du Château-d'Eau, 10th
Corner of rue de Reuilly and boulevard Diderot, 12th
2, rue François-Millet, 16th
27, rue Boursault, 17th

Square Violet, 15th

Place de Costa-Rica, 16th

Remarkable streetlamps

Pont Alexandre-III

One of a kind

Only one or two examples of certain models of streetlamps are still to be found in the capital (the one in the place de Furstemberg is unique) while others can only be seen in a particular area. That is true of the rostral columns of the place de la Concorde and the lampposts of the Hôtel-de-Ville (which unfortunately are copies) and pont Alexandre-III (they date back to 1900 and have always been electric). Others include the lamps fitted on a corner building in the place Vendôme, the ones in the place Franz-Liszt and cour Napoléon, the bronze Carrier-Belleuse torchères at the foot of the great stairway of the Opéra, and the Félix Chabaud lamp-women who surround the palais Garnier. The lamppost with its great lyre and fitted clock in the square Louise-Michel below the Sacré-Cœur is also a rare specimen.

Also

Place de la Concorde, 1st
Place de l'Hôtel-de-Ville, 4th
Opéra-Garnier, 9th
Square Louise-Michel, 18th

Telescopic lampposts

The green art deco obelisks set at the four corners of the pont du Carrousel are telescopic lampposts, designed to be raised from 12 to 22 meters in height by a remote-controlled electric motor. Devised by the wrought-iron sculptor Raymond Subes and installed in 1946, the system had the advantage of leaving the view of the Louvre unobstructed during the day. At night, the light from the lamps covers the entire bridge from above.

Pont du Carrousel, 1st

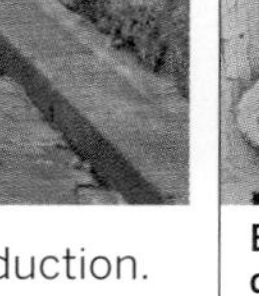

Lighting landmarks

A twofold rarity

The lamppost in the passage Vandrezanne is noteworthy because this kind of console streetlamp with a bracket to keep the lamp away from a facade is rare and also because there is no real reason for it (there is no house nearby, only a wall). It is a rather quirky modern reproduction.

Passage Vandrezanne, 13th

Stamped with the city's seal

This lamp bracket (*below*) at 104, rue Mouffetard is extremely rare since it is one of the last —together with the one in the passage Saint-Paul (4th)—that feature the arms of the City of Paris.

Between 41 and 43, rue de Provence, 9th

Between 2 and 4, rue Gazan, 14th

Let there be light

When the American Thomas Edison presented his incandescent electric light bulb at the International Electricity Exposition in Paris, Parisians were literally and figuratively dazzled. Electric lighting was very costly at the time and so was only to be found in a few very elegant public places: the Théâtre-Français, place de l'Opéra, Grands Boulevards. Subsequently, a few private buildings went electric and little cast-iron hatches began to appear at the foot of facades. These fuse covers were marked with the stamp of the Compagnie Continentale Edison and only electricians, using a special key, were allowed to open them. During renovation work they are usually removed; these hatches are now few and far between. The ones on a building in the parc de Montsouris simply bear the words *Distribution d'électricité*.

Top to bottom
18, rue Saint-Séverin, 5th
44, rue Notre-Dame-de-Lorette, 9th

Pioneering plaques

Plaques providing such information as *Électricité force motrice* (Electricity, driving force) or *Eau et gaz à tous les étages* (Gas and water on every floor) advertised a building's modern conveniences. Others supplied information for the benefit of technicians searching for the cause of a power outage.

The Pigeon family grave

This is one of the most startling tombs in the cimetière du Montparnasse. Monsieur and Madame Pigeon are shown in their marital bed wearing street clothes. She is lying down while he is half-sitting. Why? Because Charles ordered the tomb on the death of his wife Léonie in 1909, while he was still alive. Although Charles Pigeon did not invent the gasoline lamp, he was the first person to market a portable gasoline lighting appliance, which was patented in 1884. Non-inflammable and non-explosive, it was presented at the Universal Exposition in 1900.

Montparnasse Cemetery, 14th (22nd division)

Mr. Ara surrounded by his oil lamps, which are all rare and, above all, in working order. From left to right: a "solar" lamp, a Quinquet lamp, a small lighthouse lantern, an adjustable lamp (white), a tin pump lamp in candlestick form, and a Carcel-type lamp (in brass).

Museum of Antique Lighting

The affable Monsieur Ara collects and lovingly restores kerosene lamps and broken gas burners. His ceiling is a maze of chandeliers, wall lamps, fittings with beaded fringes, lamp-post heads, and opaline lampshades dating from between 1825 and 1925. He knows all there is to know about the different models of lamps and types of combustion: flat wick, stable flame, butterfly burners, fan flames, Auer burners, "bulb" effect incandescence, and more. His visitors leave much enlightened and with a radiant smile.

4, rue Flatters, 5th (lumiara.perso.neuf.fr)

3 On the trail of the city walls

For a very long time, Paris's gender has been the subject of much debate. Masculine or feminine? Is Paris a he or a she? In past centuries, the city was walled many times (seven to be precise). Like a latter-day Helen of Troy, it was lusted after and besieged. Later, it grew stout and matronly, and burst its corsets when it annexed its suburbs in 1860. Paris's current physiognomy is closely linked to the real or abstract presence of the walls and ramparts that were once built around it for military or fiscal purposes.

Map of the successive walls of Paris

6, rue de la Colombe, 4th

The Gallo-Roman era

The only remaining traces of the fortifications that protected Lutetia in the 4th century are in the rue de la Colombe on the island that is now known as the île de la Cité. Its ancient inhabitants had to guard against barbarian attacks, especially Germanic raids, so they raised ramparts all around the island (which was smaller than it is today). They were 8 meters high and 2.7 meters wide, and equipped with parapet walks and battlements. Today a double row of cobbles on the ground marks their position and width.

The tenth and eleventh centuries

Rue des Barres, 4th

Rather than a wall, there was probably just a simple embankment of earth with a palisade surrounding three natural areas of high ground that were safe from flooding on the Right Bank of the Seine. There were three gates: the porte de Paris (now the place du Châtelet), the porte Saint-Merry (near the church of that name), and the porte Baudoyer (where the eponymous square is situated today). At the time, the fortifications enclosed the église Saint-Gervais-Saint-Protais with its elm (*see p. 62*) and market. Although we know little about these fortifications, the steps in front of the church and the layout of the rue des Barres tend to confirm their existence.

Place Saint-Gervais, 4th

The walls of Philippe Auguste (1190-1670)

In 1190, Philippe Auguste was preparing go on a third crusade, but he was concerned about the presence of the English in Normandy. To deal with the threat, before he gave the order to depart, he decided to fortify a number of his towns. They included Amiens, Gisors, Évreux, and Paris, where he ordered the construction of unprecedentedly large fortifications. The rampart was 8 to 10 meters high, more than 5 kilometers long and 3 meters wide. It had some 70 guard towers, including four particularly massive ones near the Seine. Every evening, a chain was stretched across the water to prevent any river-borne attack. Now the King of England was welcome to try his luck—he would get more than he bargained for!

The colossal fortifications did not only surround houses, churches, and palaces, but also fields, meadows, vineyards, and orchards, which would be needed to feed the population were there a siege. The walls protected the city for about 150 years. After that time, they were not demolished, but rather "swallowed and digested" by new buildings. The great fortifications became boundary markers and were used as supporting, dividing, and foundation walls. The towers were turned into homes, workshops, and even chapels, which explains why so many remnants have survived. Unfortunately, they are mainly on private property and so difficult to visit. Even so, the curious can still follow the perimeter of Philippe Auguste's wall (preferably by bicycle).

(See map of the walk on the following page)

Palais Royal-Musée du Louvre
Place du Palais Royal
D
Rue St-Honoré
Musée du Louvre
Louvre-Rivoli
RUE DE RIVOLI
Rue du Louvre
RUE DU LOUVRE
RUE J.-J. ROUSSEAU
RUE MONTMARTRE
Rue Coquillière
Bourse du Commerce
Les Halles
Rue Berger
Rue Tiquetonne
E. Marcel
RUE E. MARCEL
RUE DE TURBIGO
Arts et Métiers
RUE RÉAUMUR
RUE BEAUBOURG
RUE DU TEMPLE
Rue de Montmorency
Rue Rambuteau
Rambuteau
BVD DE SÉBASTOPOL
RUE DU RENARD
Rue du Pont Neuf
Pont Neuf
QUAI DU LOUVRE
La Seine
A
QUAI DE CONTI
Rue Guénégaud
Rue Mazarine
Rue de Seine
Rue Dauphine
Châtelet
AV. VICTORIA
Hôtel de Ville
RUE DE RIVOLI
Quai de l'Horloge
Quai des Orfèvres
Cité
Quai de la Corse
Quai aux Fleurs
La Seine
Rue des Francs Bourgeois
Rue des Rosiers
Rue du Roi de Sicile
St-Paul
Pont Marie
R. Charlemagne
QUAI DES CÉLESTINS
Quai de Bourbon
Rue St-Louis en l'Île
QUAI DES GRANDS AUGUSTINS
QUAI ST MICHEL
St-Michel
St-Michel N.D.
QUAI DE MONTEBELLO
Rue de Buci
R. St-André des Arts
Mabillon
Odéon
Carrefour de l'Odéon
BVD ST-GERMAIN
R. des Quatre-Vents
Rue de l'Odéon
Rue de Tournon
Cluny-La Sorbonne
Paris V
Paris VI
Rue Racine
Rue Monsieur le Prince
BVD ST-MICHEL
RUE ST-JACQUES
Place Maubert
Maubert-Mutualité
BVD ST-GERMAIN
QUAI DE LA TOURNELLE
BVD HENRI IV
Pont de la Tournelle
RUE MONGE
R. des Écoles
R. du Cardinal Lemoine
Jardin du Luxembourg
Place E. Rostand
Rue Soufflot
Rue Cujas
Panthéon
Rue Clovis
RUE SAINT JACQUES
Rue des Fossés St-Jacques
Rue de l'Estrapade
R. Blainville
Rue Thouin
Cardinal Lemoine
Jussieu
Rue Jussieu
Luxembourg
Rue Royer-Collard

Right Bank

→ Starting from the Louvre shopping mall and Sully mezzanine.
At the end of the 12th century, the Louvre was a very strongly built castle. The powerful fortress stood just outside Philippe Auguste's wall and its massive keep symbolized royal authority. The castle has been rebuilt so many times that today no sign of it is visible from outside the building. However, in the 1980s, an archeological dig revealed its monumental substructure: the foundations of the towers and keep that were demolished in 1528.

→ Walk via place du Palais-Royal to rue Saint-Honoré and head down the right-hand side of the street to no. 146.

We know that the buildings from nos. 146 to 150 were built along the line of the wall because of the slanted shape of the lot: instead of being perpendicular to the street, it runs parallel to the line of the former fortifications, as is shown by the angle of the chimney stacks. The same kind of layout is to be found on the boulevard Saint-Germain on the Left Bank *(see the next page).*

→ Continue down rue Saint-Honoré and turn left on rue du Louvre.

At no. 11, a concave recess shows where a tower stood on the neighboring lot.

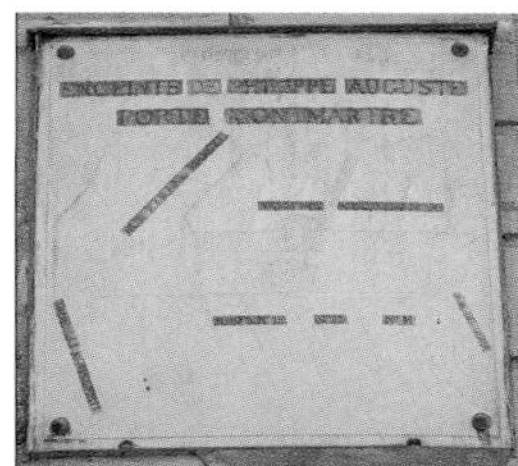

→ Turn right down rue Coquillière and then left on rue du Jour, and finally left again down rue Montmartre.
An antique plaque at no. 30 carries a sketch showing the location of the porte Montmartre.

→ Fork right on rue Étienne Marcel and head for the tour de Jean-Sans-Peur at no. 16.
The tour de Jean-Sans-Peur was built in 1409 and is partly supported by the wall.

→ Continue straight down rue Étienne-Marcel, rue aux Ours, and rue du Grenier-Saint-Lazare. Turn right on rue Beaubourg and then left down rue Rambuteau, which ends at the rue des Francs-Bourgeois. Discreetly enter the courtyard of the Crédit Municipal at no. 55-59.
A double line of cobblestones marks the path of the wall. It runs to the base of the tour Pierre Alvart, reinforced with brick and

heightened in 1885 (only the stone base was part of the old fortifications) to house a stairway leading to the adjacent building.

→ Continue along rue des Francs-Bourgeois, turn right on rue Pavée, and continue as far as rue de Rivoli. Cross it, take rue du Prévôt and, at the end, turn left on rue Charlemagne. You will see an esplanade on the right in rue des Jardins-Saint-Paul.

This is the most impressive remaining section of the fortifications: about 100 meters of wall and two towers—the tour Montgomery to the north (sadly half-demolished when rue Charlemagne was widened) and the well-conserved tour Montigny. The surfaces of the stones are engraved with the marks of workers who marked each stone to make sure they would be paid for each one they set. *(see p. 205)*.

→ Head along quai des Célestins, cross the pont Marie, continue on rue des Deux-Ponts, and cross to the Left Bank over the pont de la Tournelle.

Left Bank

Since the wall could not cross the Seine, buoys were moored to posts on each bank and chains attached to them to bar the way of any would-be invaders using the river. High watchtowers completed the defenses. There was one here, downstream, on the quai de la Tournelle. It was linked to the tour Barbeau standing opposite on quai des Célestins (no. 32).

→ Take rue du Cardinal-Lemoine. Before crossing boulevard Saint-Germain, pause for a moment.

The wall passed between today's nos. 2 and 4 on the boulevard and continued diagonally. The narrow building at 7 bis was built on the site of the wall, as the angle of its chimneys shows *(see p. 41)*.

→ Continue along rue du Cardinal-Lemoine to no. 30 bis.

In the basement of the post office is an arch 5.2 meters high, which was once equipped with a portcullis. It was discovered during a dig in 1991. Here, a channel diverted from the River Bièvre passed under the wall. It was dug to supply water to the gardens of the abbaye de Saint-Victor (which can be visited on the first Wednesday of every month at 2:30 pm).

→ Turn right on rue des Écoles, cross and take rue d'Arras.

In the 13th century, rue d'Arras ran along the inside of the wall (in fact, it was called "rue des Murs"). A section of wall about 30 meters long which remains in the garden of nos. 9-11 can be seen through a window on the ground floor.

→ Cross rue Monge and continue down rue d'Arras. At the top of the steps, turn left through the passage to rue Jacques-Henri Lartigue.

A piece of wall was incorporated into the fire station. The other side can be seen in the BiLiPo (Library of Police Literature).

→ Return to rue du Cardinal-Lemoine and walk uphill. Turn right on rue Clovis and stop at no. 5.

Very few remnants of the wall display this kind of profile, sliced like a

piece of cake. You can judge the wall's height (although the battlements have gone), thickness, and building method: a mass of rubble-stones bound by very hard cement sandwiched between two stone facings using the Roman method called "backfill." If you go to no. 7 and enter the courtyard there, you can see another vestige of inner wall.

→ Turn left on rue Descartes and go to no. 47.

Around 1200, this was the site of the porte Bordelles, named for the local landowner. A plan displayed at no. 50 shows the exact location. It was subsequently renamed Bordet and then Saint-Marcel, and was one of the gates of Paris of both the Philippe Auguste and Charles V fortifications. It was made up of a structure flanked by two large round towers, equipped with a drawbridge leading to a timber bridge with a portcullis. It was demolished in 1683. In the small yard of no. 47 (access is protected by a door code), a spiral staircase can be seen that leads to the second floor, where the top of the ramparts and the walk were once located.

→ Turn right on rue Thouin.

Rue Thouin was laid over the ditches of the fortifications when they were filled in 1685. The building at no. 14 was built just after that, in 1688, supported by the medieval rampart. When the rampart was demolished, it left an empty lot (which became a courtyard) and a sheer back wall.

→ Continue down rue de l'Estrapade to rue des Fossés-Saint-Jacques.

In 1346, the defensive capacities of the wall were improved: dry ditches were dug at its foot on the outer, rural side. Rues des Fossés-Saint-Bernard, Fossés-Saint-Jacques, and Fossés-Saint-Marcel follow these old

ditches. You can walk along part of the line of the fortifications on those streets.

→ Continue on rue Malebranche.

The very steep rue Malebranche was laid in 1585 near the Philippe Auguste wall, whose ditches had just been filled. It was initially called the "rue Sur-le-Rempart" and then "rue des Fossés-Saint-Michel."

→ Turn right on rue Le Goff, then left on rue Soufflot. Cross boulevard Saint-Michel and enter rue Monsieur-le-Prince.

This street also has a sharp gradient linked to the wall. It runs along the line of the counterscarp between the porte Saint-Germain and the porte Saint-Michel. It was formerly known as "rue des Fossés-Monsieur-le-Prince."

→ Note the gradient in rue Antoine-Dubois on the right and then turn right on rue Dupuytren. Crossing boulevard Saint-Germain, head on into the cour du Commerce-Saint-André.
This passage was opened in 1735 when the ditch of the fortifications was filled. Inside no. 4, in the restaurant dining room, you can see a massive tower that was set in the wall. It has two doors—one that led to the city side and the other to the country side. The wall protected the abbaye de Sainte-Geneviève, but not the abbaye de Saint-Germain-des-Prés, which was itself fortified, so the village of Saint-Germain was divided in two.

→ At the end of the passage, cross rue Saint-André-des-Arts and go straight down rue Mazet to the corner of rue Dauphine.

A plaque at no. 44 shows the location of the porte Dauphine and tells the story of its demolition.

→ Head along rue Dauphine to the passage Dauphine. At its end, turn left on rue Mazarine and immediately enter the Mazarine parking garage and go down to level -1.
More than 50 meters of the wall were discovered intact when the underground parking garage was excavated. Today, they can be seen on two levels.

→ Leave the parking garage and turn right on rue Mazarine and then right again onto rue Guénégaud. At the end of the street, take quai Conti on the left until you reach impasse de Conti.
Above, at the end of this dead-end street, you can see a last remnant of Philippe Auguste's fortifications.

→ Return to quai de Conti.
This was the site of the tour de Nesle, linked at night by chain to the tour du Coin on the opposite bank near the Louvre. The chain crossed the Seine where the pont des Arts stands today. You have now come full circle.

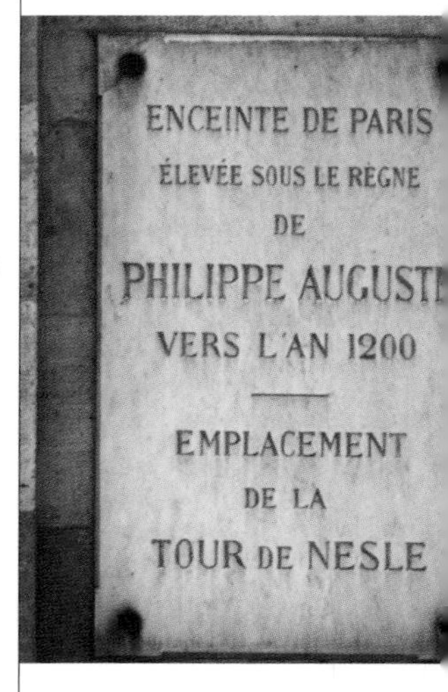

The archeological crypt of the Louvre, 1st

The wall of Charles V (1356-1634)

In 1356, the Parisians were apprehensive. Following the defeat of the French forces by the English at Poitiers, King Jean le Bon (John the Good) had been captured. The merchants' provost, Étienne Marcel, feared an attack before he gave the order to depart. Paris's defenses had to be strengthened. Philippe Auguste's wall still protected the Université district on the Left Bank, but the Right Bank was vulnerable. A new, bigger, and more efficient wall than the old one was urgently needed.

The wall was not just an ordinary rampart, but a system of fortifications 87 meters wide. They formed a series of obstacles: a triple forward-defense embankment, a counterscarp wall 6 meters high, and a main ditch 30 meters wide filled with water and rubble to provide a glacis for direct fire from artillery, which was rapidly becoming a key weapon. The wall continued to mark the boundary between the city and its surrounding districts until the 17th century. The place names of Paris still reflect this: the rue Saint-Antoine was inside the wall; the rue du Faubourg-Saint-Antoine outside. The same goes for the rues Saint-Honoré, du Temple, Saint-Denis, etc. Later, between 1624 and 1634, Charles V's fortifications were destroyed and their ditches filled by Louis XIII. There are few remnants since they were mainly earthworks, with stone playing only a very minor part.

The escarp wall

Charles V's wall incorporated the Louvre fortress. In the museum's shopping mall, a 200-meter length of the escarp wall was discovered during a dig in 1991. It was a "robust" section consisting of a stone wall supported by wooden beams and topped by an artillery platform. It also had a moat: the surface of its stones show marks made by the water.

The parapet walk

Rue d'Aboukir follows the plan of Charles V's fortifications. The even-numbered buildings run along the path of the wall; the street was laid over the filled ditch. Homes were built in the remains of the ramparts. Visit the passage Sainte-Foy: walking up its 13 steps is the equivalent of climbing the old embankment to reach the parapet walk.

The does' leap

Other uneven pieces of ground reflect the topography of the former wall. The 47 steps of the passage du Pont-aux-Biches (Bridge of Does) run between the top of the rampart and the city 7 meters below.

Boulevard Beaumarchais and rue Amelot, 11th

Multiple steps

The height difference of four meters between boulevard Beaumarchais (on the embankment that protected the wall) and rue Amelot is reflected by the steps in the rues Clotilde-de-Vaux, Scarron, Marcel-Gromaire, and Charles-Luizet.

Fossés jaunes barrier
(1634-1670)

François I had Charles V's bastioned fortifications strengthened. To the east and south of the Right Bank, new bastions were added to Charles V's ditches, which had been gradually filled by 150 years of accumulated debris thrown over the wall by Parisians. To the west, new larger fortifications were constructed. They were known as the "Fossés jaunes" (Yellow Ditches) because of the color of their earth. Today's Grands Boulevards follow the same path and their layout is the only remaining sign of the defensive works.

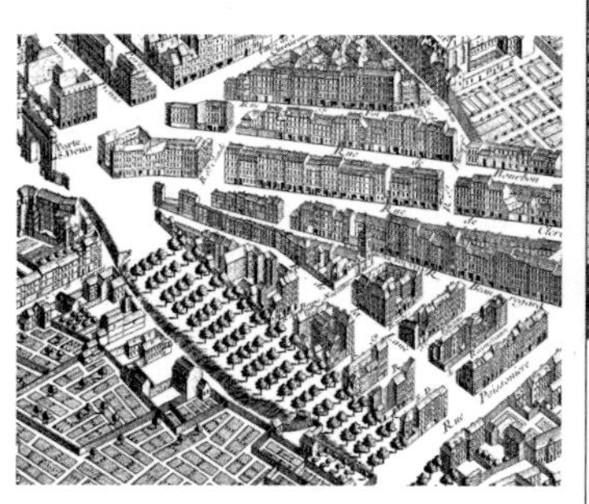

Remains of the sixth bastion of the Fossés jaunes after the development of the Cours (in the area of today's porte Saint-Denis). Turgot plan, 1734. (Private collection)

The wall of the Fermiers généraux
(1788 and 1860)

This wall was fiscal rather than defensive. Since the 16th century, tax collection had been farmed out to the Ferme générale (General Farm), a company of 40 financiers called the Fermiers généraux. They had a royal contract: each year, they undertook to pay a certain sum to the Royal Treasury and they were free to set the taxes they chose. Consequently, the Fermiers généraux amassed colossal fortunes and were bitterly hated by Parisians. Any consumer item or foodstuff entering the city was taxed: wine, straw, wood, coal, cooked fruit, joints of meat, etc. Naturally, everyone tried to evade these octroi taxes. By the late 18th century, tax fraud was so rampant that the Fermiers généraux persuaded the king to build a fiscal barrier enclosing Paris. A wall 3.4 meters high was constructed around a 28-kilometer perimeter. Its 54 gates were closed with bars and flanked by *barrières* buildings to provide accommodation and offices for the revenue staff. The wall followed the same path as today's above-ground Métro (lines 6 and 2).

Parc Monceau, 8th

The wall of the Fermiers généraux and its parapet walk followed the same concave, curved path as today's Métro viaduct. At the time, the building was flanked by two outbuildings in the form of guard posts that blocked the route du Bourget (now avenue de Flandre) and the route de Pantin (now avenue Jean-Jaurès).

Rotonde de La Villette, 19th

Octroi barriers

There were four taxation offices set up to tax goods coming into the city: Chartres (parc Monceau), Saint-Martin (La Villette), Le Trône (Nation), and d'Enfer (Denfert-Rochereau). All persons entering Paris with any kind of merchandise had to pay the octroi tax. At the rotonde de La Villette, the names of all the Parisian octrois can be seen engraved at the top of the two walls that border the esplanade.

The annexation plaque

A plaque at 86, boulevard de Rochechouart commemorates the annexation of 1860, when 11 surrounding villages were absorbed into Paris. They included this one, Montmartre, which became the 18th arrondissement. The annexation made the Férmiers généraux wall obsolete and it was demolished.

86, boulevard de Rochechouart, 18th

Thiers's wall (1846 and 1919)

In 1830, after Napoleon's defeats and the invasion of France by Austrian, Russian, and Prussian troops, the defense of Paris was a critical issue. The Fermiers généraux wall was not fit for military purpose, so the government decided to construct fortifications in the suburbs. Minister of War Adolphe Thiers supervised the work. By 1846, an uninterrupted wall 33 kilometers in length and 6 meters wide encircled the suburbs, cutting certain villages in half (Gentilly, Ivry, Montrouge, etc.) by decision of the government. Including their ditches, the fortifications were 140 meters wide and had a paved interior road (now the boulevards des Maréchaux). However, in 1870, the fortifications—the world's longest city walls—proved completely ineffective. As a result, they were demolished between 1920 and 1924. From 1945 on, the strip of now empty land was used to build housing projects, stadiums, public gardens, and a university campus.

The porte de Bicêtre of the Thiers wall. In the distance, 16, boulevard Kellermann, 13th (Fonds Lansiaux, archives de Paris)

4 In search of lost time

61-63, rue Réaumur, 2nd
(see p. 58)

Sundials

It is a little-known fact that Paris is the French city with the greatest number of sundials. There are 120 of them scattered around the capital—except in the 17th arrondissement, which curiously has none. About 80 of them give solar (or true) time, while the others are purely ornamental or not in working order. The oldest dates back to the 16th century. Church clocks and the watches of the affluent were adjusted to sundial time. The plate and the gnomon (the part of the sundial that casts the shadow) were traditionally inscribed with philosophical maxims in Latin or French. Some were epicurean ("Enjoy life while it lasts"), while others were frankly depressing ("As you look at me, you are aging" or "Alas! The hour you see may be that of your death"). You should not be surprised if a sundial does not show the same time as your watch. Three factors cause discrepancies: the equation of time (the fact that the solar day is not invariable but changes with the season), longitude correction (giving universal time), and the time zone (Greenwich Mean Time plus one hour in winter and two hours in summer in Paris). Some sundials only show the time in the morning and others the time in the afternoon. The remaining ones that still work show the time all day long.

The old-timer of Saint-Eustache

The transept of the church of Saint-Eustache was built between 1537 and 1545, and the sundial more than 30 meters up on its southern facade dates back to that time, making it the oldest one in Paris. It tilts slightly to the west. The gnomon is set just below the rose window and the hour and half-hour lines are carved into the stone. If you look further down, you can also see a noon mark on the pillar to the left of the portal. It no longer works without the metal circle formerly set at the convergence of the three bars, which enabled the sun's position at noon to be identified.

Place René-Cassin, 1st

Day and night

This sundial is high above the ground on a five-floor art nouveau building. It is framed by two allegories: Day (represented by an awakening nymph) and Night (a woman covering her head with a veil). The 1908 work is by the sculptor Jules Louis Rispal.

18, rue Perrée, 3rd

This dial photographed at noon exactly shows the discrepancy with the official time.

The amorous philosopher's sundial

In the courtyard of the hôtel Dupin (the former hôtel des Vins), a sundial in excellent condition is painted on the facade. The great Jean-Jacques Rousseau would often have glanced at it, since he was a daily visitor to the hôtel Dupin—first as a friend of Louise Marie-Madeleine Dupin, who welcomed the finer minds of Paris to her salon, and then as her *notiste* (a sort of personal secretary) from 1745 to 1751. He was helping her write a book on the subject of women. She was a beautiful, quick-witted patron and he inevitably fell in love with her. Sadly, the chemistry was one-sided: a love letter he wrote to her was icily returned.

68, rue Jean-Jacques-Rousseau, 1st

123, rue Saint-Jacques, 5th

Babylonic and sidereal time

The complex sundials in the *cour d'honneur* (three-sided courtyard) of the lycée Louis-le-Grand were used by Jesuits as a teaching aid to instruct second- and third-year philosophy students. Their systems are impenetrable for the uninitiated. Right at the top is a double sundial showing standard hours (solar hours). Below is another pair showing temporal hours (with the day divided into 12 hours between sunrise and sunset), Babylonic hours (the time gone by since sunrise), and Italic hours (the hours remaining until sunset). At the bottom, the sundial on the left shows average hours, while the curves represent variations between mean time and solar time. The one on the right displays sidereal time, used to locate celestial bodies.

129, rue de Grenelle, 7th

Peculiar spelling

The *cour d'honneur* of Les Invalides has no fewer than seven sundials on three of its four facades (the one to the north holds a clock). Installed between 1679 and 1770, they are as complex as those at the lycée Louis-le-Grand (*see opposite*). Their French spelling may seem rather peculiar, but was standard in the days of the Enlightenment: *Heurs artificielles* (artificial time), *Heurs planétairs* (planetary time), *Grandeurs des nuicts* (length of nights), *Grandeurs des iours* (length of days), *Heures babiloniques* (Babilonic time), *Heures italiques*

(Italic time), etc. Signs of the zodiac are also displayed, painted brick-red like the cave paintings at Lascaux. A notice in the gallery explains the principle of each sundial.

Chercher midi à quatorze heures

This French expression, ("seeking noon at two p.m."), which means "to look for complications where there are none," derives from a sign displayed circa 1675 at 19, rue du Cherche-Midi (Seek-Noon). It featured an astronomer in a toga using a compass to measure the degrees of a sundial. The points

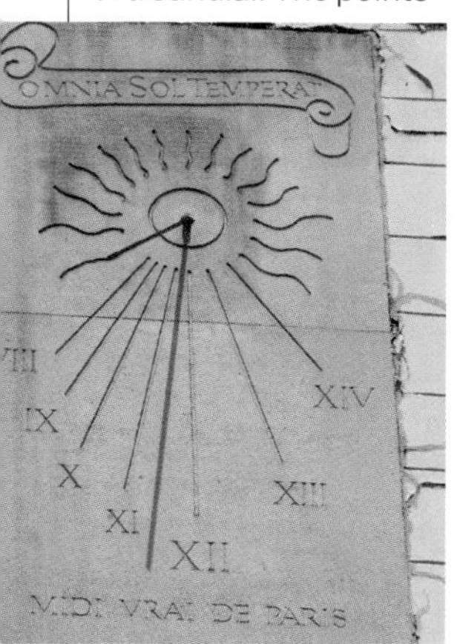

of the compass were on noon and 2 p.m. In 1874, the sign was replaced with a bas-relief showing the same design. In 1982, a sundial showing "the true noon of Paris" was added at no. 56.

19 and 56, rue du Cherche-Midi, 6th

Vespers time

All that remains of the former *couvent* (which can mean convent or, in this case, monastery) des Grands-Augustins, demolished in 1897, is a piece of facade engraved with a huge sundial. It can be seen on the level of the second and third stories from a private rear yard. Its lunar form is perfectly preserved and it features signs of the zodiac. It is a pity that a rather incongruous window was later knocked through in the middle of the dial.

55, quai des Grands-Augustins, 6th

The cock and typo

The sundial in the rue de l'Abreuvoir bears the inscription *Quand tu sonneras, je chanteray* (When you ring, I will crow). The final Y, usual in Old French, gives it a misleadingly antique air, since it was only engraved in 1924. Also, there is an inverted N in the word *Quand*, a nod to the Cyrillic alphabet. The detail is interesting given that the owner of the house who had the sundial made was Commandant Henry Lachouque (1883-1971), a French officer and historian who specialized in the First Empire and was particularly interested in Napoleon Bonaparte's Russian campaigns.

4, rue de l'Abreuvoir, 18th

From cock to clam

On the tower of the formal stairway in the courtyard of the hôtel des abbés de Cluny is a sundial dating back to 1674. Its seashell theme reflects the emblem of Abbot Jacques d'Amboise, who had the Parisian hôtel des abbés de Cluny rebuilt.

6, place Paul-Painlevé, 5th

Horizontal sundials

On the botanical promenade by the jardin de Reuilly, an integrated horizontal sundial in butterfly form covers 625 square meters. It is a specially designed modern model (1992) whose complex operation is explained on the white marble gnomon. Even more spectacular is the sundial in square Émile-Gallé, which has 10 stone sculptures to mark the hours.

Square Jacques-Hillairet, 12th

Square Émile-Gallé, 11th

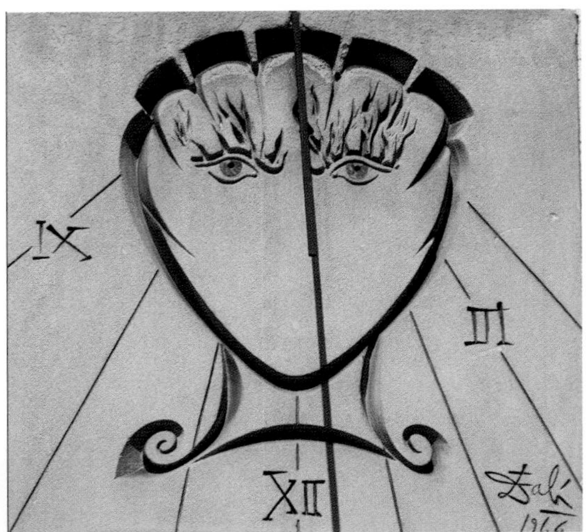

A signed Dalí

A genuine Dalí in the street! Unbelievable! Of course, this is no melting watch or other surrealistic canvas, but a sundial personally engraved by the master in 1966 for friends who had a store at 27, rue Saint-Jacques. The work was unveiled with much media-friendly ceremony. Perched in a cherry picker, Dali engraved his signature and the date for the TV cameras. The sundial is a cement molding showing a female face whose upper part suggests a scallop shell. In an allusion to the sun, its eyebrows are flames.

27, rue Saint-Jacques, 5th

Brainteaser

This afternoon sundial, added to this low rear-courtyard building in 1751 or 1757, is bewildering. It is impossible to work out what it is supposed to show.

75, cour de l'Étoile-d'Or, 11th

Noon marks

Noon marks are not the same as sundials: they only show the exact time of noon. Like sundials, they can be vertical or horizontal.

The solar cannon

The mascot of the Palais-Royal, a miniature cannon on its pedestal in the middle of the lawn, was a noon-mark gun: one that signaled noon acoustically. This was done by an ingenious system of converging lenses called a *verre ardent*, invented in

the 18th century by a Sieur Rousseau, a gnomonic engineer who had a clockmaker's store at 95, galerie de Beaujolais. Loaded with gunpowder, the small cannon was placed under a magnifying glass located between its breech and the noonday sun. When the sun reached its zenith, its rays were focused by the lens and the resulting beam detonated the gunpowder. At noon precisely, when it was sunny, walkers could check that the hands of their watch were exactly aligned on 12 and, if necessary, reset them. There were other cannons of the same kind in the city, but the one at Palais-Royal was internationally famous. It inspired the abbé Delisle to write these lines (inscribed not far from the pedestal):

At the stroke of noon,
In the garden of the Palais-Royal in Paris...
In that garden, all comes together
Except the shadows of the flowers;
Although behavior there is often remiss,
The watches at least are correct.

The cannon fired every day until 1914 and then far more occasionally: only on Wednesdays and Thursdays in summer from 1975 to 1981. In 1990, its precision and discipline were restored and it began to sound again every day at midday. A firearms specialist from the armorers Fauré-Lepage came each morning to fire it. Then in April 1998, it was stolen. By a common thief? An angry neighbor? As the subsequent investigation revealed, the cannon was not universally appreciated. A complaint register kept by the Palais-Royal janitor shows how much the gunfire infuriated some residents. A certain Monsieur J. especially complained of "this detonation at noon that frightens small children." In 2003, a copy of the cannon was installed at the Palais-Royal, but it had apparently taken a vow of silence. It remains mute to this day and its fragile lens is kept in the supervisors' office.

Jardin du Palais-Royal, 1st

Also see Buffon's gazebo in the Jardin des plantes (p. 92).

The Sulpician gnomon

In the left wing of its transept, the église Saint-Sulpice has a noon mark in the form of an obelisk 10.72 meters high. From it extends a brass line that runs nearly 40 meters across the floor. A lens set in the stained glass of the south transept's rose window lets through a ray of light at solar noon that crosses the brass line at a point that varies according to the season, depending on whether the sun is higher or lower in the sky. The scientific instrument was commissioned in 1728 by the parish priest, who wanted to be able to determine the precise moment of the spring equinox and thus when Easter fell.

Église Saint-Sulpice. Place Saint-Sulpice, 6th

The meridian of France

The Observatoire de Paris marks the position of the meridian of France, a geodesic meridian that crosses the country from Dunkirk to Perpignan. A geodesic meridian is

used as a reference in drawing a map of a large region or country, so the meridian of France served as the reference when the first map of France was made. The meridian was chosen in 1667 when the Observatoire was built. Jean-Dominique Cassini recorded his plans: "I felt a large room was needed to enable sunlight to enter through a hole and allow a description of the daily path of the image of the Sun to be made on the floor. [...] In the middle of the southern facade, a little window or opening was left that gave onto the top of the large room, and we planned to mark on the paving not only the meridian line, but also the lines of the hours." That room is today's Salle Cassini, crossed with fine copper lines set in the white marble flagstones. In 1884, an international convention standardized the Greenwich meridian, which was further to the west.

61, avenue de l'Observatoire, 14th
Inscription is engraved on a marble flagstone at the southern end of the meridian line.

The pyramid of Saint-Leu

In a corner of the second courtyard (on the left) of the hôtel des Monnaies is a stone pyramid, called the Pyramide de Saint-Leu. It is a vertical noon mark 7.8 meters high designed in 1777 by Masters Pingre and Jeaurat of the Academy of Sciences. Aside from the vertical meridian line, it features the 12 signs of the zodiac.

11, quai de Conti, 6th

Clocks

More and more public clocks appeared in the 19th century as rail transport and industry boomed. They were installed on many public buildings—stations, town halls, schools, hospitals, and so on. They were all the more useful since watches were still expensive luxury items, only affordable to the well-off.

The belfry of Saint-Germain

The clock on the belfry of the église Saint-Germain l'Auxerrois is one of the oldest still in working condition. Construction of the bell tower began in 1858. It was designed by Théodore Ballu, who had worked on the restoration of the tour Saint-Jacques shortly before (1852-1855), and this explains the resemblance. The clock is decorated with the signs of the zodiac and there are also a barometer and thermometer (on the lateral faces). All three were restored in 2004.

Place du Louvre, 1st

The first public clock

The horloge du Palais was presented to the people of Paris by Charles V in 1371. It was a timely gift! Thanks to this groundbreaking public clock, the city's inhabitants could at last find out what time it was, even at night and when the sky was cloudy (unlike with sundials). It rang on the hour and every quarter of an hour, and people came from far and away to admire it. It is decorated with two figures: Law (on the left) and Justice (on the right). It has been restored and altered many times and the dates of these works are shown at the bottom of the face (1472, 1585, 1685, 1852, 1909, and 2011). It is something of a miracle that it is so well preserved: it is not only the oldest extant public clock but also the very first.

Corner of boulevard du Palais and quai de l'Horloge, 1st

The horloge aux dauphins

We know very little of this clock, except that it was installed on the facade of the hôtel Raoul, the only remains of which are its adjacent gate (*see p. 101*). However, it is not nearly as old as the hôtel Raoul since it is believed to have been manufactured between 1850 and 1880. Two carved wooden dolphins flank the clock face, whose hands are stopped at six o'clock. The clock is protected by an unusual conical zinc shelter.

6, rue Beautreillis, 4th

The clock tower of gare de Lyon

Until 1891, there was a time difference among the cities of France. Each city had its own time, based on the position of the sun in the sky at midday: solar or true time. This meant that between Strasbourg and Brest was a 50-minute time

difference. This was not really a problem for the populace, who traveled slowly until the end of the 19th century, but with the proliferation of railways, timing became an issue. As a result, it was decided that all the country's cities would adopt a standardized, civil time. Built in 1900, the clock tower of gare de Lyon was one of the first to display that time. It is 67 meters high, has a clock face on each side with colossal hands (the minute hands are 4 meters long), and is perfectly reliable since its mechanism is synchronized with the time signal of France Inter radio.

Gare de Lyon, 12th

The exception that confirms the rule

Why do clocks and watches with Roman numerals feature a IIII instead of a IV? The question is an important issue for specialists in antique timepieces. Originally, when the use of Roman numerals spread in Europe, the four was written IIII, a symbol that the illiterate found easier to understand. The IV we know today only appeared belatedly, in the 17th century. Ever since, the guild of clockmakers has remained loyal to the old representation. Firstly, for symmetry and balance: the IIII is opposite the VIII and comparable in size. Secondly, because it allows the face to be divided into three groups of four similar signs: one with only Is, one with Vs and the last with Xs. Lastly, on the face, the figures between III and IX are upside down because, unlike Arabic numerals, they face out from the center. An inverted IV and VI could be confused. QED. A few rare exceptions confirm the rule—for instance the clock in the city hall of the 14th arrondissement of Paris.

2, place Ferdinand-Brunot, 14th

Facial transparency

The disconcerting aesthetics of the transparent clock of the musée d'Orsay have won it a certain international renown. Suspended between the museum building and the sky, it looks out over the Seine and the jardin des Tuileries. The interior clock is just as magnificent. So why such clocks in a museum? Because the building was once a rail station, built for the Universal Exposition of 1900. The interior clock overlooked the platforms in the grand concourse.

Musée d'Orsay, 1, rue de la Légion d'Honneur, 7th

© MUSÉE D'ORSAY/SOPHIE BOEGLY

A 24-hour dial

The clock of the Bergère telephone exchange has an extremely rare distinction: it displays 24-hour time. The phone exchange was constructed between 1911 and 1913, just as time zones were introduced around the world. France adopted Greenwich Mean Time and consequently a universal 24-hour time (instead of twice 12 hours) in March 1914. This undoubtedly influenced the architect François Lecœur, who designed the wrought-iron clock decorated with signs of the zodiac. It adorns a blank wall (telephone cables are attached to it inside). There are other 24-hour clocks in France, but with their figure 1 placed at the top of the dial. The one at the Bergère exchange

is alone in having the figure 1 at the bottom. This was probably so that the 12 would be at the top, where it is to be found on all the 12-hour watches and clocks that are so familiar to us.

17, rue du Faubourg-Poissonnière or 2-10, rue Bergère, 9th

Hanging in the air

Some clocks in narrow streets are suspended like a sign on a bracket to allow passers-by to stand far enough back to read the time on an ordinary clock face. They include the clock at the church of Saint-Louis-en-l'Île, which can be read from the end of the street, and the one on the bell tower of the église Notre-Dame-de-Bonne-Nouvelle.

Left to right

Église Saint-Louis-en-l'Île. 19 bis, rue Saint-Louis-en-l'Île, 4th
Église Notre-Dame-de-Bonne-Nouvelle. Facing 38, rue Beauregard, 2nd

One minute to go!

The stamp of officialdom

For the French administration, postmarks are proof of date of dispatch. So the clock of the Central Post Office in the rue du Louvre is very familiar to Parisian procrastinators and dawdlers, who wait until just before the deadline to mail their tax returns and payments. The clock governs the life of the only French post office to be open almost 24/7 (there is downtime for computer maintenance between 6 and 7:30 a.m.). People dash up to the building at a minute to midnight to make sure their letter is stamped with that day's date, even if it does not leave until the next day.

52, rue du Louvre, 1st

Everybody's time

In the square of the gare Saint-Lazare, a work by Arman features a joyously shambolic pile of clocks, all showing a different time—enough to confuse any passenger in transit! The opus has a sibling: a pile of suitcases on the other side of the square in the cour de Rome. They are respectively titled L'Heure de Tous (*Everybody's Time*) and Consigne à vie (*Left for Life*).

Cour du Havre, 8th

The flow of time

One of the most amazing clocks ever made is the work of Bernard Gitton, an artist who designs fabulous water features. He combined the clepsydra of the Ancient Greeks, which measured time by the flow of water, and the pendulum of the traditional clock, which

keeps it accurate. The complex mechanism, which includes a pump, glass pipes, a lever, and colored liquid, is constantly in motion. A ringed column graduated up to 60 shows the minute, while another, known as the "column of spheres," gives the hour.

Galerie du Claridge, 8th

The clock district

The quartier de l'Horloge, which was built in the 1970s when a condemned block was demolished, takes its name from the monumental automaton clock that artist Jacques Monestier was commissioned to create to decorate the new neighborhood in 1975. Named Le Défenseur du Temps (*The Defender of Time*), it shows a humanoid attacked by a crab, a bird, and a dragon hanging onto a rock. In the 1980s, every hour on the hour, you could see one of the three animals (symbolizing the sea, sky, and land respectively) attacking the humanoid. The struggle was accompanied by the crashing of waves, the gusting of wind, or the rumble of moving ground. At noon and 6 and 10 p.m., the humanoid was attacked by all three creatures at once. Sadly, the spectacular show is over: the clock stopped working in 2003. The quartier de l'Horloge is private property and so its owners are responsible for maintaining its buildings and streets. They do not have sufficient funding to repair the automaton.

8, rue Bernard-de-Clairvaux, 3rd

Covert restoration at the Panthéon

The Untergunther group are a collective of urban Indiana Joneses who clandestinely restore different monuments and historic artifacts neglected by the authorities. In 2004, they turned their attention to the interior clock of the Panthéon, a Wagner model of 1850 that had been out of order since 1965. For more than a year, they spent three or four evenings a week meticulously restoring it, supervised by a professional clockmaker. They were impressively organized, setting up a complete, collapsible workshop of wooden crates in an empty room in the monument. At midnight on December 25, 2005, they started the clock and evacuated the premises, leaving a mischievous note in the Panthéon's gold visitor book. The Centre des monuments nationaux sued for vandalism (sic!), but the Untergunthers were cleared. Although it is now in perfect working condition, the Panthéon clock has been stopped again, probably because it would disturb the solemn ambience of the monument with its quarter-hourly chimes.

Inside the Panthéon (5th) on the left-hand side of the nave, over the model of the building.

The rose window of Réaumur

You could loiter a long time on the odd-numbered side of rue Réaumur without noticing it, but if you cross the street, it is as unmissable as the neo-Gothic building it graces. A church? No, a building constructed in 1900, just after the repeal of the Haussmannian architectural regulations, which meant that Philippe Jouannin and Édouard Singery were able to give free rein to their imagination. The clock is the central feature of a rose window whose mosaics suggest the stained glass of a church. Its decorative theme is time: the months of the year engraved in stone form a circle around the clock face. Signs of the zodiac make up a corona and bas-relief medallions show the four seasons. Visitors can make a discreet foray into the stairway of the building (open weekdays) to admire its transparent face from the inside.

61-63, rue Réaumur, 2nd

The sentinel clock

So why is this small, low clock fitted so near the ground on the front of the police station of the 6th arrondissement? Is it for the use of the patrolmen and women? It is doubly protected by a wooden case and a small metal canopy. According to municipal officers long familiar with the timepiece, its 60s-type Schlumberger face replaced a previous, superannuated dial in 2004.

78, rue Bonaparte, 6th

The speaking clock

The Observatoire de Paris is built on former quarries. It was in its cellars 28 meters underground that the "official clock" was in installed in 1920, in the salle des Garde-Temps (now the laboratoire Foucault). There, it was protected from changes in pressure and temperature that would cause the expansion and contraction of its metal parts—disastrous for any high-precision instrument. At the start of the 1930s, so many people were telephoning the Observatoire to check the time that it was beginning to disrupt the institution's work, especially since it had only one line. To address the issue, the director, Ernest Esclangon, asked the Brillié company to supply a system to speak the time continuously. It would be synchronized with the fundamental clock and based on the new technology of the "talkie" movie (notably *The Jazz Singer*). So on February 14, 1933, the world's first speaking clock (featuring the recorded voice of Marcel Laporte, known as Radiolo, an announcer on Radio-Paris) came into service. From day one, the 20 telephone lines were overloaded: only 20,000 calls out of 140,000 got through. The number of the service, ODEON 84-00 went down in history. The original speaking clock can still be seen at the Observatoire de Paris in the salle Esclangon, together with the generations of machines that succeeded it.

La salle Esclangon is open to the public during the annual Journées du Patrimoine celebration.

©ROLAND BARILLET

At the fourth beep

The 1933 speaking clock was obviously modernized over the years. In 1991, it became fully electronic. It was accurate to 50 milliseconds or less (in continental France at least, because of the delay over long-distance telephone lines). To ensure a high level of

back-up, there was a set of four speaking clocks, one of which was connected to the France Télécom network. The three others were ready to take over if the first should stop working. The speaking clock can still be called in France on 3699.

61, avenue de l'Observatoire, 14th

5 Remarkable trees

Paris may be mainly mineral, but it has no fewer than 484,500 trees (according to a census in 2011). Obviously, if you exclude those in the major woods—the bois de Boulogne and Vincennes (300,000)—there are "only" 184,500 left, shading the city's gardens and avenues. But that is still a very respectable number compared to those on property managed by the City of London, for instance, which has only 155,460 (2002 census). Chosen for their legendary sturdiness, plane, lime, and chestnut trees cover 80% of the landscape. However, current trends favor diversification and the traditional trees are tending to lose ground, replaced by less common varieties, such as the Judas, flowering pepper, and sophora flamingo (with its bright pink blossom). More than 160 different species now populate the Parisian soil, some of them truly remarkable. Aside from the most unusual varieties, this chapter also looks at historic trees, ones that have set records, and the more mischievous specimens that grow in some very startling places.

Arboretum of the parc de la Vallée-aux-Loups, Châtenay-Malabry
(see p. 63)

Wood chips

Each avenue tree (the ones that line streets) has an RFID (Radio Frequency Identification) chip implanted in its trunk at a depth of two centimeters. This transmits an ID number that provides access to the tree's computer profile, grouping all data related to its date of planting or transplanting, pruning, diseases diagnosed, and any damage caused by vehicle impacts.

Waving hankies

In April and May, do not miss the blossoming season of the handkerchief tree (also known as the pocket handkerchief, dove, or ghost tree), so-called because of its odd, spectacular white flowers that flutter like hankies in the slightest breeze.

Alpine garden of the Jardin des plantes (5th), allée to the right when leaving the tunnel
Square Maurice-Gardette, 11th
Parc Monceau, 8th

Special species

Avenue Foch, 16th (even-numbered side)

The monkey-puzzle tree

The *araucaria araucana* is a peculiar conifer commonly known as the "monkey puzzle" because of its leaves, which are intertwined and so sharp that its branches seem impossible to climb, to the regret of primates.

Also
Garden of the hôpital de la Salpêtrière, 13th
Parc des Buttes-Chaumont, 19th (near the pont aux Suicidés)

The fau de Paris

In summer, all you can see of this tree is an igloo of foliage; in the winter, its twisted skeleton is revealed with its bent, jointed, twisted branches drooping down to the ground like the ribs of an umbrella. It is called the "dwarf" or "twisted" beech, or *fau de Verzy*, since the largest population in the world is to be found in the National Forest of Verzy near Reims (about a thousand specimens).

Square des Arènes de Lutèce, 5th
Parc des Buttes-Chaumont, 19th

Parc de Montsouris, 14th

A crying tree trunk on boulevard Saint-Michel, 5th.

Stigmatic bark

"Wait for me under the elm..."

Because of its blood-red sap, which flows heavily when its bark is cut and suggests the blood of the martyrs, the elm has been seen as a holy tree since the dawn of Christianity. In

the Middle Ages, there was an elm in every village of France, in front of churches and manor houses, and at crossroads. Initially a tradition, in 1605, this became an obligation decreed by Sully, the minister of Henri IV. People gathered there to attend trials, talk business, and pay their debts, which explains the French expression "Wait for me under the elm."

The Saint-Gervais elm was the most popular in Paris. It is so deeply rooted in the city's history that nobody can imagine the square of Saint-Gervais without it. A new one is planted when the incumbent begins to falter (today's was planted in 1936). More evidence of this arboreal affection is

Left to right

Place and church of Saint-Gervais, 4th

supplied by the stylized elm used to decorate the wrought-iron supports of the windows of the rue François-Miron and the rue des Barres. These houses, which line the northern side of the church, were built by the parish in 1737. There is also an elm pattern on four of the wooden stalls in the choir of the church.

Nos 4 through 14, rue François-Miron and 17, rue des Barres, 4th

Mulberries and silkworms

Botanically speaking, white mulberry trees are characterized by four different shapes of leaves. A single branch can grow the four types, which are lobed to different degrees. Silkworms love to feast on this foliage. The two trees here, at either end of the double row of lime trees lining the terrasse des Feuillants, are the descendants of the 20,000 mulberry saplings planted in this location in 1600 on the recommendation of agronomist Olivier de Serres. Henri IV had come up with the idea that it would be better to manufacture silk in France than import it at an exorbitant price. The rise of the silkworm nurseries was underway.

Jardin des Tuileries, terrasse des Feuillants, 1st

The cedar that crossed the Channel and arrived in a hat

Ah, jealousy, the green-eyed monster! In 1734, France did not yet have a single cedar of Lebanon, while Britain had many, following their introduction as early as 1630. Still, all was not lost: Bernard de Jussieu, a naturalist at the Jardin du Roi, crossed the Channel to secure a specimen of the sought-after variety (England being closer than Lebanon).

A weeping cedar

In the green belt that separates the 16th arrondissement from the *périphérique* beltway grows a little weeping blue Atlas cedar. Cedars are not generally known for their displays of emotion, but at the end of the 19th century, a genetic mutation in the arboretum de la Vallée-aux-Loups produced a blue cedar with a weeping posture. Today, the majestic cedar's foliage covers a ground area of 680 square meters. Its seeds produce ordinary, non-weeping cedars, but it has been possible to grow others of its kind from cuttings and grafts. The cedar in the jardin Debussy is one of its descendants.

Jardin Claude-Debussy, 16th

Arboretum of the parc de la Vallée-aux-Loups, Châtenay-Malabry

Returning home to the rue des Bernardins, he was in a hurry to plant his cedar in the Jardin du Roi, but on the way, the cracked container holding it fell apart and Jussieu had to use his hat as a makeshift plant pot for a few minutes. The story is now legendary.

Jardin des plantes, 5th (below the maze)

The oak of liberty

During the Revolution, a new tradition was born: planting a tree to symbolize newfound freedom, the Revolutionary ideal. It could either be a poplar or an oak. By the end of 1792, there were more than 60,000 in France, 200 of them in Paris. The jardin des Tuileries obviously had its own. These liberty trees were widely felled or uprooted after the Restoration, but others were later planted for the centenaries of the Revolution in 1889 and 1989. This oak of liberty planted for the bicentenary is one of the very few oaks in Paris itself. It stands apart from the garden's other trees in the middle of an allée, bracketed by two rounded stone benches.

Jardin des Tuileries, below the terrasse des Feuillants opposite 238, rue de Rivoli, 1st

A forested, deforested, and reforested wood

At the start of the 13th century, Philippe Auguste turned his eye to the bois de Vincennes and decided to declare it a royal

hunting ground. He surrounded it with a 12-kilometer wall, leaving no avenue of escape for the fallow deer, does, and stags released there. Louis XV later turned it into a public promenade, entered through one of the six gates opened in the wall. He also had many trees planted. Unhappily, after the

Revolution, it became a military exercise ground. The army cleared 166 hectares and constructed a firing range, a cartridge depot, and barracks. However, the wind of history changed again in 1860 when the

wood was conceded to the City of Paris by Napoleon III and became the eastern counterpart of the bois de Boulogne. Only two hardy specimens from the first wave of planting carried out under Louis XV around 1731 remain by the lac des Minimes. We do not know by what miracle the copper beech (near the red houses) and sessile oak (surrounded by benches) escaped the post-Revolutionary leveling.

Bois de Vincennes, route du Grand-Prieur et route Circulaire, 12th

Ten arms to hold you

This oriental plane tree planted in 1814 is not only two centuries old, it has the most massive trunk of any tree in Paris. It is no less than 7 meters around and at least five people are needed to hug it fully.

Parc Monceau, 8th

Broken records

Head in the clouds

The tallest tree in Paris (including its two woods) stands on the city's broadest avenue. Where else? It is a hybrid plane tree that rises to 45 meters. Its top overlooks the surrounding buildings although they are six stories high. Even so, its record is slightly overshadowed by the fact that the neighboring trees are almost the same height.

Facing 31, avenue Foch, 16th

The elder on crutches

Life is not easy for a tree in Paris: little soil, scarce water, a great deal of pollution, and many enemies (destructive insects, dog urine, car scrapes, graffiti carvings, and so on). The life expectancy of the average tree is 80 to 100 years, half that of its rural counterparts. Given that, we can only admire the false acacia planted in 1602, the oldest of any category, which still produces masses of blossom. A coat of ivy seems to protect it. Two concrete crutches hold up its trunk, which has itself been reinforced with injected concrete.

Square Viviani, 5th

The iconoclasts

The maple in its dacha

"I was here first, I'm not going anywhere." That more or less sums up the story of the maple that casually thrusts through the roof of the orthodox chapel of Saint-Séraphin-de-Sarov, rubbing shoulders with its blue onion dome. The place of worship was built in 1933 on the site of a shed and a garden with two trees. It was decided to spare the trees and build the wooden chapel around them because Saint Séraphin (or Seraphim) was a hermit monk who lived in the forest, communing with nature. One of the trees died (its trunk remains near the altar) but the other is still flourishing.

91, rue Lecourbe, 15th (at the back of the 2nd courtyard)

Mauve cascades

Dreary in winter, wisteria blooms with splendid mauve flowers in the spring. They run over walls, climb across railings, and bring a special fragrance to the sidewalk. Three specimens of Parisian wisteria are particularly impressive. One near the Jardin des plantes is well over a hundred years old and has taken over the facade of an entire building, even invading its roof. Another, smaller, but more floral creeper embellishes the front of the Vieux Paris restaurant on the île de la Cité. Finally, the one on the rue Ricault climbs 7 meters up a building, totally concealing some of its balconies.

14, rue Cuvier, 5th
7-9, rue Ricaut, 13th

26, rue Chanoinesse, 4th

A very thirsty ash

If you stand on the corner of the rue Amelot and rue Oberkampf, near the Vélib' public bicycle depot, you can see an ash that seems to be rising out of a brasserie called Le Centenaire (nothing to do with the age of the tree: the bistro was founded a hundred years after the Revolution). Sadly, your wonder fades as you walk down the rue Amelot.

Corner of rue Amelot and rue Oberkampf, 11th

A premonitory tree

Lying uprooted on the ground is a 30-meter oak, its trunk desiccated and rugged. Is it a victim of the great storm of 1999, forgotten by the city's arborists? No, it is actually a patinated bronze cast entitled L'Arbre des Voyelles (*The Tree of Vowels*). Ironically, the government commissioned the work from the artiste Giuseppe Penone in 1999—just before the storm.

Jardin des Tuileries, 1st (near the terrasse du Bord-de-l'Eau)

6 The Quasimodo tour

If Quasimodo, the Hunchback of Notre Dame, suddenly found himself flung forward in time to the present day, he would struggle to recognize Paris. Long ago, its medieval houses of timber and cob were burned or reduced to rubble under the pickaxes of demolition crews. Only fortified or religious structures remain, built to resist the whips and scorns of time, and the slings and arrows of invaders. The Conciergerie, Notre-Dame, and Sainte-Chapelle are, of course, prime examples. So let us meet our Quasimodo on the île de la Cité and take him to visit the Right Bank, which also has some fine relics.

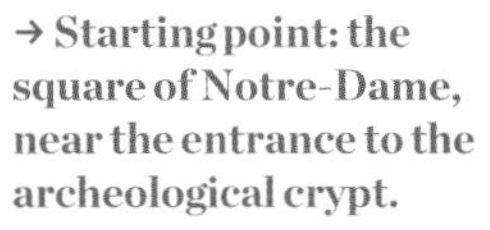

→ Starting point: the square of Notre-Dame, near the entrance to the archeological crypt.

Vanished chapels

Opposite you is Notre-Dame, whose construction began in 1163 and ended nearly two centuries later. Its original surroundings were nothing like this huge plaza. The square was very small in those days (one-sixth the size it is now) so as to heighten the cathedral's majesty. Notre-Dame was reached through a labyrinth of alleys lined with chapels and timber-framed houses. Gradually, the cathedral appeared. The visitor would first see the magnificent rose window and then the entire overpowering,

intimidating monument. When it was restored by Viollet-le-Duc in the 19th century, the decision was taken to demolish all the houses, shops, and chapels in front of it to provide a perspective and open up the view of the building. It was an unfortunate choice. Subsequently, Notre-Dame was said to look like "a huge elephant lost in the middle of the desert." Today, lines of ochre flagstones on the ground mark the locations of former alleys and 17 chapels, and provide a plan of the cathédrale Saint-Étienne that preceded Notre-Dame. The names of the chapels are engraved on the paving: Le Gros Tournoy, L'Agnus Dei, La Marguerite, la Croix-de-Fer...

→ Take the rue d'Arcole, turn right onto the rue Chanoinesse, and then immediately left on the rue de la Colombe.

A dove of legend

On the ground outside no. 4, a double row of paving stones shows the location and thickness of the ancient Gallo-Roman fortifications (*see p. 39*). The street's name—*colombe* (dove)—is a reminder of a 13th-century legend: a male dove is said to have come to the aid of his mate who was buried under the ruins of a house. He saved her life by bringing her seed and water on a wisp of straw. The story is that this ingenious conjugal rescue touched the hearts of the local population. Above the door of no. 4 and at the corner of the rue des Ursins, two bas-reliefs reflect the tale.

→ Turn right and continue along the quai aux Fleurs.

Abélard and Héloïse

On the site now occupied by no. 9 lived Canon Fulbert, the landlord of Abélard and uncle of Héloïse, the Romeo and Juliet of Paris. The star-crossed lovers are commemorated by medallions on the door and facade.

→ Walk over the passerelle Saint-Louis, take the rue Joaquim-du-Bellay, cross the pont Louis-Philippe, and continue until the end of the rue du Pont-Louis-Philippe. Turn right on the rue François-Miron.

Houses of the Reaper and the Sheep

Records of these high houses (Maisons du Faucheur et du Mouton) with their timbered walls date back to the start of the 15th century. In their original state, they could be 14th-century; they have been adapted a number of times. No. 13 originally had a projecting gable, which, like all the others in Paris, was removed by royal decree in the 17th century since it was feared they might collapse. In 1607, again like many others, the two houses were plastered to reduce the risk of fire. Finally, they were radically redesigned when they were restored in 1967.

→ Take the rue Cloche-Perce, cross the rue de Rivoli, turn left on the rue du Roi-de-Sicile, and keep going straight until you reach 24, rue des Archives.

Cloître des Billettes

The cloister of the *couvent* (convent or, in this case, monastery) of Carmes-Billettes is the only surviving medieval cloister in Paris. It is not large, but very beautiful with its polygonal pillars and keystones finely sculpted in an extravagant style.

→ Back in the rue des Archives, turn right on the rue Sainte-Croix-de-la-Bretonnerie and then left on the rue Vieille-du-Temple until you come to the rue des Francs-Bourgeois.

The turret of the hôtel Hérouet

The elegant projecting corner turret with its pepperbox roof belongs to the town house of Jean Hérouet, treasurer of France at the beginning of the 16th century. Seriously damaged by a bomb on August 25, 1944, the building was rather sloppily restored.

The turret is its finest relic.

→ Head up the rue des Francs-Bourgeois in the direction of traffic for a few dozen meters.

Impasse des Arbalétriers

This deliciously medieval, narrow, dead-end lane was once an alley leading to a training ground for crossbowmen (*arbalétriers*) outside the fortifications at the foot of Philippe Auguste's city wall. Two homes with

overhanging second floors dating back to 1620 stand on either side of it.

→ Go back the way you came and head down the rue des Francs-Bourgeois in the opposite direction to the traffic, and then the rue Rambuteau. Turn right on the rue du Temple and then left on the rue de Montmorency until you reach no. 51.

Maison du Grand-Pignon

This squat construction, which is also referred to as the *auberge* (inn) *de Nicolas Flamel* is, to our knowledge, the oldest building in Paris. Built in 1407, it belonged the writer and alchemist Nicolas Flamel and his wife Pernelle. The couple were well-known philanthropists. They took in workers for a modest but rather unusual rent: the daily recital of two prayers (a Paternoster and an Ave Maria) for the dead. An inscription on the facade written in Old French bears witness to this requirement.

→ Continue on the rue de Montmorency, straight down rue du Bourg-l'Abbé and then, after the boulevard de Sébastopol, keep going along the passage du Bourg-l'Abbé and the passage du Grand-Cerf. Take the rue Tiquetonne on the left, then turn left again on the rue Française. Once you are on the rue Étienne-Marcel, make your way to the tour de Jean-Sans-Peur.

Tour de Jean-Sans-Peur

The only completely intact example of Parisian fortified civil architecture dating back to the Middle Ages, this tower is the last remnant of the hôtel de Bourgogne, built by Jean-Sans-Peur (John-without-Fear). As his name fails to suggest, Jean took great precautions over his personal safety after ordering the assassination of his cousin and enemy Louis d'Orléans in 1407. A visit holds some wonderful surprises: a winding stair whose crowning vault is a splendid piece of stone lacework and sophisticated chambers equipped with comfortable pit privies.

→ When you reach Étienne-Marcel Métro station, head along the rue Pierre-Lescot to the junction with the rue de la Grande-Truanderie.

Cour des Miracles

The name of the rue de la Grande-Truanderie (Great Scam) refers to one of the Paris's 12 *cours des Miracles*, so called because when the most severely crippled beggars returned there at the end of each working day, they suddenly found themselves cured, lively, and nimble. Each had their specialty: the *francs-mitoux* pretended to faint at street corners, the *piètres* hauled themselves about on crutches, the *coquillards* claimed to be pilgrims in need, the *sabouleux* were phony paralytics or epileptics, the *rifodés* crawled on deformed limbs, the *mercandiers* affected to be war victims, and so on. They had laws, a language, and a leader called Le Ragot (today, slang for gossip), who was succeeded during the reign of François I by Le Grand Coësre. Every night, the beggars gave their chief a percentage of their gains and then spent the rest on a feast, since their law required them to keep nothing for the next day, but eat, drink, and be merry until all their money was gone. Towns within the town, the cours des Miracles had as many as 40,000 inhabitants in 1560. The Police Lieutenant La Reynie cleared them in 1667.

7 Springs eternal

From the Middle Ages to the 19th century, Parisians drank water from the Seine even though the contents of the city's sewers poured directly into the river. The alternative to this dubious supply was well water, which could also be foul. Paris is located at the center of a geological basin with impermeable strata at various depths (4 or 5 meters down in lower areas and 6 or 7 where the ground is higher), so many wells were sunk. Their water was generally better than the river's, but not necessarily clean (it was sometimes polluted by animal carcasses, domestic waste, cesspits, etc.).

Since Ménilmontant and Belleville were perched on hills, their villagers were fortunate enough to have local springs, which were channeled over aqueducts at the end of the 12th century to private and public drinking fountains on the Right Bank. Paris had barely 17 public drinking fountains on the eve of the 15th century, but today it has 230—some modest, some monumental. Most were built during the Second Empire when the capital was supplied with copious clean water by Haussmann's radical redesign of the city. Together with engineer Eugène Belgrand, director of the service des Eaux, Haussmann created a state-of-the-art system based on the separate sourcing of spring water for domestic supply, and river water for public use (fountains, fire plugs, street cleaning, etc.). The city's drinking fountains are familiar objects to Parisians, but some of them have highly distinctive designs.

Avenue d'Ivry, 13th *(see p. 76)*

A sinister cross

Installed in 1529, the fontaine de la Croix-du-Trahoir was the scene of many public punishments and executions—not only of mere run-of-the-mill felons. Counterfeiters were boiled there, while indiscreet servants had their ears sliced off (according to records, this continued until 1739). A wheel (on which the condemned were "broken") and a gallows (*arbre sec* or dry tree) also served their dreadful purpose as passers-by looked on. Next to them was a cross where prisoners could kneel to say their final prayers. A few butchers and fruit and vegetable sellers laid out their produce on the fountain's steps.

Corner of rue Saint-Honoré and rue de l'Arbre-Sec, 1st

Heads and tails

Medici on one side, Leda on the other: the jardin du Luxembourg has a two-faced fountain. On one side is the fontaine Médicis, whose majestic 50-meter-long basin is lined with urns. In her cave, the nymph Galatea lolls in the arms of the shepherd Acis under the raging eye of Polyphemus. In 1856, the fontaine de Léda was installed behind it, on the junction of the rue de Vaugirard, rue Saint-Placide, and rue du Regard. It had to be removed to open up the rue de Rennes.

Jardin du Luxembourg, 6th

An F in Natural Science

The main feature of the fontaine Cuvier is a monumental group in bronze by Jean-Jacques Feuchère. Made in 1840, it shows an allegory of Natural History seated on the flank of a lion. At its feet frolic various amphibious creatures: crocodiles, otters, and seals sculpted by Pierre Pomateau. Unfortunately, the artist does not seem to have been a naturalist by nature and must never have examined a crocodile in his life. Who has ever seen the reptile rotate its neck around 90 degrees, a posture physically impossible for the great predator?

Corner of rue Cuvier and rue Linné, 5th

A man, not a monarch

The fontaine Molière (1844) was the first monument commemorating a man who was not a sovereign. It stands near the house where the actor and playwright died (40, rue de Richelieu). Two allegories attend his statue: La Comédie sérieuse and La Comédie plaisante, each holding a parchment engraved with the titles of Molière's works.

Place Mireille, 1st

Regard des Religieux de Saint-Martin. 42, rue des Cascades, 20th

The regards of Belleville

Many streams flowed over the impermeable clay soil of Belleville hill. The monks of Saint-Martin-des-Champs kept vines there and, as early as the 12th century, they decided to channel the streams to tanks connected to an aqueduct. It supplied their priory, which was located on the site of today's Conservatoire des Arts et Métiers (3rd). The complex network was equipped with *regards*: small stone edifices from which the channeling could be examined. Provosts (merchants and magistrates) were responsible for inspecting the channels one by one every year. They visited every *regard*, checked the water's purity, tasted it, and made sure that no locals had set up their own personal unofficial branch supplies. Only eight of the 18 remaining *regards* are visible. The others are concealed or covered by buildings. The most accessible are the *regards* de la Lanterne, des Messiers, de la Roquette, and des Religieux de Saint-Martin. The last three line the rue des Cascades (at nos. 17, 41, and 42).

Regard de la Lanterr. 213, rue de Belleville, 20

Local street names offer a reminder of the former rivers and streams of Belleville and Ménilmontant (20th): rues des Cascades (waterfalls), de la Mare (pond), des Rigoles (rills), de la Duée (a gushing stream), de la Cour-des-Noues (a *noue* is a brook) and so on.

Place Paul-Verlaine, 13th

Ferruginous water

In the 1830s, technological progress enabled the sinking of half a dozen artesian wells in Paris. The work involved boring deep through the subsoil to the Albien water table about 600 meters down. The idea was to supply Parisians with pure water, slightly rich in iron. The first shaft was sunk at Grenelle (1841) and then it was Passy's turn (1861); its well was to irrigate the bois de Boulogne and fill its lakes. In 1866, work began on another at la Butte-aux-Cailles to provide a water supply for the newly annexed neighborhood. The surplus was to be used to feed the Bièvre river, which often dried up in the summer heat. The drilling work ran into many problems, however, and the well was only opened in 1903. Meanwhile, local buildings had been equipped with piped running water and the Bièvre partially built over. To use the 6,000 cubic meters produced daily, public baths were inaugurated in 1924. Showering was compulsory on entry and swimming lessons were available (the pool is still open today). Nothing remains of the Grenelle well, but those at Passy and la Butte-aux-Cailles continue to supply lukewarm ferruginous water.

Square Lamartine, 16th

The best of intentions

In 1895, the builders of the gare de Port-Royal were thoughtful enough to cater to the many expectant mothers who would be using the station to get to and from the new maternity unit of the Baudelocque clinic, the second faculty of obstetrics in Paris, opened in 1890. A large recess was opened up on the platform with a cast-iron drinking fountain in its center. However, the pregnant women's thirst was not slaked for long. The water quality apparently deteriorated over the years, given the notice in red that warns "Water dangerous to drink." Today, the drinking fountain has run dry.

RER Port-Royal station, on the platform direction Châtelet, 14th

A soda fountain

Opened in September 2010, one public drinking fountain dispenses sparkling water. No miraculous spring supplies it, though: the carbon-dioxide gas is added artificially (inside the shed) to ordinary precooled Paris tap water to make it sparkle. The aim of the service is to encourage Parisians to drink water from the fountain instead of less ecologically-friendly bottled water.

Jardin de Reuilly, 12th

Place Stravinsky, 4th

The wackiest water feature

The fontaine Stravinsky (aka fontaine des Automates) leaves nobody indifferent. In fact, that is precisely its point. It pays tribute to the Russian composer Igor Stravinsky, who caused a scandal himself on the first night of his "Rite of Spring" at the théâtre des Champs-Élysées on May 29, 1913. With its avant-garde rhythms and inflammatory choreography, the work outraged the critics of the day, who called it "The Massacre of Spring." In the fountain, everything shifts, twirls and splashes. The 16 creations moved by the water were dreamt up in 1983 by Jean Tinguely and Niki de Saint-Phalle, who were partners in life and sometimes in commissions. She created the opulent, colorful, papier-mâché-style polyester sculptures, while he designed the whimsical machinery. Each part refers to one of Stravinsky's scores: the key of G, the nightingale, the firebird, the elephant playing the clown and waving his trunk, the snakes nestling in a coil, the red heart of love turning in circles...

Also see The Dance of the Emerging Spring (p. 146).

Wallace fountains

The Prussian siege of Paris in 1871 left the citizens drained and literally plagued by thirst. Many of the city's aqueducts had been destroyed and drinking water had become scarce and expensive—dearer than wine, in fact—so citizens were tempted, especially the poorest, to simply get drunk. Fortunately, Sir Richard Wallace, a rich Francophile heir and owner of the Château de Bagatelle in the Bois de Boulogne, provided Parisians with 50 drinking fountains. He designed the models himself and had them made in cast iron, which was solid and suited to mass production. The parts were cast by the Société anonyme des hauts-fourneaux (Blast Furnace Corporation) of the Val-d'Osne. When the first fountain was opened on the boulevard de La Villette in 1871, there was much pushing and shoving: everybody wanted to taste the water from this *brasserie des quatre femmes* (it was decorated with four caryatids). The project was an immediate and lasting success. In 1876, passers-by in certain neighborhoods were still complaining about having to stand in line for a good five minutes to get their cup of water. Indeed, the fontaines Wallace were originally equipped with tin cups secured by a chain, but they were removed in 1952 for reasons of hygiene.

Four models of fontaines Wallace can still be found in the public places of Paris: "large," "small-column," "wall-fitting," and "hydrant" drinking fountains.

Métro Sèvres-Lecourbe, 15th

Grand modèle

This design is 2.71 meters high and very distinctive with its scaled dome supported by four caryatids, each one different (eyes open or closed, the position of the knee, the draping of the tunic). They symbolize Kindness, Sobriety, Charity, and Simplicity. Paris has 108 models of this type.

Rue Alain-Chartier, 15th. Two examples of Wallace fountains (a small and a large model) within a few meters of each other.

Small-column model

This kind is less widely known and for a good reason: there are only two left. On this smaller model (2.5 meters), the nymphs were replaced by narrow pillars to reduce manufacturing costs.

Corner of rue de Rémusat and rue Mirabeau, 16th

Below: **Place Tristan-Bernard, 17th**

Facing 59, rue Geoffroy-Saint-Hilaire, 5th

Wall-fitting model

Only one wall-fitting model remains, in the rue Geoffroy-Saint-Hilaire. It has a shell-shaped basin decorated with tritons. On its base is the mark of the foundry in the Val-d'Osne. In fact, these drinking fountains were so successful that competitor foundries moved into the market and produced copies.

Hydrant model

At the entrance of garden squares, 21 hydrant drinking fountains with a pushbutton faucet quench the thirst of passers-by. They bear the arms of Paris (except for a few exceptions). The ones in the place des Invalides and the jardin de Reuilly, for instance, have blank sides.

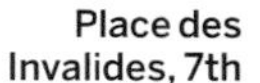
Place des Invalides, 7th

Color-coded

When Richard Wallace announced his decision to donate the drinking fountains to the City of Paris, the authorities accepted the gift gratefully, but insisted on the color: they had to be dark green to fit in unobtrusively and harmoniously with the vegetation of the garden squares that were appearing everywhere at the time. So Parisians got used to seeing them in that shade. What a surprise it was, then, when they suddenly came across a firetruck-red, mailbox-yellow, or shocking-pink Wallace! The daring initiative was launched by the local authority of the 13th arrondissement in 2011. Three models were installed in colors directly related to their location: red in the heart of the East Asian quarter and wheat yellow in the district where the great mills stood. However, the pink one not far from the French National Library is something of an enigma. Is it a nod to the *bibliothèque rose* collection of children's books... or even to erotic literature, which is associated with the color pink in France? In 2014, a Smurf-blue newcomer joined the trio.

Avenue d'Ivry, 13th ***(see p. 70)***
Esplanade Pierre-Vidal-Naquet, 13th
Rue Jean-Anouilh, 13th
Place Pierre-Riboulet, 13th

Place Jean-Anouilh, 13th

1

Wells

The number of wells in Paris reached its peak in 1875, when there were more than 30,000. From that point, the number fell as more and more buildings were connected to the water main. The Commission française pour la protection du patrimoine historique et rural is producing a remarkable inventory (a work in progress) and it puts the number at 358 today, visible above ground or concealed in private cellars. They can be filled in or not, with or without edging, round or oval, equipped with or lacking a hoist...

A complete list may be found on the site http://cfpphr.free.fr

2

3

4

1 16,rue Michel-le-Comte,3rd. An ivy-shrouded shared well in a rustic courtyard, formerly that of a 14th century inn.

2 Hôtel de Cluny (in the courtyard), 24, rue du Sommerard, 5th. The edging and metalwork came from a manor near Amboise belonging to François Sauvage, keeper of Charles VIII's silverware. The gargoyle in the form of a "wild man" was the "canting arms" (arms that form a visual pun) of François Sauvage. All were brought here in 1871.

3 The Alpine garden of the Jardin des plantes, 5th. One of the very few Parisian wells still in use, since the gardeners draw water from it to water the plants. Its hoist (out of order) is hidden by a clematis bush.

Water pumps

In neighborhoods where the water table was less than 10 meters down (Marais, Temple), pumps were in general use at the end of the 16th century. They were more practical than using a bucket and hoist to haul up water from a well. Water pumps supplied drinking-water fountains (there were 2,000 of them circa 1880). Most were in the courtyards of buildings for the use of the residents, but they were also found in streets and squares. The supply of running water to the higher floors of buildings at the start of the 20th century steadily made them obsolete. They were massively destroyed during the First and then the Second World War so their metal (the cast-iron mechanisms and copper housings) could be recycled. No Parisian pump has survived in working condition, but 83 "relics" (more or less intact and with or without handles) remain in a few courtyards and backyards.

A complete list may be found at http://cfpphr.free.fr

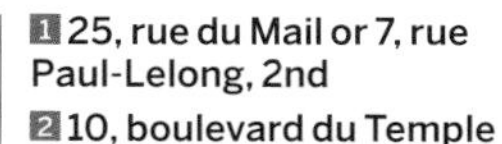

1 25, rue du Mail or 7, rue Paul-Lelong, 2nd

2 10, boulevard du Temple (in the courtyard), 11th

3 47, rue Saint-André-des-Arts, 6th

Also:
58, rue du Faubourg-Poissonnière, 10th
Square du Cardinal-Verdier, 15th

4 25 and 27, rue Dussoubs, 2nd. Set in the street facade, two small masonry wells. One of them still has its wooden hoist.

5 Square Viviani, 5th. A half-moon well from the former House of Lions.

6 Cour de Rohan, 6th. This one has an iron hoist. Its edge is decorated with a gargoyle. Since the ground has been raised by a meter, the gargoyle is now flush with it.

Also
35, rue de Picpus, 11th

1

5

6

2

3

8 Urban signage

The architecture of a building or the decoration of a facade are not the only surprises in store when you take the trouble to look around as you wander through Paris. Street nameplates also have a lot to say about the city's tumultuous history, and the design of the building numbers can be very revealing, too. A little practice and you will catch yourself looking for and nodding familiarly at the city's enameled plaques with their old-fashioned air.

14, rue Montcalm, 18th
(see p. 87)

Street-name plaques

Rue Poulletier (4th) was originally named Poultier for a businessman, an associate of Christophe Marie, real-estate developer of the île Saint-Louis.

Stone tablets

In 1729, a decree made it compulsory for buildings to display a stone tablet engraved with the street name… but not just any old way: the letters had to be two and a half inches high with their grooves darkened, and the tablet had to be bordered by a channel that formed a frame. Any plaques you may see that fit this description date back to that time.

Former names

Paris streets have often changed their names. Two periods were particularly eventful: the Revolution and the annexation of 1860. During the Revolution, any mention of kings or saints was frowned on. Those unfortunate plaques that broke the rule were systematically defaced (*see the following page*). The annexation led to another general upheaval. When Paris absorbed its neighboring villages, it found itself with 10 rues de l'Église, five grand-rues, etc. Today, streets can be renamed in honor of an illustrious figure or simply out of common decency: who would want to live in the rue du Poil-au-Con, now the rue du Pélican? In all these cases, every single nameplate is supposed to be changed. If not, things can get very confusing. Yet on occasion, we see streets with two different names: the old one and the new one. Mischief or carelessness on the part of city workers? No, just a (commendable) desire to preserve a piece of historically or aesthetically remarkable signage.

Also

Corner of rue Legendre and rue Nollet, formerly rues Saint-Louis and d'Orléans (17th).

Left to right

Rue de la Mortellerie became rue de l'Hôtel-de Ville (4th) —a plaque can be seen at no. 95.

Rue Vieille-du-Temple (4th) was once called Vieille rue du Temple.

Voltaire's injunction

Dead-end streets were once called *culs-de-sac* (or bag-asses) until the father of Candide intervened. "I do not see that a street resembles either an ass or a bag. I would ask you to use the word *impasse*, which is noble, sonorous, intelligent and necessary," Voltaire resoundingly demanded in 1760. His wishes were respected, but a few cul-de-sac signs slipped through the net. They can be seen next to newer *Impasse* plaques.

Top to bottom

The cul-de-sac du Bœuf (4th) was never turned into an impasse. Impasse de l'Hôtel- d'Argenson, 4th

Also

Impasse de la Poissonnerie, 4th
Impasse Élise-Drivon (formerly de la Sallembrière), 5th

Revolutionary removal

On August 14, 1792, the Convention nationale passed a decree ordering "the elimination of signs of feudalism and superstition." Consequently, the symbols of royalty (above all the fleur-de-lys) were removed from public monuments and the word "Saint" from street signs, including the underground signs in quarries! Kings and saints were two sides of the enemy coin, since kings were supposedly God's representatives on Earth. Traces of the subsequent statutory chiseling remain today. Later, as a sign of reconciliation, Bonaparte allowed saints' names to be restored in April 1802. The stonecutters re-engraved the S's and T's where they had been removed, although they did miss some signs, as in the rue Saint-Séverin (5th) on the corner of the impasse Élise-Drivon.

1 Rue Saint-Jacques, in a subterranean passage, 5th

2 Rue Saint-André-des Arts, 6th

3 Rue Saint-Martin, at the corner of rue de la Verrerie, 4th

4 Rue Saint-Séverin, 5th

Districts and sections

In 1789, Paris was divided into 60 districts, which were in turn replaced by 48 sections in 1790. Then the law of October 11, 1795 created 12 arrondissements, each of which consisted of four of the former sections. Certain street signs engraved in stone still show the number of the district or section.

Rue du Vide-Gousset, 2nd . Formerly part of the Le Mail section.

Survivors

Few royal symbols escaped the carnage. The two fleurs-de-lys engraved at the corner of the rue Bailleul and the rue de l'Arbre-Sec were miraculously spared. They can be seen above the "SG" mark, which was made when the streets were inventoried on the orders of the king in the 18th century. At the corner of the place de la Concorde and the rue Boissy-d'Anglas on the facade of the hôtel Crillon, a protective glass sheet covers a sign marked "Place de Louis XVI," the name of the place de la Concorde from 1826 to 1828. It is one of the last surviving painted signs dating back to the Restoration.

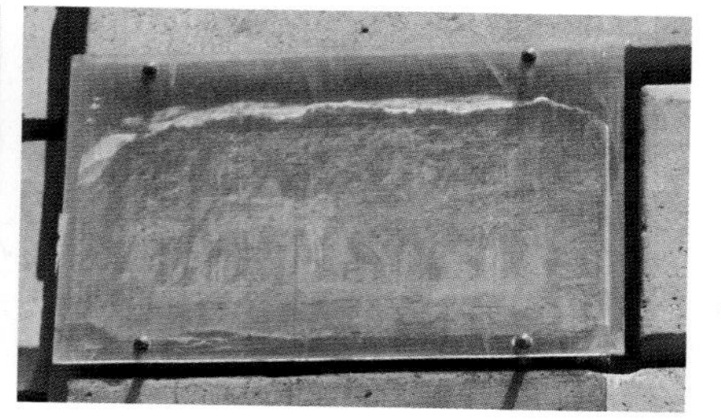

Left to right

Corner of rue Bailleul and rue de l'Arbre-Sec, 1st
Corner of place de la Concorde and rue Boissy-d'Angla, 8th

A touch of fancy

Some signs have a rather more unconventional appearance then others. Dreamt up by the architect or owner, they are added to the statutory sign and can mainly be found in the more elegant neighborhoods of Paris. When the avenue Mercedes became the avenue du Colonel-Bonnet, nobody had the heart to remove its delightful street sign in blue and gold mosaic. The rue Agar was almost completely the work of Hector Guimard, who lavished attention on every detail, including the street sign, whose design reflects his distinctive style. Then the sign on the front of the Paris-Drouot post office is, as usual, written in white against a blue background, but around it... could that be the sun of Provence?

22, rue de Provence, 9th

Lava-rock, sheet-metal and... wooden signs

In 1823, engraved stone tablets were replaced by iron signs with white letters against a black background and then, in 1844, by enameled Volvic lava-rock tablets with white letters against a blue background. A decree of 1876 ordered the addition of the number of the arrondissement above the street name. Later, in 1932, the model changed again: the dark blue became lighter, the framing

28, rue Saint-Paul, 4th. Plaque of Volvic lava-rock.

bronze-green and black-and-white shadow effects and corner roses were added to the signs, now made of enameled sheet metal. Very understandably, the authorities never suggested wooden signs, so the presence of one in the Marais district comes as a surprise. The much-weathered panel is clearly old, since it is set in the stonework of the wall.

The battle between old and new

Before computers existed, street signs were virtually craft-designed. Their makers made every effort to achieve a harmonious balance between the size of the sign and the length of the name. However, today's standardized models are computer-designed, produced by a machine with no inkling of aesthetics. Legibility does not seem to be a priority either, as is shown by the sign on the corner of the rue du Faubourg-Montmartre and rue de Châteaudun, which cannot be read from the opposite sidewalk. The letters seem to have been scrunched up to fit them into the blue box. The multisyllabic rue Notre-Dame-de-Recouvrance has suffered the same fate. Shortage of space is clearly a very Parisian issue.

Typos set in stone

Stonecutters do a tough job that demands skill, precision, and steadiness. The one responsible for the sign on the corner of the quai des Grands-Augustins and the rue Séguier must have been exhausted when he engraved the final N back to front. Then the man who worked on the sign in the rue Jean-Beausire got his math wrong when calculating the space available and was forced to place the final E of Beausire above the R. Finally, the craftsman given the task of restoring the abbreviation of "Saints" on the sign of the rue des Saints-Pères would not have won any spelling bees: he left the word in the singular.

124, avenue Victor-Hugo, 16th

"Mr. Hugo, in his avenue"

The great writer was the only person to receive mail addressed in this way; the only figure to have been "streetified" in his lifetime. Shortly after his 80th birthday, a national holiday, the avenue d'Eylau where he lived was renamed in his honor. A sign and medallion of Hugo at no. 124 remind us that he was a resident there from 1881 to 1884 (at that address, but not this building, which was demolished).

Corner of quai des Grands-Augustins and rue Séguier, 6th

Subterranean typos

Quarries are not exempt from signage slipups: they have their own linguistic and typographic irregularities. There is a story behind this sign, which reads "Under the pavement…". The first four lines were cut straight and properly centered in the workshop before the sign was installed underground. By that time, though, the boulevard had been given a name, which a stonecutter added lopsidedly. Stonecutters were often illiterate and copied writing letter by letter. If they forgot one, their supervisor corrected the sign. There are plenty of these blunders to be found underground. One of the most impressive is a figure: the date "1874" anagrammatically given as "8174"!

A lack of imagination?

Voie AA/12… A curious name for a pedestrian alley. It sounds more like the serial number of an asteroid. Yet surprising as it may seem, the municipal authorities have never gotten around to renaming this passage 60 meters long and 6 wide, which links the avenue Daumesnil and the rue de Charenton. When a thoroughfare is created but no name immediately suggests itself, the councilors assign it a code name

made up of one or two letters, a forward slash and an arrondissement number. This rule is often applied to identify périphérique beltway entry and exit ramps, but is extremely rare within the city itself.

Voie AA/12, 12th

Street numbers

A color code to find your bearings

Until the 18th century, houses were not numbered; street signs were the only guides. Then in 1779, a numbering system was introduced. It was very different to the one used today. The numbers painted on houses went up one side of the street and then back down the other. Adjoining alleys and dead-end streets were numbered as if their houses were in the main street. In 1805, the system was entirely revised by Prefect Frochot, who placed odd and even numbers opposite each other, beginning with the end nearest the Seine or starting upstream of the river for thoroughfares parallel to it.

2 and 4, place de la Concorde, 8th

People struggled to master the new system. To help them, the numbers of streets parallel to the river were painted red against an ochre background, and those of perpendicular streets in black with the same ochre background. Examples of this color code still survive, with an anomaly in the place de la Concorde where the numbers are white instead of black.

Also
167, rue Saint- Jacques, 5th
2, rue des Saints-Pères, 7th
6, 6 bis, and 8, place de la Concorde, 8th

2, rue Garancière, 6th

1096 rue Garancière

How can there be such a large number in such a short street? Half-erased, it dates back to the Revolutionary period when streets were numbered by district (*see p. 80*). In this system, numbers could quickly rise very high indeed, for instance 1096, the only one of its kind, which can be found on the église Saint-Sulpice.

The ghost of the Bièvre

In the days when the River Bièvre still flowed above ground, the rue Guyton-de-Morveau ran at a right angle from its bank. Once the Bièvre was covered, the street was extended and gained 10 new numbers over the river. The old numbering system (15 and 19) can still be seen at nos. 25 and 29. So today's no. 11 was the old no. 1.

25 and 29, rue Guytonde-Morveau, 13th

82, rue Blanche, 9th

Custom numbers

Numbers painted in oils were soon erased by the elements, so they were replaced by blue enameled signs in 1847. Many numbers engraved in the stone or cut in relief have survived, though. Individuals could express their personal tastes and the City had no issue with the results as long as they were legible. Sometimes, streets were so narrow that they needed sideways-facing numbers on brackets —for instance in the impasse Saint-Denis. However, others are to be found in the rue d'Anjou and the rue des Mathurins, which are reasonably wide.

7, impasse Saint-Denis, 2nd

Also
16, rue de Tolbiac, 13th
52, rue de l'Hôtel-de-Ville, 4th
11 et 13, rue des Filles-du-Calvaire, 3rd
53, rue des Mathurins, 9th
170, rue de la Convention, 15th

Innumerate thoroughfares

Parisian streets sometimes move in very mysterious ways. The best-known example is the rue de Rennes, which should have started by the Seine once the Left Bank was remodeled, but began at Saint-Germain-des-Prés. So it starts at numbers 41 and 44, the first numbers that were originally reserved. Similarly, on the rue

Saint-Jacques, the numbering jumps from 33 to 55 because of the gap opened by the boulevard Saint-Germain. The same goes for the rue d'Anjou, which leaps without warning from 39 to 51. Another eccentricity: 34, rue Sainte-Marthe is suddenly followed by 26, rue du Chalet. Then the rue des Vinaigriers begins at 20 and 23 because the first section became the rue Jean-Poulmarch. Proof of this takes the form of superimposed signs at the corner of the rue de Lancry. At 14, impasse Saint-Denis, there is a number… but no door. 110, rue Vieille-du-Temple also displays the engraved number 126. On the rue Saint-Dominique and the rue de Bretagne, it was thought wiser to mention both the new and old numbers.

Opposite, top to bottom

5, rue Saint-Dominique, 7th
44, rue de Bretagne, 3rd

Also

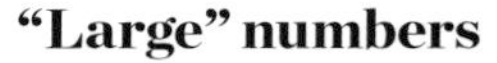

41 and 44, rue de Rennes, 6th
33 and 55, rue Saint-Jacques, 5th
39 and 51, rue d'Anjou, 8th
34, rue Sainte-Marthe and 26, rue du Chalet, 10th
20 and 23, rue des Vinaigriers, 10th
14, impasse Saint-Denis, 2nd
110, rue Vieille-du Temple, 3rd

Rue du Faubourg-Poissonnière was almost continuously lined with "hotels of ill-repute." This one became a hotel, period.

36, rue Saint-Sulpice, 6th. This was originally a bordello. A large numberin gold and sky blue advertised the fact.

"Large" numbers

Before bordellos were prohibited by the Marthe-Richard law, they were identified by special number signs. Although administrative regulations forced the *maison closes* to remain relatively discreet, potential customers could recognize these "houses of ill-repute" from certain clues at the front: a red lamp or neon light, frosted-glass or opaque windows with Persian blinds, or a door with a mesh-covered "Judas hole"… or a "large" number above it. This could either literally be bigger in size than those on the neighboring buildings or an "aesthetically-styled" number added to the official plate.

Also

3, rue Laferrière, 9th
32, rue Ballu, 9th
47, rue du Faubourg-Poissonnière, 9th

Artists' heaven

If one goes by the names on the entry-code panel restricting access to 3, avenue Junot, Modigliani, Rodin, Renoir, Goya, Fujita, Raphael, and many other artists live at the address. Quite a hall of fame! So is the building an artists' heaven? Not as such. It is more a haven for its resident contemporary movie and theater VIPs, who came up with this subterfuge to protect their privacy.

3, avenue Junot, 18th

Archaic enameled signs

At right, from top to bottom
18, rue Mouton-Duvernet, 14th
9, rue Beautreillis, 4th

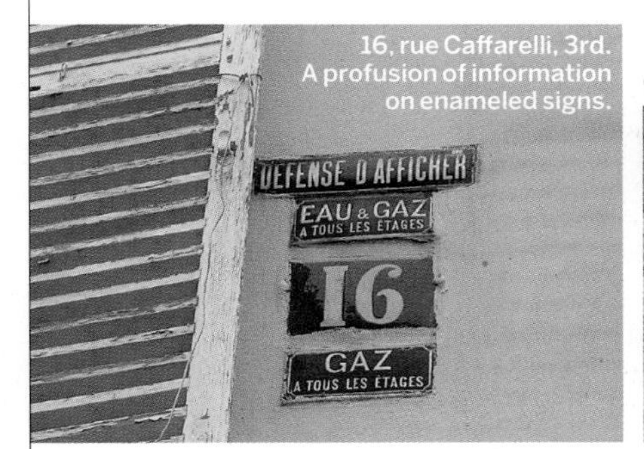

16, rue Caffarelli, 3rd. A profusion of information on enameled signs.

9, rue Notre-Dame-de-Lorette, 9th

Water and gas on every floor

Town gas was once limited to homes on the ground floor, the building lobby, and any workshops in the courtyard, but then risers were installed to supply individuals on every story. Suddenly, more and more tenement buildings were displaying signs that read "Gas on every floor" to advertise the good standing of the apartments and their comfort and modern conveniences. This initial hint of luxury attracted tenants. The same was true of water, which reached all the floors of buildings on the Right Bank in 1865 and on the Left Bank in 1875. The advent of running water was accompanied by water main drainage (which became compulsory in 1894), making both trips to a water supply in the yard, and the repellent draining of a cesspit, things of the past. "Gas on every floor" signs are very common, but those advertising water mains are less frequent. Signs for the two together are very rare. They were probably stolen to be sold, since their wording was famous well before Serge Gainsbourg immortalized it in a song.

If there were no running water on the upper floors of a building, residents had to go down to fetch it from a fountain, which was located in the courtyard or even at the bottom of the stairs, as here in passage des Deux- Pavillons, 1st.

Also
84, quai de Jemmapes, 10th
52, rue Sambre-et-Meuse, 10th
160, rue de la Croix-Nivert, 15th
8, rue Tardieu and 8, place Jean-Baptiste-Clément, 18th
17, avenue Gambetta, 20th
13, rue du Faubourg-Poissonnière, 10th
41, rue Notre-Dame-de-Lorette, 9th

Homes with every comfort

Near Pigalle, an enameled blue plate proudly advertises the fact that the building has water, gas, electricity, and even *calorifère*, a kind of central heating (a coal stove was installed in the cellar and its heat supplied to the upstairs through a network of built-in air conduits or via water pipes). Tenants in the Grenelle neighborhood were proud to have electricity, while some lucky souls in the 11th had a supply of "Seine and spring water on every floor." Others in Belleville and the Marais were fortunate enough to live in a hygienic *Maison salubre*. The living standards of certain inhabitants of the Alésia district seem to have been less elevated, in their *Maison en partie meublée* (part-furnished building).

12 and 14, rue Pétion, 11th

93, rue Saint-Honoré, 1st

Comprehensive insurance

The first insurance companies were founded in the 18th century, but it was not until the start of the 19th that they really took off. Many establishments appeared and were often highly specialized, dealing with shipwrecks, loss caused by hail or epizootic diseases, and so on. One such company founded in 1838, La Seine, provided insurance covering accidents caused by horse and carriages; Le Phénix (1819) guaranteed against fire; L'Union (1828) was a life-insurance company; La Préservatrice (1864) insured against all kinds of accidents. The nameplates of these companies appeared everywhere on the buildings they insured. This was a good way to advertise and at the same time reassure potential tenants. Some of these signs were more explicit than others. For instance, who knew that a "MACL" plate, for instance, marked a Maison Assurée Contre l'Incendie (building insured against fire)? La Confiance's chosen logo was a young woman standing and leaning on a cippus (half-column) with her feet to the left, a bundle of goods and, on the right, agricultural implements.

Also

Corner of rue Pernelle and rue Saint-Martin, 4th
34, rue Étienne-Marcel, 1st. Building owned by L'Union.
7, rue Lagrange, 5th
24, rue Saint-Séverin, 5th
15, rue de Maubeuge, 9th
33, rue de Paradis, 10th
61, rue Lecourbe, 15th
15, rue Montmartre, 1st

45, rue de Richelieu, 1st

29, rue Madame, 6th. Along with the phoenix, the dragon was a much-prized logo for insurers specializing in fire.

Pont Alexandre-III, Right Bank, 8th

Warning: prohibitions!

Whether or not they remain valid, certain warnings can still bring a smile to our faces. Woe betide the careless driver who tries to turn his cab with an overloaded roof under the coach entrance of 226, rue Saint-Denis, at the risk of damaging his merchandise. And let those impudent enough to beat their rug under the pont Alexandre-III beware! Then what dreadful fate may await anyone entering the passage Barrault with a vehicle weighing more than three tons: riddled with quarry excavations, the ground could open up beneath them. Finally, the south tower of Notre-Dame carries the dire warning: "It is very expressly prohibited to write on the lead or walls, to ring the bells, to throw anything from the tops of the towers or to leave any kind of waste, on pain of a fine." This notification is displayed in two places and dates back to the building's restoration by Viollet-le-Duc in the 19th century.

Passage Barrault, 13th

226, rue Saint-Denis, 2th

Impasse du Tertre, 18th

Slow: urchins ahead

Motorists, slow down, beware of street urchins. Today, the notice to the right, installed by the Automobile Club de l'Île-de-France on the impasse du Tertre, is a source of amusement: no sane motorist would attempt to drive through the packed crowd. It reflects the former links between Montmartre and the French automobile industry. Another plaque at the corner of the rue Norvins and the place du Tertre commemorates a great achievement. On December 24, 1898, a small gasoline-powered "car" driven by its constructor, Louis Renault, managed to climb the steep rue Lepic and ended up here, panting like a winded marathon runner. Renault had just developed the vehicle, which was a Dion tricycle with an added wheel and gearbox. After Renault's triumphant achievement, orders poured in at his workshop, heralding a great industrial saga.

Top to bottom

Corner of rue de Castiglione and rue Saint-Honoré, 1st
53, rue des Francs-Bourgeois, on the door of the church of Notre-Dame-des-Blancs-Manteaux, 4th

Also
Corner of rue Norvins and place du Tertre, 18th

Suspicion abounds

Security concerns have been with us for quite a while. The first security companies that were founded at the end of the 19th century employed watchmen to patrol or stand guard at their customers' premises. Here and there, round white-enameled plaques about 10 centimeters across show that the building was under surveillance. They generally bear the name of the Société parisienne de surveillance (SPS) or Surveillance Générale BP, which both used keys as emblems.

Plugging fireplugs

Enameled plaques carrying codes once showed firefighters exactly where to find a *bouche d'incendie* (BI) or fire hydrant. The one top right, for instance, mentions a 100-millimeter diameter hydrant (there were also 150-millimeter ones) connected to the drinking-water network (a cream-colored background meant non-drinking water) via a supply conduit 150-millimeters in diameter from the Vanne river, a tributary of the Yonne. The red line shows the direction of the exact location of the hydrant (here, facing away from the plaque, 0.7 meters ahead and 2.4 meters to the right). All these old enameled plaques are steadily disappearing, removed to be sold as curios. There are also more recent, less ambiguous second-generation plaques, on which the information BI 100 or BI 150 is marked clearly top center. Firefighters can now check detailed plans with GPS in their trucks, enabling them to find hydrants more easily. In Paris, 100-millimeter hydrants are located on the same sidewalk about 100 meters apart. On the sidewalk opposite, there is the same spacing, but staggered 50 meters, so on a Paris street, there is a 100-millimeter hydrant every 50 meters to supply firetruck pumps.

9 Architectural oddities

Tilted and stepped houses, buildings that form a hollow or ridge, lopsided windows, anachronistically layered facades: sometimes the architect's rationale takes an unexpected turn and the logic escapes us.

8, rue Henri-Barbusse, 5th.
A mysterious lack of symmetry on the third floor. Is the view prettier to the west?

Something not quite right

The acacia recess

In the 19th century, a large garden by today's boulevard Raspail extended as far as the distinguished Grande-Chaumière academy of painting. The garden was itself known as the "Grande-Chaumière" and was famous for its alfresco balls and hidden spots, perfect for romantic frolics. As time passed, urban development gradually took hold and then one day, plans were announced to construct a building on a particular lot where an acacia stood. For some unknown reason, the tree was associated with Victor Hugo. We know that the writer lived close by at no. 177, but there is no reason to believe he planted the twisted tree himself. Even so, the locals were so attached to it that the owner of the land had to promise not to touch it. That explains the curious design of the house's concave facade set back from the tree. The original acacia has gone, but another tiny one has been planted in its place.

229, boulevard Raspail, 14th

©ALBERT HARLINGUE/ROGER-VIOLLET

19, rue Pierre-Demours, 17th

An eviscerated château

A street running through an opening in the ground floor of a noble building? This absurdity is the work of Samson-Nicolas Lenoir, an architect and speculator who purchased the magnificent, richly decorated château des Ternes *(see p. 101)* in 1778. Lenoir had absolutely no qualms about stripping the château of its precious furniture, dividing the grounds into a number of lots to be sold to different speculators, and gutting a section of the ground floor to make way for a passage, which was so narrow that pedestrians had to flatten themselves against a wall when a carriage passed.

Brick-à-brac

It leaps to the eye as you enter the passage des Récollets from the rue du Faubourg-Saint-Martin. On the brick building, a number of zinc-roofed cottages have sprung up, like weeds sprouting from the gaps between paving stones. The strange additions could be straight out of a graphic novel by Tardi or a Sylvain Chomet movie: *The Triplets of Belleville* or *The Illusionist*. The building's architect was Louis Bonnier (1856-1946), the same man who designed the Butte-aux-Cailles swimming baths.

18, passage des Récollets, 10th

A unique configuration

A surprise awaits strollers reaching the peak of the butte Bergeyre, a hill topped by a discreet, charming residential village totally hidden from the eyes of less curious passers-by. It was built around 1925-1930 on the ruins of a former carnival, the Folles Buttes, which entertained the public with its rides and exhibitions of curiosities until 1914. Some of the steps heading up the hillside are as steep as those in Montmartre. The houses in the rue Barrelet-de-Ricou are supported by a very high tilted wall, which forms the back of the courtyards of the buildings standing below. This massive piece of engineering was needed to shore up the foundations because of local geological faults.

Rue Barrelet-de-Ricou, 19th

15, quai de Bourbon, 4th. A lopsided window: a flaw in the fine architectural harmony of the île Saint-Louis.

An advent calendar

Imagine an advent calendar—the kind whose windows children excitedly open each day to find out what surprise they conceal. By mid-December, some of the many little shutters are open and some remain closed. The frontage of the rue Dalayrac looks very like one of these calendars with its chaotically positioned windows of various sizes—tiny, medium, or large—with half or quarter shutters Even the color of the plaster varies! The effect is startling and amusing. The other side of the building is on the passage Choiseul.

28 - 38, rue Dalayrac, 1st

Anachronisms

A mismatched layer cake

Commissioned to add extra floors to a building in 1967, the architect Paul Chemetov followed to the letter the instructions drawn up by the curators of the Monuments historiques authority: "a stone facade, vertical windows and a Mansard-style roof." The intention was to add stories to a pre-existing Haussmannian building dating back to 1904 (the construction of its upper floors had been postponed because of the First World War). Basing his plans on these specifications, he designed this startling structure. The appalled City Planning officials could do nothing to stop the project since it fully complied with the terms of the contract.

12, rue de l'Épée-de-Bois, 5th

1-3, rue des Ursins, 4th

Genuine fake medieval houses

This building in the rue des Ursins is not nearly as ancient as it looks. It is a kind of patchwork constructed in 1958 using various medieval parts (wrought-iron grilles, stained glass, ogive windows) found here and there by the architect Fernand Pouillon. The tiny door to the right of the steps is bewildering. What kind of pixie was it designed for? In the recess at no. 5, there is a remarkable "medievalized" garage door. Another hoax can be seen in the rue Volta: a house that was long thought to be the oldest in Paris. However, research conducted in 1979 revealed its true date of birth: it is another imitation commissioned by a bourgeois gentleman of Paris in 1644.

Also
3, rue Volta, 3rd

Replicated remains

An architect's folly, yes, but with a hidden purpose. Looking at these obviously bogus ruins forming the base of a contemporary building constructed in 1979 by the ED Architecte firm, passersby are reminded that it was here, in a chronologically distant chapel, that Saint Denis preached to the very

first Christians of Lutetia. As the story goes, the evangelist from the South of France came to convert the local population and stayed in the area, living in a hole in a nearby quarry pit adjoining a vast Gallo-Roman necropolis. It was here that he was arrested by the Romans and martyred *(see p. 123)*.

11 bis, rue Pierre-Nicole, 5th

Record holders

Family feuds

This tiny shop with its narrow upstairs window squeezed between two six-story buildings has won its place in the record books as the smallest house in Paris. Exactly how small is it? 1.10 meters wide and 5 meters high! It was built in part of a passage that had previously connected the rue du Château-d'Eau and the rue Faubourg-Saint-Martin. Following a quarrel over an inheritance, the owners blocked the path by constructing this diminutive house at its entrance. So cramped as to be uninhabitable, the building is used as storage space by the shop on the ground floor.

39, rue du Château-d'Eau, 10th

Buffon's gazebo

We know of Buffon the naturalist and administrator of what was once the Jardin du Roi (after the Revolution, it became the Jardin des plantes). We are less familiar with Buffon the metalworker. Very much a Renaissance man, he was fascinated by the science of metals. When he inherited a forge in the Burgundian town that bears his ancestral name, he kept it running full-time. In 1786, it was there that he ordered the manufacture of metal parts to build the gazebo that stands on a maze of a hill in "his" garden. It is actually the oldest metal structure in France. From 1786 to 1793, it sheltered an acoustic noon mark (*see p. 53*) in the form of a gong that sounded at true noon. Its hammer, a terrestrial globe that struck 12, was operated by a counterweight that was released when a magnified sunbeam burned through a hair. The hair had to be replaced each day to rearm the mechanism.

Jardin des plantes, 5th

Rue Berton, 16th

Be it ever so narrow...

The rue du Chat-qui-Pêche (5th), which is 2.5 meters wide at its most constricted point, is often said to be the narrowest street in Paris. Wrongly, because there are actually even narrower alleys: the rue du Prévôt in the Marais (1.8 meters), the rue Berton in Passy (1.5 meters), and especially the sente des Merisiers (0.87 centimeters) near the porte de Vincennes. These three thoroughfares seem even narrower because of their lengths: 104, 206 and 100 meters respectively. Passersby feel they are walking along the bottom of a ravine whose walls are closing in. The impasses Saint-Denis (1st), Élise-Drivon (5th), and Bouvart (5th), which are hardly more than an arm's length wide, are also contenders.

Rue du Chat-qui-Pêche, 5th

Abnormal accommodations

The Concorde "gatehouses"

On the perimeter of the place de la Concorde with its rumbling traffic, trenches 20 meters wide once surrounded the place itself, which was a raised octagonal esplanade. Balustrades ran along the top of these trenches, six stone bridges crossed them and at the corners were "gatehouses" with steps providing access. At the start of the 19th century, Parisians were very fond of strolling around the trenches, and those two-floor "gatehouse" homes

were greatly prized. Their top level was lit by three bull's-eye windows and a spiral stairway led down to their "garden" level. They were occupied by a sergeant of the police, an employee of the neighboring naval ministry, a justice of the peace, and a café owner. All enjoyed their little rustic paradises without asking anything of anybody and nobody questioned their right to live there. Indeed, for 30 years (from 1798 to 1828), the former place Louis XV—known as the place de la Révolution by that time—had no recognized owner. It no longer belonged to the City of Paris after the Revolution. The cadastral conundrum was finally resolved on August 20, 1828, when a law was passed to return the square and the avenue des Champs-Élysées to the City. In return, the municipality accepted the responsibility of renovating them within five years. In 1838, the architect Hittorff installed allegorical statues representing the main cities of France on the gatehouses, which were set around the square in roughly the same configuration as the cities on the map. In 1853, Napoleon III ordered the trenches to be filled. The people of Paris missed them—not as much for the ladies of negotiable virtue who had plied their trade there each night as for the refreshing cool of the greenery, which delighted amblers in the summer. Today, the stone balustrades mark the ghostly outline of the long-gone trenches. As for the gatehouses, they now house only the brooms and hoses of city employees, except for the Brest and Rouen ones, which today provide access to underground parking garages.

Place de la Concorde, 8th

A tragic past

The high gate at 40, rue Durantin opens onto a superb, long, majestic courtyard, surrounded by Restoration-period buildings reached by a dual stairway. It is known as "Jews' Yard" in memory of a raid during the Second World War, when all the

Jews living there were rounded up and taken to the Vél' d'Hiv' (Winter Velodrome) and then the camps. The yard has served as a location for many movies, notably La Rafle (*The Round Up*), directed by Roselyne Bosch (2010).

40, rue Durantin, 18th

A Paris commune

The cité Napoléon program launched in 1851 by the president, Prince Louis-Napoléon Bonaparte, was the first workers' housing project in the capital. It was built to house the employees of a new neighboring gasworks. Inspired by Charles Fourier's phalanstery, the philanthropic construction was ultramodern for its day: well-ventilated housing surrounding a courtyard at a rent of 60 to 180 francs. There were common facilities on the ground floor: a laundry with a dryer, a day-care center, a free dispensary, a bathhouse, etc. The remarkable project had its downside, though: approximately a hundred strict rules, including the closing of the gate at 10 p.m. (it was impossible to get in after that time) and a regular visit from an inspector who was responsible for keeping an eye on the tenants' morality. Because of this, the cité Napoléon (dubbed the "Rochechouart barracks") was avoided by the workers and plans to build one in every neighborhood were soon dropped. Subsequently taken over by a number of co-owners, the cité still has its water fountain, modest lean-tos, and worn wooden stairs.

58, rue de Rochechouart, 9th

Rue des Immeubles-Industriels, 11th

Honey, I'll be downstairs working

Modern ground-floor and mezzanine workshops and, above, apartments with all modern conveniences for the worker's families, all supplied with energy by a powerful, 200 horsepower steam engine under the pavement: this was the brilliant idea of locomotive constructor and real-estate developer Jean-François Cail, who cared about working-class comfort. Yet another disciple of Fourier! Cail realized the project in 1872 in the faubourg Saint-Antoine, the bastion of Parisian woodworkers. The result was a perfectly aligned set of 19 industrial buildings, their facades punctuated by slim, open, cast-iron columns. Shortly before, in 1866, Cail had already built a vaguely similar but much less ambitious project in the 10th arrondissement to provide housing for rail staff who worked at the gare du Nord. It was in a street that was later named for him.

The Gruby observatory

In 1865, Hungarian scientist David Gruby, a pioneer of medical microbiology, had a private observatory constructed on the terrace of his Montmartre building. He would spend his time observing the extreme: from the extraordinarily small (when he worked

during the day) to the enormously distant (at leisure in the evening). During the war of 1870 and the Prussian siege of Paris, Gruby loaned his observatory to the French army so that soldiers could use powerful telescopes to monitor enemy troop movements.

100, rue Lepic, 18th

Slim buildings

Vast numbers of Haussmannian buildings in Paris are square and squat, solidly seated on their foundations and tidily aligned in close ranks along the city's avenues. However, the Haussmannian genre stretches to other, frankly startling constructions: shallow or narrow buildings as sharp as a razor. Their design is bewildering. What could fit into their rooms? A single table or a bed wedged sideways? Who lives there? Maybe LPs (little persons) or ghosts, as Roger Caillois suggested in his Petit Guide du XVe arrondissement à l'usage des fantômes in 1977. The sociologist and writer had noticed that the 15th arrondissement had a fine collection of these sharp-edged buildings. A warning, though: to enjoy the full shock effect of these architectural phenomena, make sure you approach them on the appropriate sidewalk.

Ghost seeks apt.; 15th if poss.

The largest arrondissement of Paris has a wealth of these deceptive frontages. Viewed from the correct angle, they seem two-dimensional, as if hanging there unsupported. For instance, 1, rue du Laos (when you stand in front of no. 2 in the same street), 91, avenue Émile-Zola (seen from 56, rue de Lourmel), or a building in the rue Auguste-Dorchain (viewed from 55, rue de la Croix-Nivert). On the edge of the last, the words *bains-douches* (public baths) are marked vertically in capital letters almost as wide as the wall.

Also
Rue Auguste-Dorchain, 15th

1, rue du Laos, 15th
91, avenue Émile-Zola, 15th

The maze of Mouzaïa

The quartier de la Mouzaïa, a series of flower-lined dead-end streets and through-alleys, owes its beauty to the construction-stone quarries that were worked here from the 13th to the 19th centuries, down in the belly of the butte de Beauregard. The mining weakened the subsoil of the hill, hollowing it out like a Swiss cheese, so there could be no question of constructing heavy buildings on its slopes. However, the ground was just firm enough to support low houses with a garden in front and a yard behind them. They were originally homes for blue-collar workers, but are greatly sought-after today and worth astronomical sums. Paved with large flagstones, the villa Bellevue provides the most striking view of la Mouzaïa's remarkable layout with its stepped houses that seem to be clutching each other to stop themselves sliding down the slope.

Villa Bellevue, 19th

Pointe Trigano

Already in 1900, this narrow building at the prow of the Sentier district fascinated Eugène Atget, who developed a portrait of it in his darkroom. It stands at the junction of the rue de Cléry and the rue Beauregard, and the rue des Degrés, the shortest in Paris, carelessly crosses its path. At its sharp end, a single

Pointe Trigano, 2nd

shared apartment occupies six floors, with a kitchen in the basement, a living room on the ground floor, one bedroom per floor (three), and a bathroom in the attic. No cardiac patients or arthritics, please! The poet André Chenier lived on the top floor in 1793 and there was once a wine shop on street level. A few dozen meters away at the corner of the rue Beauregard and the boulevard de Bonne-Nouvelle stands another building with a very keen edge.

Also
Corner of rue Beauregard and boulevard de Bonne-Nouvelle, 2nd

An accidental or planned effect?

A sharp wedge of a corner building may also have been deliberately designed that way because of certain urban constraints. When you stand in front of 203 bis, rue Saint-Honoré, for instance, all you can see of the building opposite is an ochre slice, carefully rounded by the architect to avoid any eye injuries. However, in other places, the effect is obviously unintentional, resulting from the demolition of a neighboring construction. For example, at 8, passage des Récollets, it looks as though the back of the building has vanished into thin air, leaving behind a forlorn, abandoned facade—a phenomenon that leaps to the eye when you are coming from the rue du Faubourg-Saint-Martin. The same goes for the building on the corner of the rue des Saules and the rue Francœur. Standing in front of 24, rue Francœur, you can see fine, exposed toothing stones, which seem to be desperately pining for their lost counterparts.

8, passage des Récollets, 10th

Corner of rue Saint-Honoré and rue Duphot, 1st

Corner of rue des Saules and rue Francœur, 18th

Left hanging

The rue Thouin was built on the ditches of Philippe Auguste's fortifications when they were filled in 1685 *(see p. 49)*. One of the houses that line it (no. 14) was built immediately after in 1688 against the medieval wall. Given the narrowness and triangular form of the lot, it had no room to extend its walls further. But later, the rampart was demolished, leaving an empty space (which became the yard) and a sheer face. The effect is striking when you come from the rue de l'Estrapade.

14, rue Thouin, 5th

Notable doors

The models of doors shown below seemed to have been designed to encourage the curious to pay more attention to the ornamental details that discreetly enhance the city.

3

4

1

5

2

6

1 58, rue deVaugirard,6th

2 94, quai de la Râpée,12th
This massive 84-ton glass door slides on rails to close the entrance of the DASES (Department of Social Action for Children and Health). The system was created by the architect Aymeric Zublena in 1992.

3 20, rue Durantin,18th
It is rare for a door to be decorated with such lavish care.

4 29, avenue Rapp,7th
The architect Jules Lavirotte, an advocate of sexual symbolism,struck a blow for his cause with this door in the form of an inverted phallus (1901).

5 24, rue du Sommerard, 5th
The ornate door next to the entrance to the musée de Cluny has remarkably decorative fittings and a dog's-head doorbell.

6 40, cours Albert-Ier, 8th
The door of the town house of master glassmaker and jeweler René Lalique is in molded and pressed white glass with a pattern of pine branches weighed down with snow.

10 Romantic ruins

What story does this unlikely, solitary gate have to tell? What sequence of events led these truncated columns and dismembered capitals to end their days at the bottom of a garden? Pediments, parts of facades... all these old, forsaken stones lend a romantic touch to their resting place. Over the centuries, Paris has constantly been built, demolished, and reconstructed in a permanent evolutionary process that began long before Haussmann's great redesign of the city. In the 1830s especially, many old buildings were razed—churches and town houses, some of which had remarkable architectural features. So what could be done with these artifacts? When it proved impossible to leave them where they were, they were removed from their original buildings and reused on others or stored in improvised stonework depots.

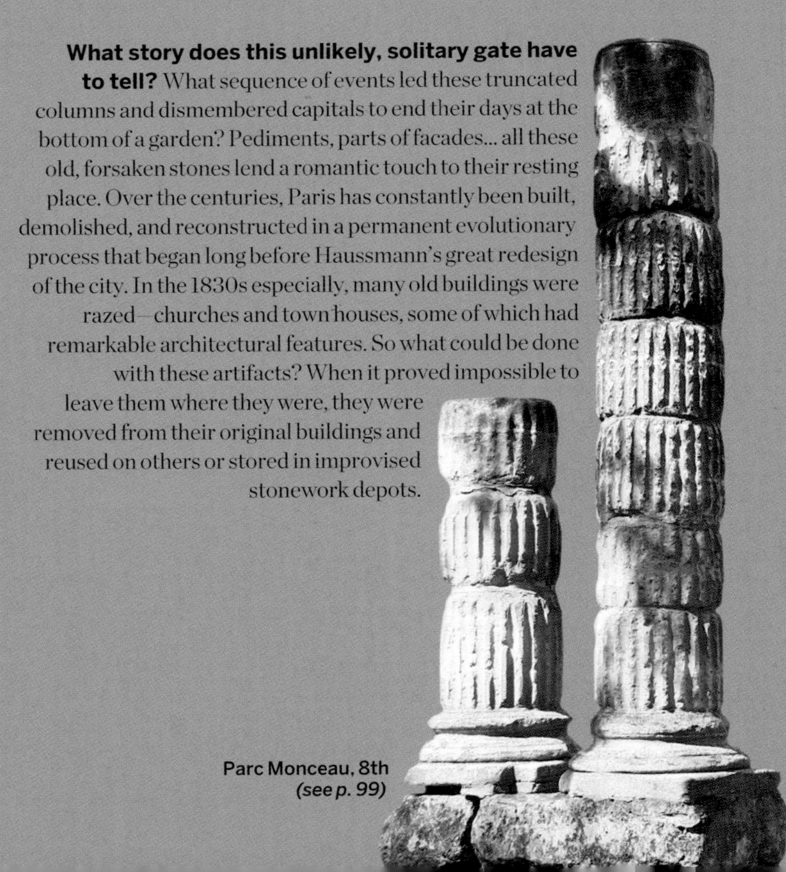

Parc Monceau, 8th
(see p. 99)

Top to bottom
École des Beaux-Arts. 14, rue Bonaparte, 6th
Square Georges-Cain, 4th

Stonework depots

Four main sites were used as stonework depots. In the 1880s, various sculptures from the palais des Tuileries (destroyed in a fire in 1871) and the remains of demolished town houses were sent to the école des Beaux-Arts. A few doors taken from defunct churches were stored in the garden of the hôtel de Cluny. The square Paul-Langevin nearby provided a resting place for some Renaissance niches from the former Hôtel de Ville (burned during the Commune). In the jardin Georges-Cain next to the musée Carnavalet, other remnants from the palais des Tuileries were stockpiled. However, these locations are guilty of one great sin of omission: they have few signs or notices to show where these vestiges came from.

Also
Square Paul-Langevin, 5th
Jardin de l'hôtel de Cluny. 6, place Paul-Painlevé, 5th

The lost Rival of Sainte-Chapelle

The chapelle de la Vierge on the rue de l'Abbaye was very beautiful. The architect Pierre de Montreuil "practiced" on this first building in around 1245, just before he built the Sainte-Chapelle, so it was actually a dress rehearsal for that flamboyant masterpiece of gothic art. After the Revolution, it was used as a grain silo before being purchased in 1802 by Doctor Salbrune, who demolished it and reused a number of its architectural features on the front of the house he had built for himself on rue de l'Abbaye. Other fragments were found during a dig when a parking garage was constructed in the place de Furstemberg. They were stored in the square next to the église Saint-Germain-des-Prés.

Square Laurent-Prache, 6th

Memories of Monceau

By the end of the 19th century, the remains of the former hôtel de Ville, burned down by the Communards in May 1871, were scattered and stored in a number of public places belonging to the City of Paris, such as the parc Monceau. The park displays fragments of columns and the archway of one of the two entrances of the defunct City Hall, which stands like a portico near the naumachia. This colonnade in the Corinthian style came from the rotonde des Valois, a funeral chapel commissioned by Catherine de Médici to hold her tomb and that of her husband Henri II (although it was still unfinished when she died). It should have adjoined the basilique Saint- Denis. In 1719, Philippe d'Orléans had the marble columns transported to his parc Monceau property where Carmontelle was creating an illusionary landscape full of ornaments and ruins.

Parc Monceau, 8th

The table de Plaisanterie

Where did this massive round table, cut from a single block of limestone and displayed in the jardin des Plantes, come from? Apparently, it was "found" in a forest near Chantilly around 1885 by a particularly intuitive mare named Plaisanterie. She was walking in the forêt du Lys when she suddenly stopped, stared at the ground and scraped the earth with her hoof.

Jardin des plantes, 5th (enter at 18, rue Buffon, and it's at the end of the allée, on the right)

After digging at the spot, the party found this circular table two meters across buried two meters under the ground. Was it used to butcher carcasses and share them during a hunt? Did it come from the medieval château de Beaularris, destroyed in the Hundred Years' War? Then it was a case of now you see it, now you don't: nobody knows what became of it between 1885 and 1950, when the animal painter Henri Camus, who specialized in racing and hunting scenes, left it to the musée d'Histoire naturelle. It is a genuinely odd artifact resembling an unfinished millwheel, polished on the edge, rough above, and, furthermore, amazingly resonant when you tap it with a finger.

Exotic ruins

On the edge of the bois de Vincennes, a rather decrepit carved wooden portal leads to the old gardens of tropical agronomy created in 1899 to study species (cocoa, vanilla, banana, and coffee plants) from France's distant colonies. In 1907, the pavilions of the Marseille Colonial Exposition of 1906 were moved to the site. It was then that the gardens were divided into two parts: Africa and Asia. Indochinese and Congolese villages, a Sudanese farm, and a Tuareg camp were set up. As the years passed, the Chinese pagoda, tiger trap, Khmer bridge, Dahomey greenhouse, and Guyanese pavilion fell into disrepair. Then in 2003, the entire site was purchased from the government by the City of Paris, which is rehabilitating the garden and ruined pavilions at a very slow rate.

45 bis, avenue de la Belle-Gabrielle, Nogent-sur-Marne

The great washhouse of the marché Lenoir

Washerwomen's shouts and laughter no longer echo behind this facade, now as two-dimensional as a stage set. In the 1830s, a washhouse was built at 9, rue de Cotte. It had a wooden and metal framework, shutters for ventilation, an oak-heartwood drying rack, a boiler and a brick fireplace, and, to signal its presence, the usual French flag painted on sheet metal that was common to such establishments. It was a public washhouse but charged a fee. It could be used by both launderers and housewives, who visited regularly until 1960, when—the last of its kind—it was

turned into an industrial laundry. When that business closed in 1987, there was talk of building a housing project on the site, but the locals campaigned to prevent the building's demolition. A compromise was reached: the facade was given historic designation, moved 40 meters and incorporated into the outer wall of a neighboring school. It was not transported stone by stone, but on rails, held in a metal frame. The operation took one morning.

3, rue de Cotte, 11th

The couvent des Cordelières

The convent of the église Sainte-Claire-l'Ourcine, founded in 1289 to house the nuns of the order of the Poor Clares, became very familiar with the slings and arrows of outrageous fortune. The rural convent located in the village of faubourg Saint-Marcel was flooded every time the waters of the neighboring Bièvre river rose, was ravaged by the troops of Henri IV during the siege of Paris in 1589, and then dissolved after the Revolution. What remained of the buildings was occupied by tanneries and laundries, and then the hôpital de Lourcine in 1834. In 1972, the hospital was reorganized and became the hôpital Broca. It was at this time that the remains of the gothic refectory of the old convent were renovated, along with the bay windows of the former dormitory and the pillars and capitals of the columns visible in the garden. A paved way marks the site of the church.

Jardin de l'hôpital Broca. Corner of rue Pascal and rue de Julienne, 13th

The château des Ternes

On this spot was a large walled farm with two towers, a drawbridge, barns, a farmyard, vines, a dovecote, a press, a fishpond, a vegetable garden, and an orangery. It was known as the château des Ternes. In 1778, the property fell into the hands of the speculator Samson-Nicolas Lenoir. He emptied the château of its furniture, ripped out a section of the ground floor to make a passage *(see p. 89),* and split up the grounds into a large number of lots that he sold to different developers. A gate standing on its own with no wall is a lone remnant.

17, rue Pierre-Demours, 17th

The late lamented hôtel Raoul

The solitary gate of 6, rue Beautreillis is a sad sight: decrepit and covered in graffiti. It once led to the courtyard of a town house built around 1606 by Paul Ardier. The house had many influential owners (most of them senior officials) before it was finally purchased in 1810 by Jean-Louis Raoul, a file manufacturer with a patent that made his fortune. The industrialist installed the forges, workshops, anvils, and bellows of his trade in the courtyard. Around 1845, the hôtel Raoul was divided into a number of rented apartments, housing up to 21 families by 1926. Over time, still owned by the heirs of Jean-Louis Raoul, it grew dilapidated and was demolished in 1960. The gate was saved at the last moment, but its future remains uncertain. The lot where the gate stands is independent of the new condominium, so it and the land it stands on are still the property of Jean-Louis Raoul's descendants. This means that its restoration is awaited in much the same way as Godot: it will not materialize until the different protagonists (heirs, sponsors, artisans, etc.) can agree on its terms.

See also The horloge aux dauphins (p. 55), Migrant stones (p. 105) and Sinister slabs (p. 224).

6, rue Beautreillis, 4th
Complete information can be found at http://cribier.net/Hotel-Raoul

11 Revolutionary Paris

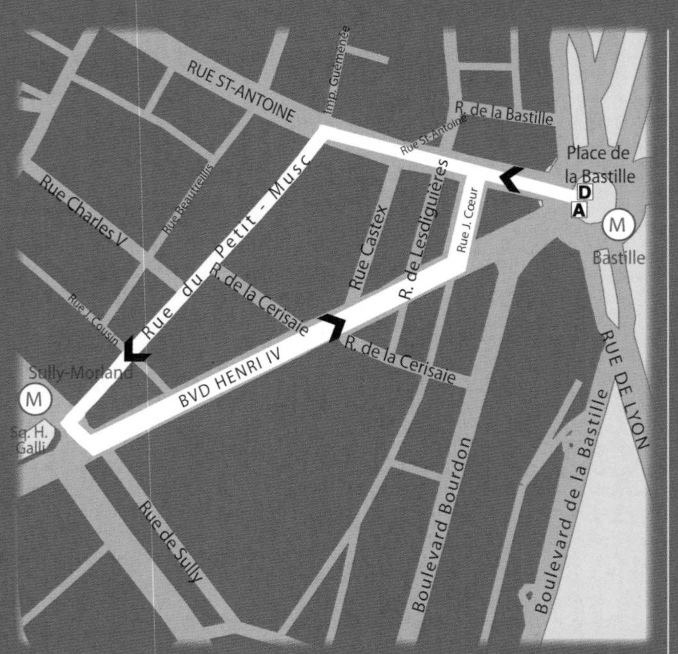

Obviously, there are plenty of remnants of the French Revolution in Paris around the Bastille district. But they can also be found in other areas, in the faubourg Saint-Antoine neighborhood and as far as the Latin Quarter on the Left Bank.

The ghost of the Bastille

The fortress prison was razed to the ground, but discreet clues to its presence remain in the form of fragments and references. Let us set out to examine them, beginning with the Bastille Métro station, which is where you will probably arrive at the start of your tour.

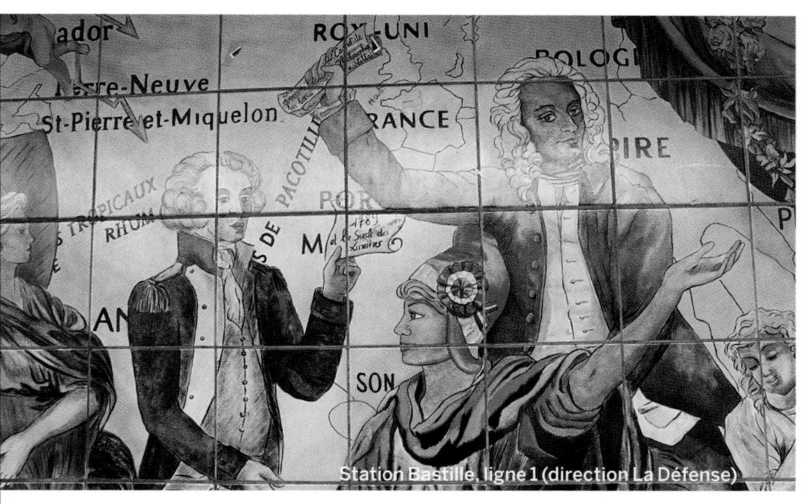

Station Bastille, ligne 1 (direction La Défense)

Top to bottom
Station Jaurès, ligne 2 (direction Nation)
Station Concorde, ligne 12
Station Bastille, ligne 5 (direction Bobigny)

Métro memories

If you come on a line 1 train, you will see a mural fresco along the platform with figures in relief. Its five scenes illustrate key moments in the Revolutionary era from the first ideological stirrings to final victory, including the storming of the Bastille and the people's march on Versailles. The polychrome work was created by Liliane Belembert and Odile Jacquot. Opposite, looking out, you can see the docks of the bassin de l'Arsenal, which is a widened version of the trench that once channeled the water of the Seine to the moat of the Bastille. On the platform of line 5, you can see a remnant of the counterscarp (part of the outer wall of the fortress's ditch) marked in yellow on the ground. Elsewhere, other references maintain the memory of the Revolution in the Métro: the billowing flags on the stained glass of the above-ground Jaurès station and the letters of the Declaration of the Rights of Man decorating the vaults of Concorde station. The punctuation marks are assembled below on a frieze: it is up to you to work out where they go.

→ Leave the Métro station and take the rue Saint-Antoine. Stop at the corner of the rue Jacques-Cœur.

Entrance of the fortress

The fortress was not actually located on the site of today's place de la Bastille as you might think, but slightly to the west. The forecourt of the Bastille (the entrance stormed by the people on July 14), was just where the rue Saint-Antoine begins today, on the odd-numbered side. A plaque at no. 5 reminds passers-by of this.

49, boulevard Henri-IV, 4th

Outline of the towers

On the ground, a line of paving stones larger than their neighbors marks the contours of the Bastille. Examining this outline, which runs from the rue Saint-Antoine to the corner of the boulevard Henri-IV, you will see that the fortress was actually quite modest in size (about 66 by 30 meters). The curve of the tour de la Liberté is marked in front of the bus stop at 1, rue Saint-Antoine. The tour de la Bazinière stood at 49, boulevard Henri-IV. Heading out into the place de la Bastille, you will find a plaque with a plan of the fortress on the facade of no. 3, in the very place where the tour du Trésor, the Bastille's treasury, rose.

A cannonball con?

Not far from the plan of the prison, in a recess at second-floor level, there is a crater in a stone that looks like the mark of a small cannonball. An engraved explanation calls it: "A relic of July 14, 1789." However, a little further to the right, the keen observer will notice another inscription: "Builder A. Duclos, May 26, 1871," the date of completion of the building (such precise chronograms

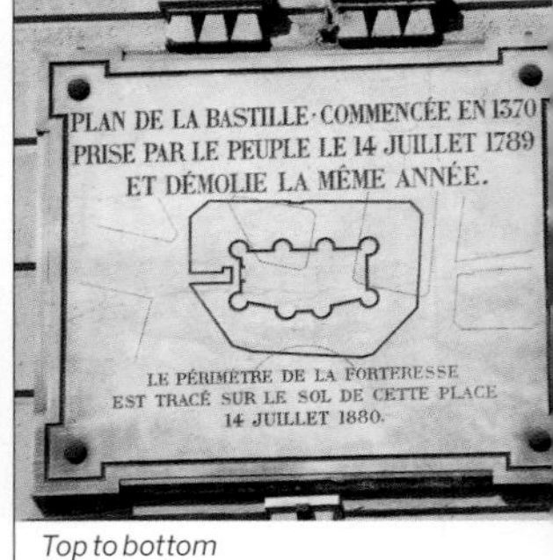

Top to bottom

1, rue Saint-Antoine, 4th
3-5, place de la Bastille, 4th

are actually quite rare). The anachronism leaps to the eye. So nobody knows whether the relic is a poor joke or if a stone chipped by a cannonball during the fighting in 1789 was really used in the construction of the building.

→ Take the boulevard Henri-IV towards the Seine. Just before you reach the quay, stop at the square Henri-Galli.

Migrant stones

When the first Métro line was dug in 1898, the foundation stones of the tour de la Liberté were uncovered 7.5 meters down under the rue Saint-Antoine. You may think "Liberté" was an odd name for a prison tower, but it was so called because the (distinguished) prisoners incarcerated there enjoyed certain privileges. In particular, they were "free" to go out on the top of the tower overlooking the city to get some fresh air and wave to friends. The Marquis de Sade was one of those favored inmates. The stones, which were the largest remnant of the fortress, had to be moved here. Another relocated vestige is less obvious but extremely iconic: the pont de la Concorde, completed in 1791. The upper part of the bridge was built using stones from the demolished fortress.

→ Take the rue du Petit-Musc back to the rue Saint-Antoine and stop at no. 17.

Square Henri-Galli, 4th

Pont de la Concorde

17, rue Saint-Antoine, 4th

Laws and acts of public authority

The chapel of the couvent des Visitandines was confiscated after the Revolution. A Republican club met here for a while before it became the temple de la Visitation-Sainte-Marie. An almost obliterated inscription on the facade reminds the passer-by of the days when citizens' meetings were held in the building: *Loix et actes de l'autorité publique*. The inscription is above a surface once used to post laws voted by the Assemblée for the public to read. It was more or less the ancestor of France's government publication Le Journal officiel. There were several such "notice boards" in every city.

Also
l'église Saint-Merri, 1st
l'église Saint-Louis-en-l'Île, 4st
l'église Saint-Gervais -Saint-Protais, 4th
l'église Saint-Séverin, 5th
l'église Saint-Philippe-du-Roule, 8th
le ministère de la Marine, 2, rue Royale, 8th

→ The tour ends at its departure point: the place de la Bastille.

Other Revolutionary relics

Left to right

46, rue Jacob, 6th

Rue des Colonnes, 2nd

Recession in the building sector

Few constructions date back to the Revolutionary period (naturally: political turmoil is not particularly conducive to a building boom). No. 46, rue Jacob is a rare specimen. Its decoration includes a Marianne wearing a Phrygian cap (symbolizing the Republic) set in a niche. The rue des Colonnes near the Bourse (Paris's stock exchange) provides another example of Revolutionary architecture in the neoclassical style.

A far from royal court

The cour du Commerce Saint-André was a hive of activity in Revolutionary times. Schmidt's workshop *(see the next page)* stood next to Marat's printing shop, where his publication L'Ami du people (*The People's Friend*) came hot off the press from 1793 onward. The passage, which was gutted in the 19th century when the boulevard Saint-Germain was opened, extended as far as today's Odéon Métro station. There, a few meters from the statue of Danton, was the house where the Jacobin lived from 1789 until his arrest on March 30, 1794. Finally, the café, Le Procope, was a meeting place for the Encyclopedists and then the Revolutionaries. It was there that the order was given to storm the Tuileries Palace on June 20, 1792 and the first Phrygian cap was worn.

Cour du Commerce-Saint-André, 6th

A Mirabeau, a Mirabelle

This was one of the nicknames of the guillotine, along with Louison, Vasistas (transom), Veuve (widow), Rasoir national (national razor), or Monte-à-regret (Climb-to-regret). It was built in 1792 in the workshop of a German carpenter called Schmidt at no. 9, cour du Commerce-Saint-André, following plans drawn up by a certain Dr. Antoine Louis (which is why it was also known as the Louison: "Little Louis"). At the time, it was pitched as a "philanthropic decapitation machine." A physician, Dr. Guillotin, was responsible for persuading the Assemblée to systematically use this egalitarian method of execution, which was neat and efficient (as tests on sheep in the cour de Rohan made extremely clear). A genuine steel guillotine blade weighing nearly 9 kilos that was used in the place de Grève (now the place de l'Hôtel de Ville) during the Revolution is part of the collection of the musée de la Préfecture de police. Next to the antiquity is a miniature replica of a guillotine which, according to the curator, has never worked (the blade is mercifully blocked halfway down).

4, rue de la MontagneSainte-Geneviève, 5th

Once Louison had done its gruesome job...

...the decapitated victims had to be buried. Executed in the place de la Bastille in June 1794, 93 of them were interred in the former parish cemetery of the church of Sainte-Marguerite, now the courtyard of the presbytery (which can be visited by appointment from the church reception office). Among the graves is that of a certain L... XVII *(see p. 118)*. The Picpus cemetery was the final destination for the remains of those unfortunates guillotined in the place du Trône

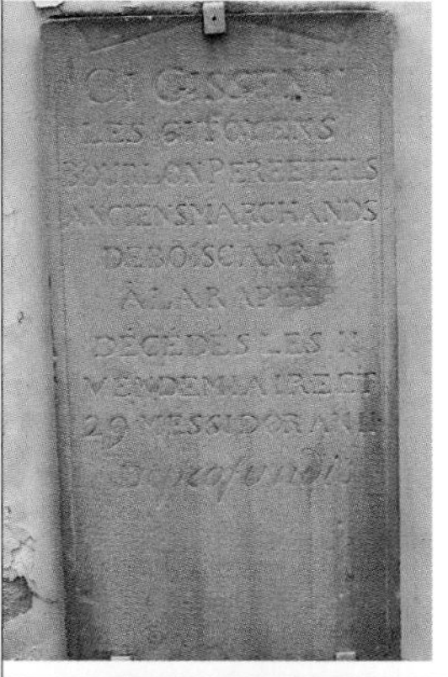

(now place de la Nation) in the summer of 1794. In total, 1,306 persons were hastily buried in two mass graves. When night fell, tumbrils loaded with bodies entered through the cart gate (whose frame is still standing). The executioners' assistants then stripped the bodies of their clothes in an artificial cavern equipped as an oratory, traces of which can be seen in the grass. It is impossible not to feel a certain emotion in such a place.

See also Revolutionary removal (p. 80).

Top to bottom

Église Church of Sainte-Marguerite.
40, rue Saint-Bernard, 11th
Cimetière de Picpus.
35, rue de Picpus, 12th

12 Wounds of war

History books are full of accounts of battles, invasions, and military conquests. Yet however well documented they are, these narratives do not have the immediate power of suggestion held by the physical presence of a relic of war or fighting. Paris still shows the scars of its bloody past. These marks may be faint and barely noticeable, but remain deeply moving for all that. For reminders of the Revolution, see the previous chapter, which is entirely devoted to that period.

(See p. 115)

The royalist insurrection of 1795

The Saint-Roch volley

Although they could be mistaken for flaws in the stone, the marks on the porch of the église Saint-Roch are actually bullet impacts. When the Republic was proclaimed, the royalists refused to admit defeat. They attempted to revolt on October 5, 1795, but the uprising was immediately crushed by General Bonaparte. The insurgents beat a hasty retreat and took shelter on the steps of the church. Soldiers posted in the cul-de-sac Dauphin (a continuation of the rue Saint-Roch to the south) fired on them. Two hours later, a total of 400, on both sides, had been killed.

296, rue Saint-Honoré, 1st

Revolutionary days of 1830

A fitted cannonball

Stuck in the eastern facade of the hôtel des archevêques de Sens, a small cannonball has survived the passing years and various refurbishments. It apparently ended up there during the July Revolution at some stage of the attack on the Ave Maria barracks on July 28, 1830 (the date engraved in the stone above the missile). Following the events of those Revolutionary Days, Charles X was forced to abdicate in favor of Louis-Philippe I, "King of the French." However, caution is needed: the suspiciously artistic positioning of the ball casts some doubt on the accuracy of the inscription explaining it.

1, rue du Figuier, 4th

The Commune

Jardin des plantes, 5th

Graffiti on the gazebo

In September 1870, the Commune had not yet been declared, but anger was already brewing. As the Prussians began to surround Paris, the citizens laid in supplies. Entire herds of livestock were penned in the Jardin des plantes under the watchful eyes of shepherds and cowherds. One of them may have written the meticulously inscribed graffiti on the fluting of one of the columns of the Buffon gazebo (the one opposite as you enter). The words are a prayer for divine assistance: "Lord God Eternal, make us victorious. Confound the Prussians." The spelling is poor, but the calligraphy precise: the letters were sculpted in dotted lines using a sharp tool. The base is marked with other, less legible supplications.

103, rue Mouffetard, 5th
A plaque commemorates the siege of Paris by the German army.

The construction of the basilique du Sacré-Cœur (18th) was decided in 1873 to atone for the Commune.

Notes in the nave

On May 22, 1871, just after Adolphe Thiers's Versailles troops entered Paris, a group of communards occupied the church of Saint-Paul-Saint-Louis, a favorite target of anticlericals. They remained there for two days before deciding to leave when the Versaillais advanced from the Hôtel de Ville. Before they left the church, they wrote a raging slogan in blood-red ink on the second pillar on the right in the nave: "The French Republic or death." These words of defiance have resisted every attempt to erase them.

99, rue Saint-Antoine, 4th

The First World War

Where it all began

On July 31, 1914, at 9:40 pm, the Socialist leader Jean Jaurès was sitting at a table in the La Chope du Croissant bistro, quietly rounding off his meal with a slice of strawberry tart. Suddenly a gunshot rang out, fired at close range by a nationalist named Raoul Villain. Jaurès slumped across the table, but then summoned up the last of his strength and clambered to his feet. He staggered along the counter before collapsing near the door. A mosaic with the date shows where he fell. To one side, a

small commemorative altar holds a bust of Jaurès and press clippings from the time. Located in the heart of the newspaper district, the café was a meeting place for journalists

and politicians of every persuasion. Jaurès, the founder of the newspaper L'Humanité and a committed pacifist, was a regular there. Three days after his assassination, Germany declared war on France.

146, rue Montmartre, 2nd

Notice of mobilization

"The Mayor of the 8th arrondissement informs his constituents that general mobilization is declared..." The die had been cast. Mobilization was declared on August 2, 1914—but the notice is not an original. It is obviously a photocopy that was put there in the 1970s and left to yellow in peace behind a dusty pane.

1, rue Royale, 8th

The soldiers' departure

That is what the public call the fresco decorating the concourse of the gare de l'Est. Its real name is "In August 1914," since it shows the departure of the *poilus* (or hairies), as the French soldiers were known, from the gare de l'Est on August 2, 1914. Albert Herter, an American decorative and fresco painter, created this 5- by 12-meter picture in 1926 in an empty room in the château de Versailles and then presented it to the Compagnie des chemins de fer de l'Est (Eastern Railroad Company). The work was personally very important to Herter: his son Everit-Albert, a volunteer, was killed on June 13, 1918 at Bois-Belleau near Château-Thierry. Herter himself is shown on the right of the painting, holding a bunch of flowers. His wife is on the left with her hands clasped. Her son is probably the central figure waving his kepi.

Concourse of the gare de l'Est, 10th

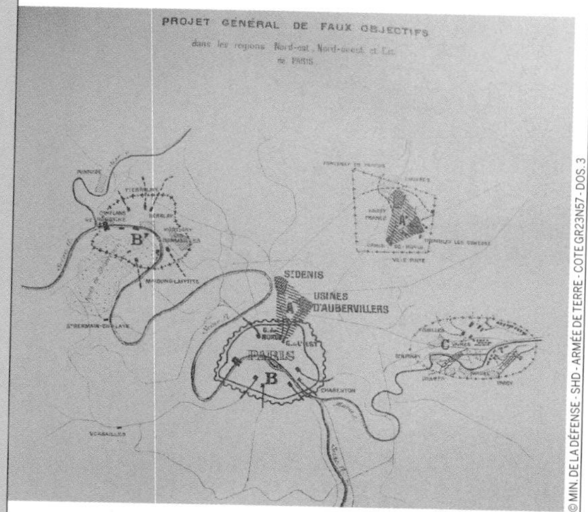

© MIN. DE LA DÉFENSE - SHD - ARMÉE DE TERRE - COTE GR23N57 - DOS. 3

Map of the passive defense project known as "fake Paris."

Fake Paris

During the First World War, the greatest ever passive defense plan was launched. The idea was to build a fake Paris in the suburbs, using special lighting effects to fool German bomber pilots. The project's code name was "Camouflage by false objectives." The first trials were conducted in August 1917 in the Orme de Morlu region near Saint- Denis. Acetylene site lamps were set up along earth tracks to suggest lit avenues. Translucent sheets lit from within simulated the glass roofs of rail stations. A sequence of yellow, red, and white lamps lighting clouds from smoke generators gave the impression of furnaces in operation, and so on. The aim was to mislead the enemy as to the exact position of Paris by installing lit objects in certain places that could be mistaken for locations in the capital that had not been blacked out. After the trials, the zone finally chosen for the mockup was to be to the south of Pontoise, where a loop of the Seine looks very much like the section of the river that crosses Paris. However, the Armistice ended these fantastic experiments and they were no longer feasible when the Second World War began because of progress in techniques to locate targets.

Shell marks

On the facade of the Ministry of War, where Georges Clemenceau was leading the government of the Republic, shell damage offers a reminder of the violent bombardment launched on March 11, 1918. An inscription engraved in the stone tells the story. The same goes for the facade of the école des Mines, bombarded on January 20, 1918 and also scarred by the Liberation battles of August 1944.

Top to bottom

231, boulevard Saint-Germain and r de l'Université, 7th
École nationale supérieure des Mine de Paris. 60, boulevard Saint-Michel 6th

Traces of shelling on the wall of Crédit Lyonnais, facing 15, rue de Choiseul, 2nd

The Second World War

École nationale supérieure des Mines de Paris. 60, boulevard Saint-Michel, 6th

Bullet marks

On the eve of the Liberation in August 1944, the first tanks of General Leclerc's armored division were approaching the city, where barricades had been built in the streets. The fighting was fierce. Bullets whined through the air and struck facades, leaving ineradicable marks.

The shells and bullets that hit the front of the école des Mines and the back of the théâtre de l'Europe shattered the stone. There is also a spectacular bullet mark on one of the recumbent bronze lions guarding the porte Jaujard at the Louvre. Distinct and round, it could only have been made during the Liberation: all the bullets used at the time of the Commune were made of lead. They could have chipped stone, but not bronze.

Théâtre de l'Europe. Place de l'Odéon, 6th

Musée du Louvre, 1st (Denon wing, Jaujard entrance, near the lions)

Panzer caliber

Two deep impact craters left by direct shellfire in the lateral facade of the Hôtel-Dieu commemorate a key moment of the Liberation. On August 19, 1944, at 8:30am, FFI police officers (French Interior Forces, the united Communist and Gaullist Resistance) occupied the Préfecture de police next to the Hôtel-Dieu, entering through a door left ajar by a mobile guardsman. The French flag was raised on the roof and Colonel Rol-Tanguy set up his headquarters in the barracks. At 2:30 p.m., the first shots were fired from the courtyard. The Germans sent heavy machine guns, cannon, and then two Panzer tanks. One rumbled down the rue d'Arcole to position itself at the turn, exactly opposite the entrance to the Préfecture de police.

The rue d'Arcole is relatively narrow for a tank of that size and its crew must have felt a bit vulnerable. Possibly sensing a threat from the gates of the Hôtel-Dieu as they came, they opened fire. However, they were too close and missed their target. Their two 88-millimeter (impressively large) projectiles buried themselves in the wall.

Hôtel-Dieu. Facing 15, rue d'Arcole, 4th (above the blue gate "Sortie SAMU")

Paul-Émile's blockhouse

One of the city's last blockhouses was concealed in the lush "no-man's-land" near the porte Dauphine. It was a genuine concrete fortress of 386 square meters on two levels (ground and basement), built in 1941 to house a German naval command post. In 1952, the Préfecture de la Seine lent the building to the explorer Paul-Émile Victor, who prepared his expeditions to the North Pole there for 50 years. In the huge basement, he bundled the material for his explorations into many little packs that could easily be carried on a man's back. On the surrounding wasteland, he tested his polar shelters. In 2010, Paris City Hall announced plans to demolish the bunker and replace it with a housing project. The locals protested fiercely and managed to stop the program.

Facing 45, avenue du Maréchal-Fayolle, 16th

Hôtel Crillon. 6, place de la Concorde, 8th

Beware the fifth column!

In military language, "the fifth column" is a colorful expression referring to an underground civilian group supporting traditional armed forces with covert action—attacks from the rear, sabotage, espionage, etc. On August 26, 1944, there was a carnival atmosphere in the place de la Concorde. The Parisians gathered there were waiting for the arrival of General de Gaulle, who was marching down the avenue des Champs-Élysées cheered by a jubilant crowd. One of the onlookers was looking rather less exhilarated, though. FFI Lieutenant René Toureng had just noticed something very suspicious: dozens of men in street clothes who looked like very Teutonic toughs were entering the Automobile Club and the Crillon. Convinced of the threat, Toureng shared his concerns with an armored division commander, who laughed in his face as he pointed out the tanks lined up in a square on the place. But Toureng refused to back down and the angry commander finally ordered his men to aim the cannons of the four closest tanks at the target identified by the worried officer: the hotel Crillon, whose balconies were packed. De Gaulle's company had barely entered the square when it came under heavy fire from one of those balconies. The tank quartermasters reacted immediately, sweeping their fire across the center of the facade and—the fifth column, literally and figuratively! That fifth column of the Crillon was rebuilt, but the stone used was of poorer quality than the original. Less resistant to air pollution, it has turned darker than its neighbors.

A German shelter 20 meters underground

Passive defense shelters were generally installed in the cellars of buildings, but some were constructed even lower, in former quarries. In particular, the Germans occupied a section below the headquarters of the

Luftwaffe in the lycée Montaigne high school. Whenever there was an air-raid warning, the staff officers gathered there, together with their humbler personnel. One of the French employees left a lot of graffiti giving the precise dates and times of the warnings, as well as various personal remarks. "Bombing March 5, 1944—The hairdresser is a jerk." On the walls, stencil-painted notices offer a reminder of the rules: "Ruhe," "Rauchen verboten" (Silence, No Smoking). A latrine is still there in a corner: a sort of rusty cylinder operated with a crank handle. Only the ceramic seat is missing.

Beneath the lycée Montaigne, 6th

Lest we forget...

The appeal to the French people

Between June 18, 1987 and June 18, 1990, more than a thousand enameled commemorative plaques inscribed with the text of the appeal of General de Gaulle to the people of France, made on BBC radio from London on June 18, 1940, were put up by the association des Français libres. In Paris, examples can be seen on arrondissement city halls, certain high schools, and in main squares: place de la Bastille, place Saint-Michel, etc.

"Bashed-in mugs" and guerrilla Resistance fighters

The musée de la Seconde Guerre mondiale brings to life events in France, from the General Mobilization Order in 1939 to the slogans of the Liberation, through documents and symbolic objects: ration cards, letters of denunciation sent by collaborators, the equipment of the perfect guerrilla Resistance fighter and so on. The musée du Service de santé des armées (Army Medical Corps Museum) presents the everyday life of military doctors: a Field Surgical Unit and its collection of stretchers, a Behind-the-Lines Hospital dedicated to corrective surgery, especially operations that attempted to reconstruct the faces of the *gueules cassées* (literally "bashed-in mugs") of 1914-1918. However, there was even deeper trauma: those of the shell-shocked, who were initially treated as hoaxers and malingerers before their disorder was finally recognized as "war hysteria or neurosis."

© MUSÉE DE L'ARMÉE, PARIS

© MUSÉE DE L'ARMÉE, PARIS

Top to bottom

Musée de la Seconde Guerre mondiale. Hôtel des Invalides, 6, boulevard des Invalides, 7th
Musée du Service de santé des armées. Hôpital du Val-de-Grâce, 1, place Alphonse-Laveran, 5th

13 Curious tombs

Avoiding the most famous cemeteries such as Père-Lachaise or Montparnasse, let us set off to explore other, more secret or eccentric places of rest.

The catacombs

There are three times more Parisians under the ground than above it, in the form of skeletons with scattered limbs. It all began with a grotesque accident in 1780: the walls of a cellar gave way under the pressure of the thousands of skeletons packed into the cimetière des Innocents, which was filled to bursting. The event pricked municipal consciences and led to a decree of 1785, which ordered the emptying of the cemetery for sanitary reasons. Thirty more Parisian cemeteries followed. From 1786 to 1814, gloomy processions headed along the boulevard Saint-Michel to the disused quarries of la Tombe-Issoire, where the remains were stacked. Then the Inspector-General of Quarries, had an idea: the bones would look much better if arranged artistically. Soon, there was a wall of femurs, crossed tibias there and a frieze of skulls above. A few well-chosen adages were added to to set the right tone. However, the meticulous arrangement was only superficial: behind it was a heap of tangled ribs and miscellaneous vertebrae up to 30 meters deep.

1, avenue du Colonel-Henri-Rol-Tanguy, 14th

© EMMANUEL GAFFARD

© EMMANUEL GAFFARD

© EMMANUEL GAFFARD

Val-de-Grâce, first courtyard to the right, 5th. It is near this small edifice, dating from the 18th century, that Philibert Aspairt was to be swallowed by the quarries that became his grave.

Philibert's tomb

Philibert Aspairt was a porter at the Val-de-Grâce. On November 3, 1793, he ventured down into the subterranean levels of the military hospital armed only with a small candle, spurred on by curiosity or—they say—the hope of finding the treasure of the Chartreux (Carthusian) monks: their finest bottles of "long life elixir." So what happened then? A fall, a sudden draft... who knows? The incautious explorer found himself lost in the darkness, wandering through tunnels that would become his sepulcher. His skeleton was found eleven years later, on April 30, 1804, under the rue d'Enfer (Hell Street!) a few meters from a door separating the tunnel from the Chartreux cellars. His remains were identified by the keyring he had been carrying and he was buried on the spot. On Philibert's anniversaries—November 3 and April 30—catacomb-goers pay tribute to the deceased by pouring a few drops of liquor over his mausoleum.

Approximately beneath 1, rue Henri-Barbusse, 5th

A hidden Jewish cemetery

At the end of the 17th century, Jews (who could not be laid to rest in municipal cemeteries) were searching everywhere to find places to bury their dead. In 1691, they reached an agreement with an innkeeper called Camot, who allowed Jews to be interred in his garden in exchange for a payment of 50 livres for an adult and 20 for a child. After

© BRUNO LAPEYRE

Camot's death, the inn was sold to a flayer named Matard in 1765. The man continued the funereal trade, but buried the carcasses of horses and oxen in the same piece of ground. Shocked by this profanation, the Portuguese Jewish community of Paris started up a subscription. With the money they collected and permission from the authorities, they were able to acquire two small lots of neighboring land. That cemetery (the property of the Consistory) is one of the oldest, most secret, and most forgotten graveyards anywhere. Thirty-one somber, black, anonymous slabs are lined up in the gravel.

49, quai de la Seine, 19th (in the interior courtyard)

L. XVII

In June 1794, the bodies of 73 people guillotined in the place de la Bastille were interred in the Parish cemetery of the church of Sainte-Marguerite *(see p. 107)*. The cemetery was closed in 1804 and a gravel yard now covers the buried bones. However, a few gravestones remain along the outer wall, including one dedicated to the citizens Bourlon, father and son, former timber merchants at La Râpée who died on 2 vendemiaire and 29 messidor in year II of the Republic. Next to their stone is another, tiny one: a child's tomb. Its Latin epitaph reads: "L. XVII (1785-1795)—Stop and see if there is such pain as mine." It was long thought to be the grave of a child who died at the Temple and was buried there on June 10, 1795: the son of Louis XVI and Marie-Antoinette. However, when the remains were examined in 1894, they proved to be the skeleton of a teenager of 15 to 18. So who is buried here? The mystery remains.

36, rue Saint-Bernard, 11th. Visit upon request at the church office.

Here lies Coco

Lost in the lawn of the garden of the ministère du Commerce et de l'artisanat, an unobtrusive tomb slab carries the words "Here, in the shade of a palm tree, was buried Coco, the dog of Her Majesty Marie Antoinette, who, on her arrest, had entrusted him to Madame de Tourzel, governess of the children of France." A fine story, but not quite true. Coco, a dwarf spaniel, seems not to have been the queen's pet, but that of her son, Louis XVII. The dog kept the prince company in the prison du Temple. After the martyred child's death, Coco was given to the sole survivor of the royal family, Marie-Thérèse, Louis XVII's sister, and she took him with her to Austria. When she brought him back to Paris in 1814, the journey proved too exhausting for the dog, now aged 22. He passed away shortly after and the former governess of the king's children had him buried. The slab is a copy: the original is kept in a safe in the Ministry.

© ANNE-MARIE MINVIELLE

80, rue de Lille, 7th. Open during the annual Journées du Patrimoine festival.

Place Saint-Blaise, 20th

Parish cemeteries

The cemeteries of the église Saint-Germain-de-Charonne and the église du Calvaire-de-Montmartre have something in common: they are the last two parish graveyards in Paris. The abbesses of Montmartre gifted their orchard to the parishioners to serve as a cemetery in 1688. The tiny graveyard (80 tombs) is entered through a forbidding bronze gate, which is only opened one day a year on November 1 (All Saints' Day). However, the Charonne cemetery is popular with local inhabitants who use it as a shortcut between the chemin du Parc-de-Charonne and the rue de Bagnolet.

Monumental recycling

Every church had its parish cemetery in the Middle Ages. The île de la Cité had no fewer than 18. Although the Haussmannian reconstruction of Paris involved comparatively few demolitions and clearances in the area around Notre-Dame, most of those churches and chapels are long gone, together with their graveyards. Gone... but not completely. Since tombstones were an excellent construction material, they were used here and there as flagstones. The ones at 26, rue Chanoinesse were recycled in the 18th century to pave

47, rue Descartes, 6th

an open-air passage providing access to a number of buildings. Their inscriptions in Gothic letters have survived, but would certainly have been worn away if more people had used that route. The passage at 47, rue Descartes is also paved with tombstones, taken from the former cemetery of Saint-Étienne-du-Mont. The serial numbers engraved on them probably corresponded to a register of persons buried in a common grave.

Tombstone of the Little Corporal

Concealed by bushes, this gravestone has ended up in a garden, its presence unsuspected by the crowds of tourists who flock to Les Invalides to see Napoleon's tomb. It is the defeated emperor's original stone, the one that marked his initial resting place on the island of Saint Helena. In 1840, it and the body were repatriated to France on the frigate La Belle Poule and placed here outside the église Saint-Louis, in a garden closed to the public but clearly visible from the windows of the corridor de Nîmes.

Hôtel des Invalides, 7th

Pasteur's mausoleum

When Pasteur died in 1895, it seemed fitting that he should be buried in the Panthéon. However, his widow formally opposed the plan and

© MUSÉE PASTEUR

sent a special petition to the highest authorities. As a result, she received a presidential dispensation that enabled her to inter her scientist husband in a crypt in the basement of his Institut. The chamber, inspired by the Mausoleum of Galla Placidia in Ravenna, has columns and a sarcophagus in porphyry, Carrara marble capitals, and a vault decorated with a white and gold mosaic whose patterns reflect the great man's work: sick dogs, sheep, hop and vine leaves, etc.

25, rue du Docteur-Roux, 15th

14 The people's devotion

Religious fervor often crystallizes around a nucleus —an object of worship and veneration. Relics (artifacts or bones) are very popular with Christians. Every Catholic church should have a relic or relics to its name. Yet compared to the cities of Spain or Italy, Paris is rather poor in relics: a single church in Rome may have more than all the churches in the French capital combined. Again, this is because of the Revolution. During the Terror, the vast majority of reliquaries were melted down and their contents burned.

The veneration of relics

Chapelle Sainte-Thérèse de la fondation d'Auteuil. 40, rue La Fontaine, 16th

Saints of choice

In every age, relics have had their zealous believers convinced of their power to miraculously heal the sick. So much so, in fact, that con artists used to mass-produce them, flooding the market with various holy remains: pieces of Saint Lawrence's charbroiled flesh, drops of the Virgin's milk, and so on. The more popular the saint, the greater the abundance. The gold medal for grifting, though, must go to a preserved breath that Saint Joseph drew while he was chopping wood (kept near to the French city of Blois). In 1847, a bibliographer took time out to inventory all the body parts preciously venerated in various places. The catalogue is instructive indeed: no fewer than 11 index fingers of John the Baptist, 10 heads of Saint William and so on.

©PAROISSE SAINT-MARCEL

In the reliquary of the church of Saint-Marcel, one of the saint's knuckles, together with relics of Saint Andrew, Saint Maxim, Saint Felix, Saint Anthony, Saint Louis, Saint Stanislas, Saint Francis de Sales, Saint Jane of Chantal, Saint Columba...

In Paris, there are a lock of hair and a bone said to belong to Saint Theresa, and one of Saint Marcel's knucklebones. Naturally, there are also relics of the Passion. They are displayed on the first Friday of every month at Notre-Dame: a crown of thorns (a ring of woven rushes seen as the second most important relic of Christendom after the shroud of Turin) and a piece of the cross and a nail (treasures protected by the Knights of the Order of the Holy Sepulcher). Although the Catholic Church cannot categorically confirm the authenticity of these three relics, it still exhibits them for the faithful to venerate.

Église Saint-Marcel. 82, boulevard de l'Hôpital, 13th
Trésor de Notre-Dame. Place du Parvis-Notre-Dame, 4th

Chapelle de la
Médaille miraculeuse

Catherine's medal

Catherine Labouré is to Paris what Bernadette Soubirou is to Lourdes. In 1830, the Virgin Mary is said to have appeared to the 24-year-old novice and entrusted her with a mission: to have a medal inscribed with the following prayer: "O Mary! conceived without sin, pray for us who have recourse to thee!" The Virgin is said to have added, "All who wear them will receive great graces." The medal was struck in 1832 and many cures and conversions followed. Every year, more than two million pilgrims come to kneel before the shrine that holds the wax-covered remains of the saint and purchase the medal.

140, rue du Bac, 7th

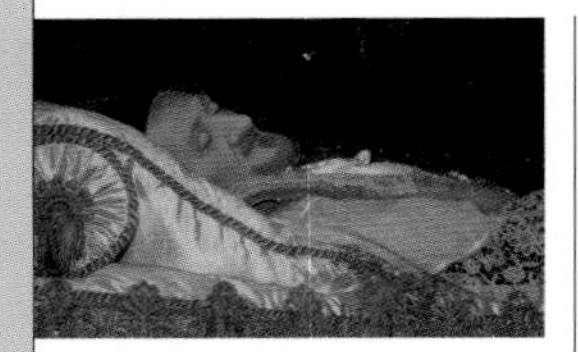

Vincent's cape

The "Vincentian museum" is devoted to the main events in the life of Saint Vincent de Paul (or "Monsieur Vincent," as he is known) the founder of the Lazarist Mission (which trained missionaries who would evangelize rural communities and provinces abroad) and that of the Sisters of Charity (the first order of nuns not confined to a convent). The museum also displays relics. They include the cape under which the saint sheltered abandoned children, a medal painted with the blood of his heart after his death, his last shoes, his umbrella, his hair shirt, and the alb in which he was buried and then found intact (his body uncorrupted) 52 years later. There are also relics of missionaries persecuted in China (three hairs from the beard of Father Perboyre, a coffin nail and more). Covered in wax, the saint's remains are kept in a solid-silver shrine in the chapel.

95, rue de Sèvres, 6th

The missionary's farewell

The Hall of the Martyrs of the Far East is both a museum and a place of contemplation. It holds relics of martyrs who fell victim to the wave of persecution in the Far East in the 1830 and 1840s. In 1843, the Mission received a case containing the remains of Father Pierre Borie, beheaded in Vietnam in 1838, along with other mementos of the martyr. It was the first repatriation in a long series, since many missionaries were persecuted during the events in Korea, China, Cochin China, and Tonkin. Since then, it has been the custom for missionaries leaving for distant lands to pray here in the presence of the remains and possessions of their martyred brothers, including the cane of Saint Théophane and the spyglass of Saint Chapdelaine.

128, rue du Bac, 7th

In the very unique église Sainte-Rita, Michael Jackson also has his altar.

Rita, Expedite, and Bonaventure, the holy matchmaker

Patron of lost causes, Saint Rita shares her church with Saint Expedite, who is said to have the same powers. Unfortunately, Expedite was decanonized by Vatican II and his statues removed from many churches. But not from this one, which is rather out of the ordinary. It is Church of England (a denomination that allows its clerics to marry and ordains women) and Monsignor Philippe occasionally holds masses here for animals. But back to Expedite. West Indians are very fond of him and call him Ti Bon Dieu (Little God) because he is so obliging that more or less any favor can be asked of him. In this church, he shares the limelight with Saint Bonaventure, a French theologian who specialized in matrimonial affairs. Lonely singles pin their petitions to two cushions placed at the feet of his statue.

Église Sainte-Rita. 27, rue François-Bonvin, 15th

Faith springs eternal

In around 250, Denis, along with his companions Rusticus and Eleutherius, preached the Gospel in Lutetia *(see p. 91)*. Prefect Fescennius Sisinius was not amused and had them beheaded in front of the temple of Mercury in Montmartre. But then there was a miracle! Stowing his head under his arm, Denis continued to climb the hill to a thick wood where a spring ran (today's square Suzanne-Buisson). After a quick wash, he continued walking. Heading down the north slope, he finally died in the presence of a widow, who buried him. Wheat immediately sprang up on his grave to hide it from profaners. In 475, Saint Geneviève took the martyr's coffin to a new tomb on the col de La Chapelle and built an oratory over it (on the site of today's church of Saint-Denys-de-La-Chapelle). King Dagobert later had the

coffin moved to the royal abbey of Saint-Denis, the necropolis of the Capetian dynasty. The martyr's brook became a place of pilgrimage. Its water was said to cure fevers and also to prevent wives from cheating: "The girl who drinks from the fontaine Saint-Denis will remain true to her husband." In 1810, it was engulfed by a plaster quarry and, with it, the hopes of many uneasy spouses.

Square Suzanne-Buisson, 18th

Thanks a million

The basilique Notre-Dame-des-Victoires was founded in 1629 by Louis XIII to offer thanks for the victory of the royal troops over the Huguenots at La Rochelle. Since then, it has been seen as the ideal place to petition saints. Successfully it seems, given the number of ex-votos

covering the walls inside. These marble plaques are engraved with requests for intercession or, more frequently, expressions of gratitude for a grace granted. The reasons given for these petitions or thanks are highly varied: ("For the release of Marceline 1942," "The student had recourse to you, the young doctor thanks you 2006," and so on). More than 37,500 are plastered absolutely everywhere, even on the vaulted ceiling and the nosing of the steps. Other offerings were provided by those who had suffered the torments of war: military decorations and items, sabers, heart lockets, plumes from the hats of Saint-Cyr cadets, and gemstone crowns are all displayed in four raised showcases on the columns of the choir, nave, and transept.

Place des Petits-Pères, 2nd

Saint-Sulpice shopping

Rather irreverently, shops selling religious objects are nicknamed *saint-sulpiceries* (a play on words: "*épiceries*" means grocery stores) because they were once very common in the shadow of the church in the Saint-Sulpice quarter. By extension, the label is also applied to such stores in other areas.

La Pastorale et Thuillier. 8 and 10, place Saint-Sulpice, 6th
Au Cœur immaculé de Marie. 8, place des Petits-Pères, 2nd

A mystical marathon

The Sacré-Cœur is the only church in Paris (and one of the few in France) to practice perpetual Eucharistic adoration. This type of worship involves the faithful coming to pray in turn before the holy sacrament (the consecrated host) without interruption, day and night. Begun in 1885, this perpetual praying has been put on hold only once or twice, during Second World War air-raid warnings. Are you tempted to join in? You simply have to register on www.sacre-coeurmontmartre.com. Once their hour of adoration is over, volunteers can rest in a dormitory or individual room in the basilica.

Sacré-Cœur, 18th

Street-corner Madonnas

One barely notices these unobtrusive niches set in facades, above a door, between two second-floor windows or at the corner of two streets. Whether they hold a statuette or not, they reveal the presence of a former oratory. Independent of any place of worship, these oratory niches are quite modest, like the statuettes they sometimes hold, which are made of plaster, wood, or painted metal. Originally, the back of these niches was painted Marian blue (the color associated with Mary) and the statuette is sometimes protected by a grill or glass. The figure mainly represented is the Holy Virgin of Protection wearing her veil or crown, alone or with the infant Jesus. Other niches hold or held saints whose patronage is linked to local history. When these statuettes are restored, they are covered with spikes to keep off pigeons and this makes them look rather like voodoo dolls.

1

Lone Holy Virgins

2

1 This slender ochre statue with its head and hand raised seems to be listening to a heavenly voice. It is the Notre-Dame-de-Toutes-Grâces. Below its corner niche are Latin words engraved in the stone: Ecce Mater Tua (Behold Your Mother).

Corner of rue Aubriot and rue Sainte-Croix-de-la-Bretonnerie, 4th

2 This painted plaster statue of Notre-Dame de Lourdes is protected by glass.

28, rue de Tournefort, 5th

3 On rue de Bercy, this Madonna is in an offertory pose behind a fine black grille.

235, rue de Bercy, 12th

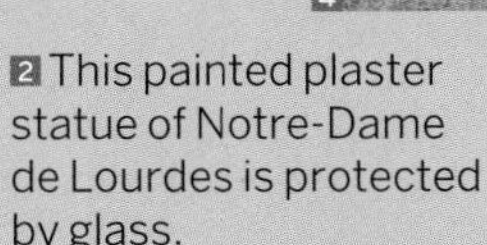

3

4

Virgin and Child

4 Quarrymen had a special Madonna: Notre-Dame-Dessoubs-Terre, installed in 1671 in the quarries under the Observatoire. The antique statue now slumbers above ground in storage at the Observatoire. A more recent statuette installed in the Capucins quarry in the 2000s perpetuates its predecessor's memory.

Carrière des Capucins, under l'hôpital Cochin, 14th

Saints and Saints

5 The back of this freestone niche painted blue shows a starry sky.
4, rue de l'Abreuvoir, 18th

6 A monumental 17th-century corner niche in sculpted stone.
Corner of rue de Turenne and rue Villehardouin, 3rd

7 This skewed Virgin is holding a remarkably unprepossessing infant Jesus in her arm.
Corner of rue De Sèvres and rue Saint-Placide, 6th

8 La Maison Bleue, a religious items store.
4 and 6 bis, place des Petits-Pères, 2nd

9 A Madonna and child crowned with silver in a niche under an ornamental canopy; behind is a starry sky.
82, rue du Faubourg-Saint-Martin, 10th

10 This more cheerful Virgin Mary has her own little metal balcony.
Corner of rue Cassette and rue Honoré-Chevalier, 6th

11 A crowned Virgin and child.
202, rue Saint-Honoré, 1st

12 The rue de la Madone was called ruelle Notre-Dame (from 1704) and then rue de la Vierge (in 1834). It became rue de la Madone in 1867 when Paris annexed its neighboring villages and homonymous streets had to be renamed.
Corner of rue des Roses and rue de la Madone, 19th

13 This statuette set in a red wall shows Saint Michel. Engraved on the base, his name has been strangely semi-Anglicized as Mickaël. Was this chance or coincidence in a very English-speaking area?
13, rue Charles-V, 4th

14 This statue of Saint Anthony overlooks what was once the pork butcher's store of Dodat, esquire (who, together with Vérot, built the passage that bears their names). Dodat's store was named after Saint Anthony the Great, patron saint of pork butchers. At his side is a pig, said to have followed him everywhere.
2, rue du Faubourg-Saint-Denis, 10th

15 Saint Andrew, the patron of fishermen, was also the patron of crossbowmen, so the inscription reads: "patron of Arc[her]s." A church nearby was consecrated to the saint. Bow merchants opened stores in the street that led to it, which became known as rue Saint-André-des-Arcs (St. Andrew of the Bows). Later, the traders moved out and were replaced by students who had come to study arts and letters in the colleges of the Latin Quarter. Gradually, the Arcs became Arts.
Corner of rue Saint-André-des-Arts and rue Mazet, 6th

16 Saint Nicholas's arms are benignly outstretched at one end of the street that bears his name.

Corner of rue Saint-Nicolas and rue du Faubourg- Saint-Antoine, 12th

17 All that remains of this statuette is the lower part. It was an image of Saint Nicolas, patron of boatmen, which overlooked a wharf below the quai de Bourbon. In the street perpendicular to it, there was an inn named À la Femme Sans Teste (At the Sign of Headless Woman) and the street took that name in 1690. When the Revolution came with its many beheadings, Saint Nicholas was one of the decapitated. So in a historical twist, the street name engraved in the stone perfectly matches (except in the matter of gender) the statue above!

Corner of quai de Bourbon and rue Le Regrattier, 4th

18 Saint Jean-Baptiste de La Salle is always shown in the company of a boy, since he was a pioneer of education in the 17th century. Until then, academic learning had been reserved for the elite, but Jean-Baptiste organized group lessons for commoners that were given in French (not Latin).

Corner of rue du Cherche-Midi and rue Saint-Jean-Baptiste-de-la-Salle, 6th

19 Saint Laurent, patron of the poor, is shown with a martyr's palm leaves. Next to him is a gridiron, the instrument of his torture.

60, avenue de Flandre, 19th

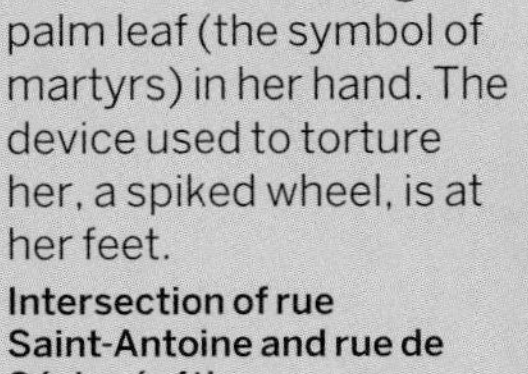

20 Saint Catherine of Alexandria is holding a palm leaf (the symbol of martyrs) in her hand. The device used to torture her, a spiked wheel, is at her feet.

Intersection of rue Saint-Antoine and rue de Sévigné, 4th

21 Saint Joan.

32, rue Beauregard, 2nd

22 The Bonnar orphanage stood here at the end of the 19th century. It was run by the Little Sisters of Saint-Vincent-de-Paul, which explains the statuette showing the saint carrying a child in distress.

Corner of rue de la Parcheminerie et rue Boutebrie, 5th

23 Saint Anne in sculpted stone, incorporated into the external decoration of a restaurant.

Corner of rue Sainte-Anne and rue Chérubini, 2nd

Keeping the faiths

Several religions coexist in Paris, some more ostentatiously than others. As you explore them, you will discover worlds that are new and different, both in their religious practices and in their places of worship.

The Orthodox priest's song

Paris has 15 or so Orthodox churches that represent different ecumenical patriarchates (Russian, Serb, Greek). Attending an Orthodox service is a memorable experience: as the priest murmurs Slavonic phrases into his long beard and swings his censer, the standing congregation bow and cross themselves in the warm candlelight. In the background are magnificent traditional chants modulated by a bass choir. Russian Orthodox churches are particularly enchanting. With its gilt onion domes, mosaic pediment, and pyramid towers, the cathedral of Saint-Alexandre-Nevski is impressive indeed. It was chosen for the funerals of Turgenev, Kandinsky, and Lifar, and Picasso's marriage to Olga Koklova. In total contrast, the church of Saint-Séraphin-de-Sarov looks more like a wooden dacha *(see p. 65)*. Elsewhere, Saint-Serge-de-Radogène rises like a mirage at the end of a steep, rustic alley frequented by Orthodox priests and cats. The church of the Présentation de la Très Sainte Vierge au Temple is particularly well lit through its glass roof (the building was formerly a typography shop).

Église Saint-Serge-de-Radogène. 93, rue de Crimée, 19th

Also
Cathédrale Saint-Alexandre-Nevski.
12, rue Daru, 8th
Église Saint-Séraphin-De-Sarov.
91, rue Lecourbe, 15th

Kippah required

There are about 25 consistorial synagogues in Paris. They are divided into two categories according to their rite: Sephardic or Ashkenazi. In the Roman-Byzantine style, the synagogue de la Victoire is the largest in France. Opened in 1874, it was a gift from the Baron de Rothschild. The synagogue is the seat of the Chief Rabbis of France and is Ashkenazi (the German rite), but still hosts Egyptian and Tunisian oratories. The Sephardic synagogue des Tournelles is a dynamic scene of life. It has a metal framework designed by Gustave Eiffel (the building was given protected status in 1987). Another great architect, Hector Guimard, created the undulating art nouveau facade of reinforced-concrete curves and counter-curves for the Ashkenazi synagogue in the rue Pavée in 1913.

Synagogue des 21 bis, rue des Tournelles, 4th

Also
Synagogue de la Victoire.
44, rue de la Victoire, 9th
Synagogue de la rue Pavée.
10, rue Pavée, 4th

The muezzin's call

Today, there are around 30 mosques and prayer halls frequented by Paris's 16,000 devout Muslims. By the start of the 20th century, the French State recognized Islam and granted it patronage in Algeria, but the religion was not established in France. There was just one little funeral mosque (now gone) near the Muslim corner of the cimetière du Père-Lachaise. However, after 1918, France owed a debt of gratitude to the 100,000 Muslims who had died fighting for the country in the First World War and this led to a project for the construction of a Muslim place of worship. In 1926, the minaret of the Grande Mosquée finally rose into the sky of the 5th arrondissement.

Grande Mosquée de Paris. 2 bis, place du Puits-de-l'Ermite, 5th

Temples and pagoda

The East-Asian communities who migrated to Paris in the 70s and 80s worship the Buddhist Triad. They pray to divinities such as the Great Compassionate One, Guanyin the Protector and the Buddha of the Future. Their everyday religious life involves many different practices, such as the cult of ancestors. The shrine of the cult of Buddha is the most secret and traditional holy place in their temples. Vietnamese grandfathers come to click their *xiang-qi* (chess) pawns around on makeshift tables. In the Olympiades quarter stands the gleaming, solemn Centre Teochew de méditation bouddhique. Finally, great religious occasions are celebrated at the pagoda in the bois de Vincennes. In a festive atmosphere, the Buddhist population comes together to lay offerings before the greatest gilt Buddha in Europe.

Left to right

Shrine of the cult of Buddha. 37, rue du Disque, 13th
Centre Teochew de méditation bouddhique. 44, avenue d'Ivry, 13th

Also

Pagode du bois de Vincennes. 40, route circulaire du lac Daumesnil, 12th

Offerings to Ganesh

Attending a puja (ritual ceremony) at the Sri Manika Vinayakar Alayam (the first Hindu temple of France) is a fabulous experience. Followed by the faithful, the priest stops at each altar, beginning with the one

dedicated to Ganesh, the elephant-headed god of knowledge. Each divinity is honored with petals, holy oil, and various colored powders. As he goes, the officiant continually chants prayers in Sanskrit and rings a bell. At the end of the ceremony, the members of the congregation are blessed with a mark on their forehead and the pouring of purifying milk into the hollow of their hand.

Sri Manika Vinayakar Alayam. 17, rue Pajol, 18th

15 Superstitions & pagan rites

Whether we believe in them or not, old customs are sometimes hard to resist. Who has never dropped a coin or two into a well for luck? Ancient beliefs die hard, and the most tenacious are impervious to time and reason. Tombs are particularly well suited to this type of pagan ritual: admiration for an artist can become a cult. Some places with a "presence" also attract loyal pilgrims.

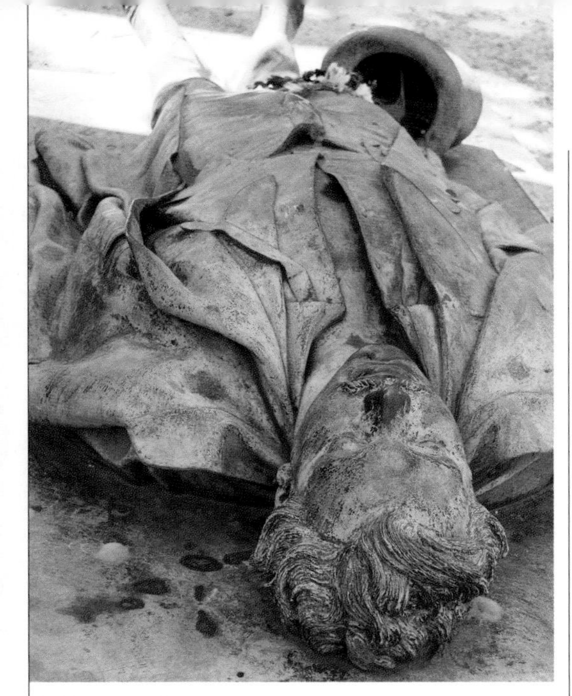

Victor's fly

How many women have come to stroke the lower torso of the recumbent figure of Victor Noir at Père-Lachaise cemetery? A lot, if the shininess of that part of its anatomy is anything to go by. In 1870, the journalist Victor Noir was 22 when he was shot dead by Prince Pierre Bonaparte following an argument. The killing triggered a wave of public protest that ended in riots, especially since the prince was acquitted. A public subscription was launched to honor the victim and Amédée-Jules Dalou was commissioned to make a bronze statue of the deceased. Specializing in realist sculpture, the artist showed Victor at the moment of his death with his shirt rumpled, a gaping wound, and his tall hat fallen beside him. Noir was to have been married the following day and was wearing his wedding clothes for the first time. That led to a legend: the recumbent statue of the former future groom was said to have great fertility powers, so women came to Victor's tomb to pray for a child, placing their hands on the figure's attractively rounded private parts. Finally, in 2004, the cemetery administration lost patience with this erotic cult and put fences around the tomb, but when the press denounced the censorship, the fences were taken down. In fact, examined objectively, Victor's manhood is not particularly striking. It is even quite modest compared to that of the statue of the revolutionary socialist Blanqui, sculpted at around the same time by Dalou.

Cimetière du Père-Lachaise, 20th. Victor Noir (92nd division) and Auguste Blanqui (91st division)

Montaigne's slipper

It is an old student custom to touch the right foot of the statue of the great philosopher Montaigne and say "Salut, Montaigne!" before an examination. The tradition is said to bring luck. The statue was originally in marble, but so many students rubbed the slipper that it wore away quickly and the city's municipal maintenance staff had to restore it constantly. So in 1933, the decision was taken to replace it with a more robust bronze copy. So the shoe became even shinier...

Place Paul-Painlevé, 5th

Married in the 13th

Before 1860, this euphemistic expression was used to describe people who were "living in sin." Before Paris annexed its surrounding villages, it had only 12 arrondissements and so it was obviously impossible to get married at City Hall in the 13th. However, when the capital was enlarged, there were 20 arrondissements. They were initially meant to be numbered like the original 12, from left to right and top to bottom (like lines of text), but that would have meant that today's very affluent 16th arrondissement would have become the 13th. That was unthinkable for the bourgeoisie of Passy and Auteuil! To their relief, the mayor of Passy, Jean-Frédéric Possoz, saved the district's honor. He managed to persuade Haussmann to number the arrondissements in a spiral from the center of the city to the outskirts. Possoz said that the idea came to him while he was eating snails.

Place Possoz, 16th

Charles, if you only knew...

Why Baudelaire in particular? Nobody knows why some writers are more popular than others after their death, aside from any literary considerations. The tomb that Charles Baudelaire shares with his mother and stepfather is frequented by often-tormented admirers who make no secret of the comfort they take from the poet's work. They cover the slab with short, anguished notes in different languages (including Urdu and Japanese). Some are folded small and slipped into the cracks in the stone at the back of the monument. All in all, it is enough to make Marcel Proust or the couple Sartre and Beauvoir, who are interred nearby and receive no such attentions, green with envy.

5, rue de Verneuil, 7th

A tribute to old cabbage head

There is absolutely no chance of missing where Serge Gainsbourg lived from 1969 (*année érotique* according to one of his songs) until his death in 1991. The facade of the house in the respectable rue de Verneuil is entirely covered with graffiti left by fans. These impromptu tributes began even before the legendary Gitanes smoker was in his grave. It amused Serge, the self-styled "Man with the Cabbage Head," but thoroughly annoyed his neighbors, who regularly demanded the removal of the offensive artwork. Gainsbourg's tomb in the cimetière du Montparnasse is also a popular pilgrimage site.

A kiss for Oscar

Wilde would be delighted to know that he (or rather his tomb) is still outraging prigs today. The monument that holds his remains was sculpted by Sir Jacob Epstein and, from its appearance in 1909, was seen as scandalous. It shows a winged sphinx (an allusion to Oscar's poem "The Sphinx"), which has the features of the great playwright. The fabulous creature had a large member (in reference to Wilde's homosexuality). That appendage so shocked many of the people of the time that the cemetery administration covered the monument with a tarpaulin until 1914. Finally, in 1961, prudish vandals emasculated the sphinx. Yet their destructive puritanism has done nothing to lessen the appeal of Oscar's tomb to those individuals—star-crossed lovers of every kind—who come to petition or thank him. Women—many of them foreign tourists—invariably kiss the stone and leave red lipstick marks.

Cimetière du Montparnasse, 14th. Division 6.

Cimetière du Père Lachaise, 20th. Division 89.

Au Bonheur des îles. 142 boulevard de La Villette, 19th

Voodoo shopping

Voodoo, a mixture of African animist rites and monotheistic beliefs, recommends "talking to the gods rather than to God." The gods in question can be pagan spirits, plants with magical powers, or Catholic saints. Specialized Voodoo stores are like esoteric, multidenominational bazaars, where Catholic icons stand side by side with Muslim amulets, Indian statuettes, Buddhist talismans, and universal aphrodisiacs. A practical cult for its believers, Voodoo provides, at little expense, solutions to all the issues of everyday life. It can reveal the answers to an examination, provide courage for those who want to ask for a raise, bring a loved one back to the marital bed, or cause a rival's downfall. Of course you must choose the right potion: Cervelle (Brain), Ce que Femme Veut (What Woman Wants), Pas Kité Moi (Don't Leave Me), Baume Juan Conquistador (John the Conqueror Balm), Case Tonnelle (Bower Hut), or Graine de Zizanie (Quarrel Seed). At the AAA emporium, potions are precisely aligned in alphabetical order according to their special powers. Bonheur des Iles (Happiness of the Islands) supplies leaves, roots, and herbs with colorful names—Miramboland, Balai de Onze Heures (Eleven O'Clock Broom)—and ritual invocations. At Comptoirs Spirituels (Spiritual Trading Posts), there are potions and sanctified amulets to suit every misfortune.

Also

Asie-Antilles-Afrique. 88 bis, rue du Faubourg- du-Temple, 11th Comptoirs spirituels.
8, rue Poulet, 18th

Locked in love

It is all said to have been prompted by the bestselling novel Ho voglia di te (*I Want You*) by Federico Moccia, published in 2006. It is the story of two lovers who follow an old custom, vowing eternal devotion by attaching a padlock engraved with their initials to a bridge, the ponte Milvio, before throwing the key into the River Tiber in Rome. So began the craze for *luchetti d'amore*, known as *cadenas d'amour* or lovelocks depending on the country—for none is now immune: lovers flock to romantic bridges everywhere. In Paris, the pont des Arts and the pont de l'Archevêché are profusely padlocked, as is a footbridge, the passerelle Léopold-Senghor (but to a lesser extent). Yet all that is nothing compared to other locations such as the Yellow Mountains Bridge of the Immortals in China or the Luzhkov Bridge in Moscow, where the authorities have installed metal jacks to lighten the load on the guardrails. The City of Paris is thinking of doing the same: the phenomenon is growing, fueled by mass tourism.

Also

Pont des Arts
Passerelle Léopold-Senghor

Pont de l'Archevêché

16 Surprising & shocking sculptures

Do we really notice the statues that preside so majestically over the center of Parisian squares and gardens? They are so familiar that we do not generally take time to examine them. A pity, because their details are often very entertaining—with the benefit of a little background information.

Hôtel-Dieu, Place du Parvis-Notre-Dame, 4th
(see p. 138)

Statues

Square Louis-XIII, 4th

A horse on a crutch

Do you see anything odd about this equestrian statue of Louis XIII in the middle of the place des Vosges? What on earth is that tree trunk doing under the horse's belly? Flashback: in 1639, Richelieu commissioned a bronze statue to form the centerpiece of what was then the place Royale and obstruct a favorite place of reckoning for duelists of the time. The statue was melted down during the Revolution, but the sculptor Cortot was commissioned to make a replacement in 1825. He chose to use marble rather than bronze and that turned out to be an unfortunate decision: the marble soon began to crack under the horse and rider's weight. That explains the tree-trunk support, which was needed to hold the whole thing up.

An officer with no kepi

Marshal Foch has been riding high in the place du Trocadéro since 1951. His back is straight, he is sporting a fine uniform but... his head is bare! Unimaginable for a soldier! Yet this is no omission but a deliberate choice by the sculptor, Robert Wlérick. His intention was to stress the marshal's intractable nature: a visor would have cast a shadow over his face, concealing his resolute expression. The general staff were not at all happy with the Marshal's sloppy appearance, but had to salute and bear it: Wlérick was backed by the Vice-President of the regional authority of the Conseil général de la Seine, a severely maimed war veteran.

Place du Trocadéro, 16th

Arc de triomphe du Carrousel, 1st

Mariole, the swaggering sapper

Dominique Gaye-Mariole, a sapper (combat engineer) in Napoleon's army, was quite a character. His name is still familiar in French since it features in the expression *faire le mariole* (to play the wise guy). A two-meter (78-inch) giant, strong as an ox, the soldier was wounded many times, but always recovered. One day in 1807 when the emperor was reviewing his troops, Gaye-Mariole had the nerve to present arms with a thirty-kilo (66-pound) cannon in his outstretched grip. News of this exploit did the rounds in barracks everywhere and Mariole became a legend. Many artists used him as a model, which is why he can be seen with his bearskin hat and sapper's apron at the top of the arc de triomphe du Carrousel (on the right when facing the Louvre).

A pantheon of masks

“Come buy my masks!” this youngster seems to be saying. But take a closer look: they are no ordinary concealments. They have the faces of famous contemporaries of the sculptor Zacharie Astruc, who created this work in 1883. They include Victor Hugo (in the figure’s left hand), Eugène Delacroix, Alexandre Dumas fils, Léon Gambetta, Jean-Baptiste Carpeaux, Camille Corot, Hector Berlioz,

Gabriel Fauré, Honoré de Balzac, and Jules Barbey d’Aurevilly. Astruc made his name with this work, which is entitled Le Marchand de Masques (*The Mask Merchant*). Sadly, it is no longer complete: the mask once held in the boy’s right hand has gone.

Jardin du Luxembourg, 6th (eastern part, on the terrace between the main pond and the école des Mines)

’Ware automobile!

In the early days of the horseless carriage, people were very suspicious of this (devil’s?) invention, which smoked and backfired and made a terrible racket. Léon Serpollet was a pioneer in the field, inventing an automobile entirely powered by steam from an instant-vaporization boiler. He also built a steam tricycle and, in 1887, became the first motorist to receive a driver’s license. Such achievements deserved recognition, which duly came in the form of a statue commissioned from the sculptor Bouchez in around 1910. However, the tribute turned out to be rather two-edged: Serpollet is at the wheel of his machine, acclaimed by admirers and surrounded by clouds of steam—but in front of the vehicle, a man is about to be run down. A shrewd, early road-safety ad.

Place Saint-Ferdinand, 17th

Morbid medicine

In a corner of the former École pratique de médecine is a mournful statue entitled La Faucheuse (*The Reaper*). Sculpted at the very start of the 20th century by Gabriel Jules Thomas, the figure has all the traits of Death and is trampling underfoot various symbols of human pride and vanity: a crown, a treasure chest, a sword, jewels, and a scepter.

15-21, rue de l’Écolede-Médecine, 6th

Caution: chariot reversing

On the roof of the Grand Palais, two miraculously balanced bronze quadrigas seem to be taking flight. A driver is standing in one ancient chariot drawn by four horses with their manes flying in the wind. A brilliant piece of work—except that the chariot is back to front. The sculptor did it deliberately to avoid hiding the figure, but the effect is quite ludicrous: the man seems to be standing precariously in a wheelchair!

Grand Palais. Avenue Winston-Churchill, 8th

A tortoise for Lafayette

To thank the French for the Statue of Liberty they had presented to the USA in 1886, 13 years later in 1899, the Americans decided to send them a statue of Lafayette, the French commander who had fought the British in the American Revolutionary War. The chosen sculptor—the American Paul Bartlett—was told to finish the statue quickly so that it could be displayed at the 1900 Exposition in Paris. Unable to complete it in time, Bartlett delivered a provisional plaster model, which he recovered after the World's Fair. He continued to work on it for eight years before he was satisfied. The sculptor had been paid in advance, so for all this time, his clients kept urging him to complete his work and pour it in bronze. When he finally did so, he added a self-deprecatory tortoise on the plinth in answer to those critics who had derided his cavalier attitude towards deadlines.

Cours La Reine, 8th (entre le Grand Palais et la Seine)

Statues of Liberty

Paris has five copies of the Statue of Liberty. The most famous is the one that stands at the tip of the île aux Cygnes (16th), a 1/5-scale model unveiled on July 4, 1889. Another, smaller replica is in the jardin du Luxembourg near the puppet theater (6th). The gilt torch above the tunnel de l'Alma (8th) is a full-scale copy of the one held by the statue in New York. Another Liberty stands below the Beaugrenelle Towers on the quai André-Citroën (15th). In the musée des Arts et Métiers (3rd) is the original 1/16-scale plaster model. Finally, a tiny reproduction of the Statue of Liberty is visible on the torso of César's Centaure. It seems to be springing from his breastplate (carrefour de la Croix-Rouge, 6th).

Top to bottom, left to right

Quai André-Citroën, 15th
Jardin du Luxembourg, 6th
Carrefour de la Croix-Rouge, 6th

Also

Île aux Cygnes, 16th Tunnel de l'Alma, 8th
Musée des Arts et Métiers, 3rd

The man who passed through walls

Le passer muraille is a collection of short stories published in 1943. It describes the adventures of a certain Dutilleul, a dull minor employee in a ministry who one day discovers that he can walk through walls. He uses his power to carry out some lucrative burglaries, signing them "Garou-Garou." The author was Marcel Aymé, a resident of Montmartre whose apartment windows looked out onto this small square (from no. 26). On his death, his friend and neighbor Jean Marais sculpted a Passe-Muraille with Marcel's features. The figure emerging from a high wall is a startling sight.

Place Marcel-Aymé, 18th

A medical mannequin

Standing in the middle of the jardin de l'Hôtel-Dieu is a startling statue. Brightly colored and disguised in different costumes from season to season, it is the unrecognizable figure of a certain Dupuytren, head surgeon at the Hôtel-Dieu hospital in 1815. The doctor—a great professional, but an obstinate, ambitious man—was not remembered kindly by his subordinates. So, since the 1980s, medical students have been using his statue (installed in 1946) as the butt of their rough humor and to let off steam. Whenever the medical team changes (in June and November), the figure is disguised as a new celebrity or even an object (Métro ticket) or country (Brazil). At various times, Dupuytren has been disguised as Mickey Mouse, Batman, Asterix the Gaul, Snow White, the rugby player Chabal, a Smurf, and Mr. Spock. Since his decorators never strip off the old paint, the figure of the baron-surgeon has grown plumper with each new coat.

Place du Parvis-Notre Dame, 4th

High & low relief

Bawdy benches

Each stall in the double rows that line the choir of the church of Saint-Gervais is equipped with a misericord (derived from the Latin word for compassion), a ledge fixed below a hinged seat to support the posterior of a cleric required to stand for parts of an endless service. The only ones of their kind, they are decorated with carvings that represent different trades: a public letter writer, an architect, a baker putting dough into an oven, a cooper, grape pickers, a cobbler, two roast-meat sellers, a boatman, and so on. Aside from these scenes of everyday life, there are other, cruder tableaus in the first row of stalls on the left. They include a couple taking a bath, a squatting man wearing a cap with donkey ears who is defecating on a doorstep, and a woman with no underwear warming her posterior by a fire.

Place Saint-Gervais, 4th

Persona non grata

With Napoleon exiled to waste away on Saint Helena, France's new ruler Louis XVIII ordered that every memento of the defeated emperor be destroyed. Masons were tasked with finding and disposing of his effigies and name. For instance, on the southern leveling marker of the parc de Montsouris, the stone has been chiseled away where Bonaparte's name was

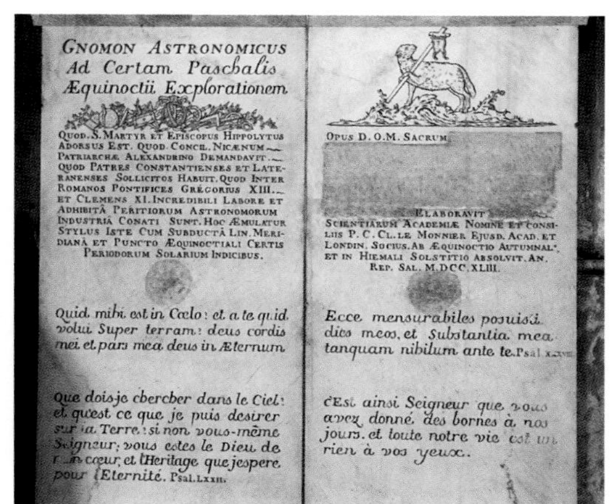

On the pedestal of the gnomon of the église Saint-Sulpice, 6th, another example of censorship, but Revolutionary this time: among the inscriptions thanking the benefactors of the Kingdom, the Church, and the Academy of Sciences, the one naming King Louis XV and his ministers was erased after the Revolution.

engraved: "In the reign of… blank." An even more absurd rewriting of history can be seen on the colonnade of the Louvre. During the First Empire, its pediment was decorated with a bust of the emperor, who had ordered the rapid completion of work on this part of the palace. So as not to detract from the whole by leaving an empty space, it was decided that a diplomatic makeover would be the best solution. A sculptor turned Napoleon's crown of laurels into a curly wig, disguising him as the Sun King, Louis XIV, and changed the inscription below. However, he missed one detail: the shield of Minerva decorated with the imperial eagle and bees so dear to Bonaparte!

Top to bottom

Colonnade de Perrault, facing the church of Saint-Germain-l'Auxerrois, 1st

Parc de Montsouris, 14th

Vengeance by visual pun

The Marquis de Louvois, Louis XIV's Minister of War, was extremely vain and keen to boast of his own achievements rather than those of others. In several places in Les Invalides, he had his coat of arms sculpted next to those of the king, who immediately had them removed. The exasperated Louvois decided that revenge was a dish best served cold. In a secret clause of his will, he left instructions that he was to be buried in Les Invalides. His body was discreetly interred in one of the tombs by a priest supporter, but the king found out and had it removed three days later. However, the monarch did not realize that the Marquis had a backup plan, a different way of ensuring his posterity at Les Invalides. Over a window in the Court of Honor, he had ordered a wolf to be sculpted. Half hidden by palm leaves, the animal's eyes were fixed on the ground of the courtyard. In other words, the wolf sees: the *loup voit*, pronounced exactly like Louvois in French. When this carefully crafted pun was explained to Louis XIV, he simply shrugged and said, "The poor man, that's just like him!"

Court of Honor of Les Invalides, eastern side, fifth window from the central pediment on the right, 7th

Église Saint-Germain-l'Auxerrois. Rue de l'Arbre-Sec, 1st

68, rue Condorcet, 9th

Canting arms

Like Louvois (*see p. 139*), the architect Eugène Viollet-le-Duc used a pithy visual signature. It was an eagle owl (the bird is called a *grand-duc* in French) perched under the cornice of a house on the rue Condorcet. The architect designed the building in 1862 and lived there until he died in 1879. It is a very simple construction without his customary ornamental extravagances. Another example of canting arms can be seen on the apse of the church of Saint-Germain-l'Auxerrois (outside). Along the cornice runs a frieze of carps in segments or *tronçons*. *Tronçon* is the homophone of Jehan Tronson, a master draper who helped to fund the church's reconstruction in the 16th century. The choice of carp may have been a tribute to the discretion and modesty of the generous donor.

A preeminent proboscis

Napoleon's Egyptian campaign in 1798 led to a wave of Egyptomania that swept through French literature, painting, fashion and architecture. A style known as Retour d'Égypte (Return from Egypt) flourished on facades, while a district dubbed Foire du Caire (Cairo Fair) appeared on the site of the former cour des Miracles in 1806. Among the pseudo-hieroglyphs on the cornice above the entrance of the passage du Caire, there is a comic profile with a colossal nose. It is the portrait of Henri Auguste Bougenier (1799-1866), a painter whose nasal appendage was so phenomenal that it was often caricatured by his artist friends. Victor Hugo mentioned it in Les Misérables and it may well have inspired Edmond Rostand as he was fleshing out the character of Cyrano de Bergerac in 1897. Below, on the frieze above the heads of Hathor, two of the central characters show the same exaggerated trait.

Place du Caire, 2nd

A Republican coat of arms on a church

From 1319, Auteuil had its own church, but once the village was annexed by Paris, a larger place of worship was needed to deal with the influx of new inhabitants. The church was completely rebuilt on a grander scale in 1877, against the wishes of the anticlerical municipal authorities. The priest at the time,

Abbé Lamazou, made every effort to speed up construction of the new sanctuary, even using his own money. However, he had to make one concession: a coat of arms of the City of Paris on the side of the building. It is crowned with stars instead of the traditional royal fleurs-de-lys of church ornamentation.

Rue Wilhem, 16th (below the entrance to the crypt)

How long can the rat in the rue Georges-Lardennois, 19th, avoid the mouser's claws?

Ball of rats

The *boule aux rats* (ball of rats) of the church of Saint-Germain-l'Auxerrois is not simply the only example in Paris, but also the only relatively optimistic one in France. A *boule aux rats* is a design dating back to the 15th or 16th century. It symbolizes an Earth ravaged by poverty or threatened by evildoers (invaders, miscreants, the ungodly, etc.). At least a dozen of them are to be found in Metropolitan France, all associated with churches. They are topped with a cross and show rats invading the ball, except for the one at Saint-Germain-l'Auxerrois, where the rats seem to be leaving.

Église Saint-Germain-l'Auxerrois, 1st (under the central gargoyle in the courtyard of the presbytery)

The *boule aux rats* of the cathedral of Mans shows the rodents entering the Earth, unlike the one in Paris, where the animals are emerging from it.

Sarah's rats

In 1876, when the architect Nicolas-Félix Escalier built a town house for Sarah Bernhardt in the rue Fortuny, the tragedian's glory was at its height and she had become very eccentric. For instance, she was permanently surrounded by rare or exotic, sometimes dangerous, pets. Are these two rats on the facade that seem to be trying to get into the wall a reference to this quirk? What we do know is that the rats are tough: they survived the refurbishing of the house in 1891. The building stands opposite the first childhood home of former president Nicolas Sarkozy and now holds the offices of ex-prime minister Dominique de Villepin's law firm.

35, rue Fortuny, 17th

Fish and fishwives

At the side of the church of Saint-Eustache, a door has a medallion in the form of a fish above it. The entrance leads to the crypt of Sainte-Agnès, the only remnant of the former chapelle Sainte-Agnès, which stood on this site until it was replaced by Saint-Eustache. The area was the terminus for the fish carts that transported seafood overnight from the Normandy coast to Paris's Les Halles wholesale market. Street names show what route the fish merchants or *poissonniers* took: chemin des Poissonniers in Saint-Ouen, rue des Poissonniers, rue du Faubourg-Poissonnière, rue des Petits-Carreaux, and finally rue Montorgueil led them to the market. Built in 1213, the chapelle Sainte-Agnès was funded by the interest on a loan. A rich merchant of Les Halles named Jean Alais had lent a large sum of money to King Philippe II Auguste. To get it back, he demanded the right to impose a tax on every basket of fish sold here. He made a fortune and, whether in atonement or to give thanks, he founded the chapelle Sainte-Agnès. The chapel was enlarged several times before it was replaced by today's building, consecrated in 1637. The fishwives of the seafood stalls at Les Halles were notorious loudmouths and believed they had a right to have a say in the running of a church they had helped to pay for by selling their fish. So the job of ministering

to the local parish was no sinecure. It was said that "nobody can be priest of Saint-Eustache if they are not mad."

1, rue Montmartre, 1st

Masonic symbols

Originating in Great Britain in 1717, freemasonry gained a hold in France in 1725, encouraged by the liberal, anglophile climate of the Regency. At first, only the high aristocracy were masons. The Consulate and the Empire were providential periods for the movement. It shared certain values and symbols with the guilds, including the rule and compass, the mallet and chisel, the level and plumb line, the rule and lever, the trowel, and so on. Parisian strollers merely have to glance up to see these masonic symbols incorporated in bas-reliefs or the ornamentation of statues, discreet signals from the builders to their freemason brothers. Such emblems mark the divide between the mysticism of freemasonry and secular life.

The shining star

A five-pointed star (pentagram) symbolizing divinity shines from the front of a building in the rue de Buci. The very first masonic lodge in France opened nearby in the rue de la Boucherie in 1725, before moving to 12, rue de Buci in 1732. It was named the Bussy lodge.

12, rue de Buci, 6th

Square and compass

Generally inseparable as symbols, the rule, square, and compass together represent equity, honesty, justice, and the spirit. They feature on a bas-relief in the rue Montorgueil showing a terrestrial globe surrounded by attributes of Arts and Letters, and on a medallion on the quai de Bourbon.

Top to bottom

43, quai de Bourbon, 4th
51, rue Montorgueil, 2nd

Pyramid

Shortly after Philippe d'Orléans, Duke of Chartres, was appointed grandmaster of the Grand Orient de France, he commissioned the painter Carmontelle to redesign the estate he owned on the outskirts of Paris. Eager to please his distinguished client, Carmontelle filled the grounds with *fabriques* representing "all times and all places" (which had been his brief) and slipped in a few masonic symbols here and there. All that remains of the "Chartres folly," as it was known, is the colonnade and Egyptian pyramid (the sign of immortality) constructed in 1773.

Parc Monceau, 8th

All-seeing eye

This eye, set in the center of a triangle surrounded by rays of light, is known as the "Eye of Providence" or "All-seeing Eye." The bright triangle is called the "delta." The design represents the eye of God watching over humanity.

Place du Palais-Bourbon, 7th (on the base of the statue of Marianne)

Athanor

Three medallions are lined up on the front of a 19th-century house on the rue de la Perle. The first features a head of Marianne; the second, a tower and bridge; the third, masonic symbols: a square, a compass, a plumb line and what seems to be an athanor, the furnace that alchemists used for their experiments. It was a kind of forge with a pipe that provided a permanent fire at a steady temperature. In masonic symbolism, the tool represents a philosophical fire.

20, rue de la Perle, 3rd

Philosophical hive

The philosophical hive represents the work ethic and, above all, community life in the lodge.

Top to bottom

23, boulevard de Bonne-Nouvelle, 2nd
64, avenue Ledru-Rollin, 12th

17 A fabulous urban menagerie

Sculptors and architects have looked to more than just the contents of Noah's Ark for inspiration when creating their animal figures. They have also delved into myth and legend to add mysterious or unsettling touches to their buildings. In Paris, the most commonly depicted real animals (horses, lions, and snakes) cohabit with mermaids, sphinxes, chimeras, and griffins. These fantastically hybrid monsters lie brazenly in wait on cornices and gates. Churches were first to adopt them in the Middle Ages. The stone iconography of places of worship played an educational role: bible stories were shown on church doors and the devil featured in the shape of a demon or dragon. In around 1240, gargoyles appeared. They were multitaskers, diverting runoff water from walls while symbolically warding off evil. Each of these grotesque figures was unique. Then, by the end of the 17th century, following archeological discoveries in Italy, Greece, and Egypt, other mythological figures such as phoenixes, sphinxes (*see p. 192-193*), chimeras, and griffins made their debut.

Notre-Dame-de-Paris, 4th (galerie des Chimères) *(see p. 146)*

Chimeras

Chimeras are monsters from Greek mythology with a lion's head, a goat's body, and a dragon's wings and tail. In everyday language, a chimera has come to mean an impossible goal.

53, rue des Mathurins, 9th *(below)*

Also

133, rue Saint-Antoine, 4th (under the balcony of the hôtel Séguier)
Fontaine Saint-Michel, 5th

Griffins and winged lions

The griffin is a Greek mythological animal that was ridden by Apollo. It has the head, wings, and talons of an eagle; the rear of a lion; the tail of a snake; and the ears of a horse. It is known as the Guardian of Justice. The winged lion is a simpler version of the griffin.

34, rue Vieille-du-Temple, 4th *(above)*
24, rue Vieille-du-Temple, 4th *(opposite)*

Also

88, rue de Rivoli, 4th
At the top of the tour Saint-Jacques, 4th
Corner of avenue de l'Observatoire and rue Michelet, 6th

Phoenixes

The phoenix, which rises endlessly from its own ashes, was the favorite symbol of insurance companies, especially those that specialized in fire coverage. It is often found on the front of buildings that belong or belonged to insurers. One example is the phoenix on the avenue Foch, which is emerging from a blaze above the porch of a building owned by life-insurance firm Le Phénix in 1892.

186, avenue Victor-Hugo, 16th

Also

22, avenue Foch, 16th

Medusas

Two sinister medusas poke their tongues out at passers-by from the door of the hôtel des Ambassadeurs de Hollande. The wooden bas-reliefs were sculpted by Renaudin.

47, rue Vieille-du-Temple, 4th

Centaurs

A creature from Greek mythology, the centaur has a human torso and a horse's body. The bearded head of this bronze centaur made by the sculptor César in 1985 is a self-portrait.

Carrefour de la Croix-Rouge, 6th

Place Augusta-Holmes, 13th

Dragons

At the start of the 19th century, the Romantic school was keen on Arthurian legend and *chansons de geste* (songs of heroic deeds)—sagas where dragons played a starring role. Two very unobtrusive dragons lurk to the sides of the stairs leading to the second floor of the Opéra Garnier. Another, more modern winged reptile with a steel and glass body writhes in the place Augusta-Holmes, above a subterranean non-potable water production plant.

This 2000 work by French-Chinese artist Chen Zhen is entitled La Danse de la Fontaine émergente (*The Dance of the Emerging Spring*). It symbolizes the energy of the water drawn from the Seine to supply the city. So where is its head? It is nowhere to be seen, giving the impression that it could abruptly surface anywhere to confront the unwary stroller.

Also
Cour du Dragon, 6th
50, rue de Rennes, 6th
53, rue des Mathurins, 9th
Opéra-Garnier, 9th
11, rue Faustin-Hélie, 16th

Unidentified creatures

Decorators have also used their fertile imaginations to create animals with no known mythological pedigree, such as the eagle-headed Atlases with human torsos on the rue des Mathurins or the weird beasts from the rue de Lota, who cling to the consoles of the facade as if their lives depended on it.

4, rue de Lota, 16th

Also
53, rue des Mathurins, 9th

A stone community

When Notre-Dame was restored in 1845, Viollet-le-Duc populated the higher levels of the cathedral with the greatest concentration of fabulous creatures anywhere—gargoyles, chimeras, and demons. The most famous of the chimeras is a strix—a night bird of ill-omen holding its head in its hands and sticking out its tongue.

Notre-Dame-de-Paris, 4th (gallerie des chimères)

Castel Béranger

Designed by Hector Guimard, the lines of the frontage of the Castel Béranger (award winner of the 1895 facade competition) are remarkable. They are so startling that they tend to overshadow the ornamental details. An incredible bestiary of fantastic verdigris animals—including cats, birds, marine creatures, insects, and reptiles, as well as indistinct forms with staring eyes—crawls over the walls. Another, unrecognizable, beast (a bat?) has strayed onto the roof. Guimard himself lived on the ground floor of the building, which was originally a housing project.

14, rue La Fontaine, 16th

Doorknockers and handles

Doorknockers are often shaped like fantastic creatures. Whether bronze or brass, in ring or in hammer form, they serve a dual purpose, enabling visitors to signal their arrival and making it easier to open or close a heavy door. They generally come in twos for aesthetic reasons, even if only one is used.

1 2, cite Malesherbes, 9th
2 6, rue Alfred-de-Vigny, 17th
3 10, rue Copernic, 16th
4 62, rue Saint-Antoine, hôtel de Sully, 4th
5 11, rue Saint-Florentin, 1st
6 22,rue de Douai, 9th
7 Rue des Mathurins, 9th
8 3, boulevard Arago, 14th
9 102, rue du Bac, 7th
10 28, rue Juliette-Lamber, 17th
11 65, rue du Cardinal Lemoine, 5th

18 Ceramics & mosaics

The multicolored ornamental ceramics and mosaics that brighten up the facades of buildings and stores are often discreet, but offer an enchanting variety of patterns and shades.

17e Arrt
RUE DES DAMES

Corner of rue Nollet and rue des Dames, 17th *(see p. 155)*

Ceramics

La céramique ornementale began to boom during the Universal Exposition of 1878, when technical progress—especially a process to prevent the glaze on ceramics from cracking—had enabled the mass production of decorative tiling. Members of the public were delighted by the range of colors on offer to brighten up their facades and the tiles' resistance to weathering. Orders flowed in at the great tile works in Ivry, the pottery in Choisy-le-Roi, and Hippolyte Boulenger's showroom in the rue de Paradis. Everybody had to have tiling to decorate his town or country house, rental property or store. People who could not afford to cover the front of the house entirely settled for a cabochon, rosette, frieze, medallion, or name tile.

Patterned with flowers, birds, arabesques, and rural scenes, these new decorative elements fueled imagination, daydreaming, and fantasies of getting away from it all. In those days of Atlantic crossings and vacations by the sea in Trouville, they suggested travel. The Roaring Twenties were the golden age of architectural ceramics, which had the added benefit of hygiene and so were used to line the walls of public baths, food stores and bathrooms. However, at the end of the decade, the Great Depression combined with fierce competition and the industrialization of ceramics production to force the two main Parisian manufacturers and many others to shut down their ovens in the 1930s.

4, rue de la Pierre-Levée, 11th

The Loebnitz manufactory

Jules Loebnitz, one of the region's tiling heavy-weights, was the man behind the ceramics process used to mass-produce monumental decorative surfaces painted in vivid, shining colors. His factory was internationally renowned and he worked with the great architects of his time: Eugène Viollet-le-Duc, Charles Garnier, Juste Lisch, and especially Paul Sédille, who became his friend. Sédille was a great proponent of colorful architecture and saw Loebnitz as a "master of fire" who could bring his dreams to life. Their partnership produced exhibition pavilions, apartment buildings, villas, hotels, and commemorative monuments. When Loebnitz had Sédille renovate his work-shops in 1880-1884, the architect decorated the facade with panels of antique scenes, based on drawings by Lévy, winner of the Grand Prix de Rome. At around the same time, Sédille asked Loebnitz to supply enameled earthenware for the sign of the new Printemps department store.

Le Printemps.
64, boulevard Haussmann, 9th

Boulenger pottery

Belonging to Hippolyte Boulenger, this other great factory had opened in Choisy-le-Roi in 1804. Boulenger had a showroom built to present his products in the rue de Paradis in Paris, the center of the crystal-ware trade. The spectacular building entirely covered with painted, unfading ceramics served as a permanent catalogue of his products. Customers simply had to choose their style: antiquity, still life, or any other genre they preferred. The hall, concierge's loge, main courtyard, and customer reception room were all decorated with ceramics. The Compagnie du métro parisien ordered its wall tiles from Boulenger (and the Gien potteries).

18, rue de Paradis, 10th

Maison Bouly

From 1867 on, this building was used as a depot by the wholesale distributors of the Ponchon (in the Oise district) potteries, which principally made china tiling. The tiles on the facade are decorated with particularly delicate patterns.

140, boulevard Richard-Lenoir, 11th

A question of hygiene

Since ceramic tiles were waterproof and easy to clean, they were particularly suitable for public baths. The bains de Châteaudun, which specialized in hydrotherapy, are now closed, but the Odessa baths, whose facade is decorated with particularly sophisticated ceramics, are still open.

5, rue d'Odessa, 14th (in the courtyard, press the "Bains-douches" button to enter)

Also
66 bis, rue du Faubourg-Montmartre, 9th

Food stores

Ceramic tiles were also ideal for food stores since their bright colors appealed to customers and their smooth surfaces were easy to wipe clean. Some of these stores are still in the same business, such as the Au Panetier bakery (2nd) or the Christ Inn's bistrot (formerly the Cochon à l'oreille), whose ceramics conjure up the everyday world of Les Halles in around 1914 with scenes of early-morning life in front of the church of Saint-Eustache, fruit and vegetable vendors, lively discussions between traders, and so on. Others have changed their specialty, such as the former fishmonger's store in the rue du Faubourg-Montmartre, whose window and interior panels of Sarreguemines tiles were inspired by the popularity of Hokusai engravings at the end of the 19th century.

10, place des Petits-Pères, 2nd

Also

15, rue Montmartre, 1st
24, rue du Faubourg-Montmartre, 9th

False pretenses

The decor of the restaurant Le Petit Zinc is puzzling. Its facade is ornamented with Sarreguemines ceramics that suggest (in writing, too) that the store not only sold farm produce (milk, eggs, fruit, and vegetables) but also had an oyster stand, all in an art nouveau style setting. That is hard to imagine at a time when stores were still highly specialized (some supplied seafood, others dairy products and eggs). In fact, the decor is a reconstruction created for Jean Bouquin, costume artist and dresser to the stars of the 1970s (most notably Brigitte Bardot), who wanted to open a 1900-themed bistro. It subsequently became Le Petit Zinc.

11, rue Saint-Benoît, 6th

3-D signs

What store in the rue Saint-Antoine promoted its business with this fine display of *Alice's Adventures in Wonderland* relief ceramics? A toy or clothing store? In any case, it is a tanning salon today. The characters include the king, the queen, a flamingo, and of course the white rabbit with his pocket watch. Near Alesia, a 1930s sign shows a character in relief offering sugared almonds for christenings, based on a drawing by the illustrator Dranzy.

32, rue Saint-Antoine, 4th

Also

51, avenue du Général-Leclerc, 14th

Portrait medallions

This building was constructed in 1881 to house the Société pour l'éducation élémentaire, the oldest and largest secular elementary school association

in France, founded in 1815. Its four medallions feature the engraver Francoeur, the geographer Jomard, and the mathematician Leroy, along with Frédéric de La Rochefoucauld-Liancourt, all active members of the Society. Their portraits are accompanied by "Art," "Morals" and "Science" belt courses, continuous rows of stones set in line with window sills, which help make the horizontal line of the sills visually more prominent. Under the upper cornice, other belt courses are decorated with olive branches and a scallop shell.

6, rue du Fouarre, 5th

Churchgoers' blushes spared!

In 1844, the painter Jules Jollivet was commissioned to decorate the enameled lava tiles covering the porch of the newly built church of Saint-Vincent-de-Paul. But when he added the final touches and the work was unveiled, the clergy was outraged: his bible scenes were far too nude, colorful, and indecent! The prefect of the Seine district and the commission des Beaux-Arts also stepped in. Finally, the order was given to remove the paintings. With a shrug, Jollivet simply put smaller copies of his bible scenes up on the front of the town house he had built in 1858. Prudes and prigs could make a detour! The opulent house held both his living quarters and studio, which were reached via separate stairs (possibly so that the artist's models would not run into his wife).

11, cité Malesherbes, 9th

Sumptuous halls

With their large wall surfaces on either side of the corridor, building entrances are a perfect place for genre paintings or variations on a theme. The four seasons, for instance, which were chosen to decorate the hall of 59, rue Caulaincourt. The scene is of four allegorical young women (in a garden, by the sea, under a vine, and in the snow). In the rue Damrémont, 12 separate tiled panels by Francisque Poulbot (1910) show children's games from month to month with the butte Montmartre in the background. Right at the end of the passage, other panels produced by the Boulenger pottery feature flamingoes in a marsh. The entrance to 8, rue Mélingue is more restrained, but very poetic.

Also
8, rue Mélingue, 19e

59, rue Caulaincourt, 18th (door-code access)

43 bis, rue Damrémont, 18th (access possible on weekdays)

The wall of I Love Yous

A work of modern art created by Frédéric Baron and Claire Kito, Le Mur des je t'aime is made up of enameled lava tiles on which the words "I Love You" are translated into nearly 300 languages. The format of the lava tiles reflects the dimensions of the sheets of paper used by Frédéric Baron to compile the vast collection of handwritten phrases.

Square Jehan-Rictus, 18th

Exhibition models

This monumental ceramic door in the square Félix-Desruelles was the entrance to a pavilion: the palais des Manufactures nationales de Sèvres (porcelain works) at the Universal Exposition of 1900. The far more modest, small ceramic panel in a courtyard of the boulevard Malesherbes came from the porch of the pavillon des Beaux-Arts at the Universal Exposition of 1878.

Also
Square Félix-Desruelles, 6th

28, boulevard Malesherbes, 8th

Métro stations

During a France-Belgium cultural exchange program in 1982, Liège station was decorated with 18 ceramic panels from Welkenraedt showing locations and monuments in that province (the Perron, the provincial palace, and so on). Porte-des-Lilas station paid tribute to the singer-songwriter Georges Brassens, whose figure was framed by two armfuls of *lilas* (lilacs)—one mauve, the other blue. In the corridors of the disused station, mosaic advertisements still sing the praises of different consumer brands (Maïzena corn flour, Jav bleach). They were installed in 1950, a few years after the station closed, to convince clients of the Métro advertising network's benefits.

Station Porte-des-Lilas (line 11, on the Châtelet platform)
Station Liège (line 13)

31 and 37, rue du Faubourg-Saint-Jacques, 14th. Signage on the facade of the hôpital Cochin.

Hanging gardens

This terraced building was constructed in 1912 by Henri Sauvage and Charles Sarazin, who apparently had little time for the preferred decorative style of the period, which tended more towards art nouveau curlicues. The facing they chose was easy-to-clean, beveled white and blue ceramic tiles similar to those used in the Métro.

26, rue Vavin, 6th

A ceramic hotel

The facade is entirely covered with sandstone ceramics. The architect, Jules Lavirotte, a disciple of art nouveau, did not pull his punches when he decorated this hotel, with its fine curved lines. He commissioned the ceramic artist Bigot, whose relief plant patterns bloom on the ivory-colored tiles.

34, avenue de Wagram, 8th

32, rue Eugène-Flachat, 17th. Turquoise tiling emphasized by a frieze of lemon trees on this building dating back to 1900.

Mosaics

Partly due to the boom in ceramics, the ancient decorative tradition of mosaics returned to fashion at the end of the 19th century. This renaissance was partly due to the presence of Italian artisans in Paris (Facchina, Salviati, Odorico, and Mazzioli), whom Charles Garnier had hired to decorate his Opéra from 1867 to 1875. The Universal Expositions gave the mosaicists an opportunity to publicize their work and secure orders. Mosaics had an image of luxury and both wall and floor versions became extremely popular inside and outside civil and religious buildings until the craze died down after the Second World War.

The maestro Facchina

Gian Domenico Facchina, a famous mosaicist from Frioul, decorated an impressive number of Parisian institutions: museums (Galliera, Grévin, Carnavalet), department stores (Le Printemps, Le Bon Marché), banks (Comptoir national d'Escompte), schools (lycée Louis-le-Grand, collège Chaptal), theaters, and so on. His execution of the flooring in the hall, galleries, and peristyle of the Petit Palais, designed for the Universal Exposition of 1900, was particularly brilliant. He created geometrical and plant patterns, such as the fine gilt water flowers against a blue background on the borders of the ponds in the interior garden. Finally, the magnificence of the galerie Vivienne owes a great deal to the Facchina arabesques and stars paving its floor.

Galerie Vivienne, 2nd

Also
Petit Palais. Avenue Winston-Churchill, 8th

16, avenue Victor-Hugo, 16th

Left to right
51, rue Ramey, 18th
24, rue des Écouffes, 4th

Colorful storefronts

Covering the front of a store with a multicolored mosaic is a smart move. It draws the customer's eye and any dirt can be wiped off in a second. In the Marais quarter, Florence Kahn's cake store decked out entirely in blue can be seen from a long way off, as can the blood-red former horsemeat butcher's store in the rue Vieille-du-Temple (*see p. 21*). The Caves populaires des Batignolles are equally striking. The former *poissonnerie* (fishmonger's store) in the rue de Seine has been opportunistically recycled as a *boissonnerie* (drinkery), but has kept its elegant red fish. Of course, fishmonger's stores kept these very practical surfaces long after they went out of fashion in the 1940s. The same goes for seafood restaurants, such as the very chic Prunier. In the rue de Londres, an entire building belonging to the Société française des eaux minerales is clothed in a bright green and blue robe shot through with sparkling-water bubbles. Then in the rue des Petits-Hôtels, there is... well, a little hotel.

Also
15, rue Vieille-du-Temple, 4th
Corner of rue Nollet and rue des Dames, 17th
69, rue de Seine, 6th
30, rue de Londres, 9th
18, rue des Petits-Hôtels, 10th

An enamel and gold fresco

To smarten up the peristyle of the facade of the Grand Palais built for the Universal Exposition of 1900, Louis-Édouard Fournier designed a fresco that illustrated great civilizations as they were imagined at the turn of the century. The idea was to glorify France's colonial empire with highly idealized images of Africa and Asia. Auguste Guilbert-Martin took on the task of turning the design into a rich enamel and gold mosaic an impressive 75 meters long!

Grand Palais. Avenue Winston-Churchill, 8th

14, boulevard de Strasbourg, 10th. Le théâtre Antoine (formerly the théâtre des Menus Plaisirs) has a multicolored facade combining enameled brick, mosaic and ceramics (1880).

Top to bottom
29, rue des Saints-Pères, 6th
35, rue Clavel, 19th

Shard signs

Mosaic signs were used to signal the presence of every kind of business: a Belleville comb manufacturer (Ets Mermet), a dance promoter with futuristic ambitions in Ménilmontant (Concert du xxe siècle), a window cleaning firm (Maison Castrique, near Bonne-Nouvelle) and bistros such as Le Comptoir des Saints-Pères or the former Café Guerbois in Batignolles, where Manet came to discuss the weighty issues of the day with his artist friends after stocking up at the store of M. Hennequin, the neighboring art supplies merchant. They gathered every Friday evening and always sat at the same table to lay down the foundations of Impressionism together.

Also
138, boulevard de Ménilmontant, 20th
22, rue Notre-Dame-de Recouvrance, 2nd
9 and 11 bis, avenue de Clichy, 17th

Cour du Commerce-Saint-André, 6th. Two side of the frontage of the Odeon Relais are faced with art nouveau floral-pattern mosaics.

Just inside

Watch where you are stepping! In various buildings, there is an entrance mosaic not far from the doormat whose theme is directly connected to the business, for instance, the "refrigerator man" carrying a block of ice in the entrance to hall A of the former refrigerated warehouses of Paris-Ivry. Behind the door of Le Temps des Cerises, a worker's production cooperative, a couple are enjoying a drink. In the rue Saint-Sulpice, the name Alys is immortalized on the floor of the hall. But are the respectable building's residents aware that they are living in a former bordello run by that Alys?

Top to bottom
Les Frigos (hall A). Rue des Frigos, 13th
Les Temps des Cerises. 18, rue de la Butte-aux-Cailles, 13th

Also
15, rue Saint-Sulpice, 6th

Dissident signs

These are a little less legible than the official enameled street signs, but so much more charming!

24, rue Saint-Victor, 5th

Also
Impasse Saint-Eustache, 1st
Avenue Victoria, 1st
Rue des Petits-Carreaux, 2nd
Rue de Grenelle, 7th
23, avenue de Messine, 8th (a building by architect Jules Lavirotte)
Rue Singer, 16th
Rue Benjamin-Godard, 16th

Building design

In 1911, the florist Pierre Orève had a building constructed at this address. It included a store set forward on the street, greenhouses in the courtyard, and a winter garden upstairs (in the glazed rotunda that can be seen on the terrace). The decor, which combines varnished bricks and mosaics showing garlands of oak and chestnut leaves, was created by Maurice Marty.

25, rue de la Pompe, 16th

Modern art

At the corner of the rue Jean-Colly and rue du Château-des-Rentiers, a multicolored street plan is displayed on a wall. But pedestrians would be well advised to ignore its directions unless they are ready to get lost: the deliberately confusing plan slyly misleads passers-by. Where are we? Rue Jean-Colly? Boulevard Masséna? And good luck searching for that nonexistent Métro entrance!

27, rue Jean-Colly, 13th

Schools

With their naïf appearance, mosaics are particularly appropriate for schools. In the Marais, a sign marks the entrance of a kindergarten. In Batignolles, the entire facade of an elementary school (the arms of the City of Paris included) is in those "broken tiles" typical of the 1925-1930 period.

Also
15, rue Truffaut, 17th

2, rue de la Verrerie, 4th

6, rue de Sèvres, 6th. Above the door of a bank,six mosaic medallions designed in 1902 show six women's faces. They are an allegory for the six continents.

19 Antique & suspended signs

Until the Revolution, signs were the only way of telling houses apart in Paris. They were everywhere in the days of the monarchic Ancien Régime. Then at the end of the 18th century, the first house numbers began to make them redundant, but they were such a longstanding tradition that they survived. Enormous pre-Revolutionary signs were made from a huge variety of materials (wrought iron, carved wood, stone, painted canvas, papier-mâché, sheet metal). Suspended from an iron bracket, they swung in the air to advertise a hostelry (with a twist of straw), a tooth-puller (a molar), or an apothecary (a mortar). In high winds, they clattered together and made a deafening racket. In 1761, Sartine, the Lieutenant General of Police of Paris, issued a decree to regulate their hanging because "they made the streets appear narrower and, in streets of shops, they considerably harmed the views from the second floors and even the light of lanterns, by casting shadows detrimental to public order." After the decree, signs had to be fixed flat to facades. Later, overhanging versions of a limited size were again permitted.

Musée Carnavalet
23, rue de Sévigné, 4th
(see p. 167)

Engraved in stone

From 1200, signs were engraved in the stone of walls to identify houses and shops. They took the form of a sculpted bas-relief above the door.

The oldest sign in Paris

As early as 1380, records mention the bas-relief of Saint Julian on the house known as "de la Heuze," making it the oldest sign in Paris. It shows the story of Saint Julian the Hospitaller, who became a ferryman after accidentally killing his parents. Jesus came to him one day disguised as a leper and Julian allowed the sick man onto his boat. In return, Jesus offered him eternal life. The bas-relief has Jesus sitting on the left, Saint Julian standing, and his wife on the right—rowing! The sign shown here is a cast. The original is in the Louvre.

42, rue Galande, 5th

Au Gagne-Petit

That is what knife grinders were once called: "small earners." In 1767, a sign in the round with this effigy could be seen at the corner of the rue de l'Hôtel-de-Ville and rue des Nonnains-d'Hyères, not far from the Seine. When the quarter was redeveloped, the building it marked was demolished and the knife grinder ended up in the musée Carnavalet, still dashing in his period costume and original colors (black cocked hat, red frock coat, and white stockings). A slightly different, unpainted copy was installed at the corner of the rue de Jouyet and rue de Fourcy. An economy department store on the avenue de l'Opéra also used a *gagne-petit* as its name and logo. The store closed a long time ago, but its sign remains: a bas-relief based on a painting by David Téniers the Younger: Le Rémouleur (*The Knife Grinder*), a 17th-century work now in the Louvre.

1, rue de Fourcy, 4th

23, avenue de l'Opéra, 2nd

22, rue des Saules, 18th

Sign puzzles

Signs that formed a visual pun were effective: they stirred the curiosity of passers-by, who remembered the address. Au Cygne de la Croix was a common name. When pronounced, it meant At the Swan of the Cross... or At the Sign of the Cross. It was used by both a former store near Saint-Lazare and a cabaret on the rue Saint-Séverin (1687). In that street, there is also a medallion engraved with a Y on a wall. The spoken version of L'Y, *lie-grègues*, was a homophone of laces used to attach pants and breeches. The letter also featured on the ironwork of balconies. Near the canal Saint-Martin was Au Lion d'or (At the Gold Lion), a phrase pronounced in the same way as "Au lit on dort" (One sleeps in bed). It was an inn and wine store. In the 17th-century, there was a wine merchant whose sign read Le Puits sans fin (Endless Well), which could also be understood as Le Puissant vin (Powerful Wine). The store was taken over by a grocer who renamed it "À la bonne source" (At the Fine Spring). Lastly, Le Lapin Agile or Agile Rabbit owes its name to André Gill, the caricaturist who painted this sign of a rabbit dancing a jig in a pot. The pun is on the phrase "le lapin à Gill": Gill's rabbit.

21, rue Jean-Poulmarch, 10th

13, rue Saint-Séverin, 5th

Also
Corner of rue Joseph-Sansbœuf and rue de la Pépinière, 8th
14, rue Saint-Séverin, 5th

122, rue Mouffetard, 5th

This bas-relief is outside the Maison de l'Annonciation. In 1682, it was the home of the Blancs Manteaux (White Coats), a mendicant order whose monks paid tribute to the mystery of the Annunciation (when Mary was informed of her divine maternity). 89, rue Saint-Martin, 4th

Guild signs

Inns and taverns

Inns and hostelries were among the first businesses (in around 1300) to use signs to catch the eye of tired, hungry, or thirsty travelers unfamiliar with the city. Their symbol was a twist of straw (fodder for horses), a fork, or a seashell (the mark of pilgrims), like this scallop sign displayed on the rue Gomboust. A famous nightclub had a crescent moon for its sign (tips pointing up).

À la Coquille d'Or.
1, rue Gomboust, 1st

Also
Au Croissant.
9, rue Montorgueil, 1st

Wine and pine

Wine merchants retailed liquor, but their stores were not inns—customers who bought wine could not drink it on the premises. A decree of 1729 made it compulsory for wine stores to have signs and bars to show their trade. The wrought-iron bars installed around the shop to protect the precious merchandise were decorated with oenological symbols: vine leaves, bunches of grapes, heads of Bacchus crowned with vine branches, or pinecones (because the insides of barrels were coated with resin pitch to make them watertight).

Hairdressers and barbers (who also acted as bloodletters) used a tricolor pole as their sign. It symbolized the rod their customers gripped to make their veins bulge. This is a new version at 62, rue de l'Arbre-Sec, 1st

Left, top to bottom
Aux Deux Pigeons.
62, rue de l'Hôtel-de-Ville, 4th
La Grille. 80, rue du Faubourg-Poissonnière, 10th

Also
La Grille Montorgueil.
50, rue Montorgueil, 2nd
Au Vieux Paris d'Arcole.
24, rue Chanoinesse, 4th
48, rue François-Miron, 4th
Au Lion d'Or.
21, rue Jean-Poulmarch, 10th

The King of Beer

One narrow facade on the rue Saint-Lazare looks very incongruous. The building used to be a brasserie called Au Roi de la Bière. With its wooden frame, small-paned windows, and stork on its chimney, it could be an Alsatian house straight out of the Petite France quarter of Strasbourg. In the center of its frontage swaggers a paunchy statue of Gambrinus, king of liquor. In fact, it is an architectural pastiche designed in 1894 for the Alsace restaurateur Jacqueminot Graff. Both the interior and exterior of the building have been given protected status by the Monuments historiques authority.

119, rue Saint-Lazare, 8th

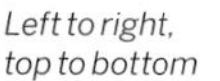

Butcher's hooks

Like wine merchants' shops, former butchers' stores can be identified by their outside grilles, which protected the goods on display while leaving them well-ventilated. Butcher shops have two features that differentiate them from wine shops: narrower gaps between the bars and a line of hooks where sides of meat could be hung, both in the store and outside. The boucherie Lalauze was in business back in the days of the La Villette abattoirs. Its storefront advertises a specialty—*foie gras rougie*—and has a line of hooks running on rails. Le Pont Traversé, now a bookstore, still has its magnificent blue and gold facade decorated with small ox and ram heads under the cornice. On a blood-red storefront at the top of the rue Mouffetard, the oxen and sheep in bas-relief are relics of a butcher's store that traded there from the 18th century until the end of the 1970s. Finally, the giant golden ox on the avenue Corentin-Cariou used to whet the appetites of workers from the La Villette abbatoirs.

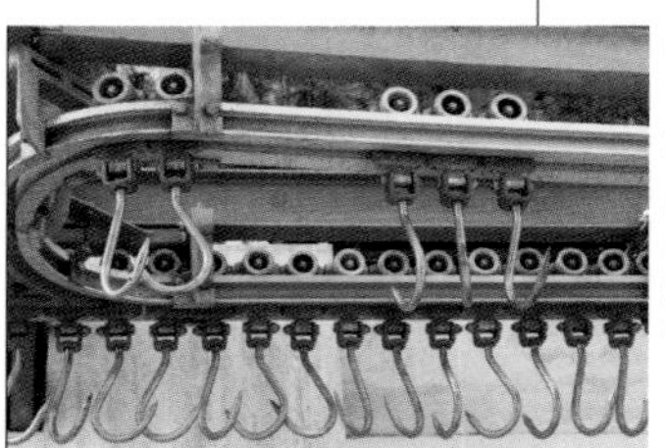

Left to right, top to bottom

52, rue Leibnitz, 18th
7, avenue Corentin-Cariou, 19th
Boucherie Lalauze. 15, avenue Corentin-Cariou, 19th

Also

Le Pont Traversé. 62, rue de Vaugirard, 6th
6, rue Mouffetard, 5th

Rue Frédéric-Sauton, 5th. Two former stores that are almost opposite each other show the differences between a butcher's store (at no. 9) and a wine merchant's shop (at no. 6).

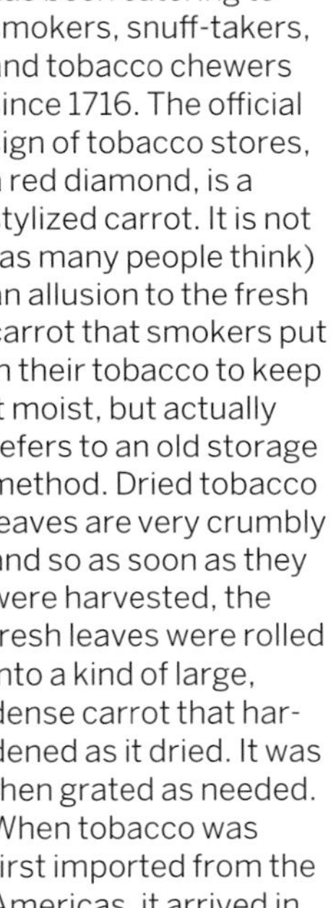

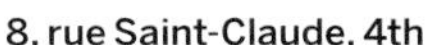

8, rue Saint-Claude, 4th

Carrot and civet

Many tobacconists chose the civet as a mascot. The little mammal's anal glands secrete a scented compound (civetone) used in pharmaceuticals, perfumery, and the tobacco industry. A little was added to snuff to give it its characteristic aroma. The civet of the rue Saint-Honoré has been catering to smokers, snuff-takers, and tobacco chewers since 1716. The official sign of tobacco stores, a red diamond, is a stylized carrot. It is not (as many people think) an allusion to the fresh carrot that smokers put in their tobacco to keep it moist, but actually refers to an old storage method. Dried tobacco leaves are very crumbly and so as soon as they were harvested, the fresh leaves were rolled into a kind of large, dense carrot that hardened as it dried. It was then grated as needed. When tobacco was first imported from the Americas, it arrived in France in "carrot" form.

**À la Civette.
157, rue Saint-Honoré, 1st**

134, rue Mouffetard, 5th. The Italian pork butcher Facchetti wanted the finest sign in the rue Mouffetard. He succeeded with this amazing display created by his compatriot Eldi Gueri in 1929.It shows game capering in a forest of sculpted stone above four panels displaying rustic scenes.

The caduceus and cross

The caduceus and green cross are the two signs of pharmacies. The caduceus is a coiled snake bending its head towards a cup—the one that Hygeia, daughter of Asclepius and goddess of health, used to give water to the serpent at the temple of Epidaurus. In 1968, the caduceus was registered as a collective trademark by the Conseil national de l'ordre des pharmaciens, but there was an issue with the cross. At the end of the 19th century, pharmacists decided to use a red cross against a white background as their sign, but in 1884, the Red Cross and Swiss Confederation began a long legal procedure to prevent this. Finally, pharmacies were forced to change their crosses from red to green in 1913.

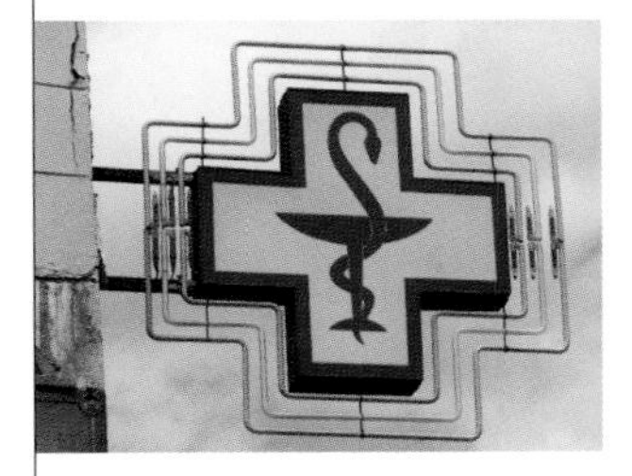

Top to bottom

**51, rue Montorgueil, 2nd
71, rue Saint-Antoine, 4th
Rue du Cherche-Midi, 6th**

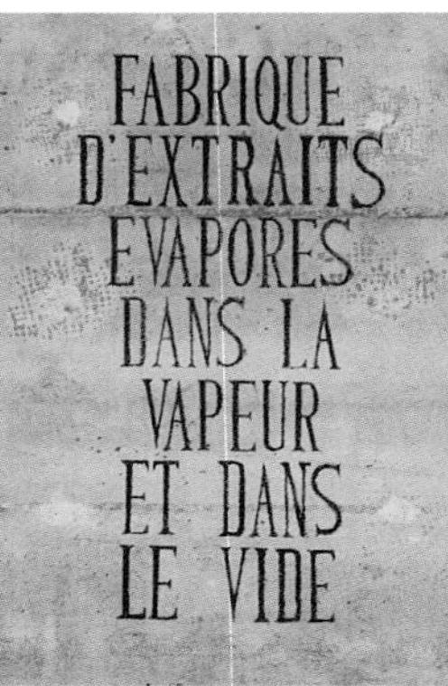

A bumblebee and rejuvenating herbal tea

In the rue Saint-Honoré, two remarkable facades stand side by side. At no. 93 is a house named Au Bourdon d'Or (The Golden Bumblebee), which has been continuously occupied by medical professionals since 1637: a midwife, an apothecary, a barber, a blood-letter (the precursor of the surgeon), and then another apothecary, who had the building renovated in the Directoire style in 1825. At no. 115 was the pharmacie du Mont-Blanc, whose wares included cacodylate (an antiasthenic remedy), "long-life" herbal tea and sympathetic (invisible) ink—which the Count of Fersen purchased there to write to Marie-Antoinette. The enigmatic inscription "Maker of extracts evaporated in steam and in a vacuum" engraved on the wall refers to a device invented at the pharmacy in 1803, which enabled the extraction of two compounds: noscapine (the first alkaloid of opium) and then morphine.

93 and 115, rue Saint-Honoré, 1st

1

Metropolitan menagerie

2

3

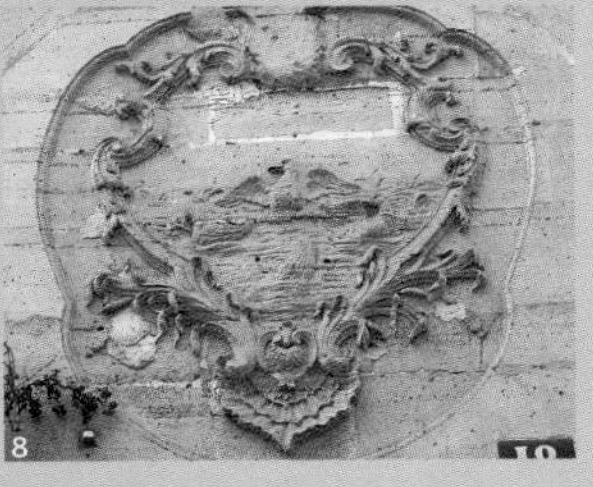

1 1, passage Rauch, 11th. A mosaic workshop (now gone) included a whole zoo's worth of wildlife in its signage in 1990: lion, dromedary, bear, panther, gazelle, walrus, and so on.

2 26, rue LaReynie, 4th. Au Chat Noir (The Black Cat), a store that once sold sugared almonds and chocolate.

3 86, rue Montorgueil, 2nd. La Fermette (The Little Farm)

4 9, rue Pierre-Lescot, 1st. At the start of the 20th century, this sculpted hive marked a honey merchant's shop.

5 5, boulevard de Sébastopol, 1st. Au Chat Noir (see below), a tobacco store

6 5, rue Xavier-Privas, 5th. This rare sign in sculpted wood is actually an old dresser door.

7 95, rue du Faubourg-Saint-Antoine, 11th. À l'Ours (The Bear)

8 18, rue des Cannettes, 6th. This sign in bas-relief that shows young ducks frolicking in a pond gave the street its name.

9 38, rueMontorgueil, 1st. L'Escargot d'Or (The Golden Snail)

10 24, rue du Four, 6th. Au Mouton (The Sheep)

11 Corner of rue du Cygne and rue Saint-Denis, 1st. Au Beau Cygne (The Handsome Swan)

Cloche and cayenne

A sign loaded with masonic symbols stands over the entrance to the *cayenne* (communal house) of the Compagnons charpentiers du devoir du Tour de France (an organization of craftsmen whose training includes a "tour" of apprenticeships with masters throughout France). The *cayenne* was founded in 1831 and is one of the oldest still in activity. The sign above the guild's bookstore behind the église Saint-Gervais is a false bell with a cord. It was once the sign of a café, À la Cloche d'Argent (The Silver Bell), where the brotherhood met.

Top to bottom

Corner of rue de Brosse and quai de l'Hôtel-de-Ville, 4th
161, avenue Jean-Jaurès, 19th

The key to commerce

Locksmiths, who were experts in the art of metalwork, took particular care over their signs, which they made themselves. They were obviously key-shaped and reflected the artisan's precision and skill.

Left to right

58, rue du Faubourg-Poissonnière, 10th
42, rue de Grenelle, 7th

Also
23, rue de l'Échaudé, 6th

15, rue du Bourg-Tibourg, 4th

Gumshoes for hire

Private eyes (members of a discreet profession if ever there was one) also have their street signs. There is no point trying to make an appointment with Lex Policindustrie, though. Founded in 1926 in the rue du Faubourg-Montmartre, the agency hung up its trench coat a long time ago. However, the one in the rue du Louvre (Duluc) and the Détectives associés in the rue du Bourg-Tibourg still tail suspects and investigate all kinds of cases efficiently and discreetly.

Also
53, rue du Faubourg-Montmartre, 9th
18, rue du Louvre, 1st

A dash of exoticism in a colonial sauce

Delicatessens supplying foodstuffs from distant lands (spices, chocolates, coffee, tea, liquor, etc.) used a tropical iconography to affirm their identity, such as these depictions of cheery and hungry "*nègres*."

Au Planteur. 10-12, rue des Petits-Carreaux, 2nd
Au Petit-Maure. 26, rue de Seine, 6th

Also
Au Nègre joyeux. 14, rue Mouffetard, 5th

Keen as mustard!

A plaque on the facade and three reproductions of medals won at universal expositions bear witness to the glories of Bornibus mustard. At the end of the 19th century, the condiment was as familiar to the public as a certain carbonated soft drink today. It was successfully marketed by pioneering businessman Alexandre Bornibus. He was one of the first entrepreneurs to fully realize the power of advertising and planned his campaigns carefully, using celebrities to plug his products: Alexandre Dumas (1872); Étienne Ducret, who wrote a lyrical opus entitled "La Bornibusiade" (1878); Georges Méliès, who made a short advertising film for the firm (1900), and so on. Once a year, Bornibus took his employees on a pleasant country outing. He also came up with dry mustard tablets (to be diluted with a few drops of water before use) for long-distance travelers.

58, boulevard de La Villette, 19th

Three Ms

The rue Mouffetard and rue Montorgueil, both pedestrian shopping streets, have another thing in common: they boast a splendid array of street signs (mainly for food and catering establishments). Antique specimens and modern variations cheerfully rub shoulders, forming an open-air museum. An actual museum makes three. The musée Carnavalet's many signs were donated by the owners of buildings destined for demolition or radical redesign.

Also
Musée Carnavalet. 23, rue de Sévigné, 4th

Rue Montorgueil, 1st and 2nd

9, rue de l'Estrapade, 5th
The sign of a coffee-roasting plant that closed about 1970. On the door of the ochre building is the monogram "BSJ," standing for "Brûlerie Saint-Jacques."

10, rue Tiquetonne, 2nd

Knock on wood

À l'Arbre à Liège (The Cork Tree) is the only known cork manufacturer's sign. The painted wooden emblem is on a building that probably dates back to the 17th century. Older still is the sign of the Vieux Chêne (Old Oak) in the rue Mouffetard, an inn that was photographed by Eugène Atget in 1911 and is thought to go back to 1592. Its worm-eaten wood was carefully restored in 2011. In fact, the only thing that is old about today's smartly varnished oak sign is the name.

Also
69, rue Mouffetard, 5th

Outsize and offbeat

Like their primitive, naïve, extra-large counterparts, a few modern signs are remarkably big and a little strange. For instance, this 10-meter-high lighthouse (an exact replica of the one at Le Croisic in Brittany), which stands on a fishmonger's store near Montparnasse. Below it is a trawler wrecked on rocks. In Bastille, a huge wine-colored bottle seems to be rising like a rocket through the roof of a bistro. Finally, in the Marais, a mammoth black and red thermometer covers almost an entire facade. In the Belle Époque period, it identified the premises of Lucien Hippolyte Bernel-Bourette, ironmaster constructor of plaques in relief and thermometers.

Left to right
Les Samouraïs des Mers. 69, rue Castagnary, 15th
64, boulevard Richard-Lenoir, 11th
Also
36, rue de Poitou, 3rd

Set under glass

Bakery storefronts were not the only ones with signs under glass. A chocolate store in Pigalle called Les Chatteries—or *catteries*, another word for candies, a name as sweet as its goods—and La Grande Crémerie de Grenelle, which sells dairy products, had signs of this kind. More spectacular (if less appetizing) is the sign of À la Renommée des Herbes Cuites (The Renown of Cooked Herbs), a former caterer and deli in the rue Saint-Honoré. Four gilt inscriptions under glass are still there on the second floor, an unusual height for signs. There is another amusing detail about the store: originally, in the 19th century, it was called À la Renommée des Épinards, but it seems that the public were not really wild about spinach. À la Mère de famille (Mother of the Family) is the oldest known confectionery store in Paris (1761). On the storefront, its business name and advertising are jumbled together in a profusion of inscriptions. Signs under glass against a marble background scattered over the belt courses, vertical shields, and low panels inventory the store's merchandise.

Top to bottom

27, rue du Commerce, 15th
8, rue Pierre-Haret, 9th

Also

95, rue Saint-Honoré, 1st
35, rue du Faubourg-Montmartre, 9th

Impermanent signs

They are almost illegible, use archaic terms and mention extinct trades and industries. A gust of wind, a sudden draft, or a rub with a cloth could send them off to sign heaven. On a worn wooden panel below an arch on the rue Saint-Denis, passers-by can just make out the words "Hats for ladies and girls." More hats "in straw and felt" are advertised on the rue Vieille-du-Temple. Then there are the "Maker of bronzes and light fittings of every style" on the rue Payenne; "A reliable firm [selling] top-quality novelty and mourning headgear" on the rue de la Roquette; "Stylish wigs and hairpieces" on the rue du Faubourg-Montmartre, and so on. Above a former plumbing supply store on the rue Jean-Poulmarch, three panels remain, their fine letters cut from white enameled sheet metal: "Basins, u-bends..." Unfortunately, the ones on the left-hand board have come unstuck.

Also

226, rue Saint-Denis, 2nd
77 and 83, rue Vieille-du Temple, 3rd
8, rue du Faubourg-Montmartre, 9th
15, rue Jean-Poulmarch, 10th

Top to bottom

13, rue Payenne, 4th
132, rue de la Roquette, 11th

Wall adverts

Many people complain of intrusive advertising today without realizing that things were even worse in the late 19th and early 20th century. There were advertisements everywhere, even on the edges of the steps in the Métro and the roofs of buses that passed under upper-floor windows. The sides of buildings were daubed with giant painted advertisements extolling the virtues of brands of polish, household appliances, chocolate, and aperitifs. This promotional enthusiasm was curbed by a decree of 1943, which limited individual advertisements to 16 square meters. That led to the standard modern billboard size of 4 by 4 meters. Although the old painted advertisements were said to be "long-lasting," they finally succumbed to the slings and arrows of the elements or exterior renovation. Fewer than 10 can still be seen, their nostalgia-tinted colors now pale and faded.

7, rue Barrault, 13th
Suze

73, rue Mouffetard, 5th
Passing time is getting the better of this sign, which invites the public to cross the street to the bowling lanes opposite.

oulevard Pasteur, 15th
paper store

1, rue Marx-Dormoy, 18th
Rozan chocolate

1, rue Auguste-Colette, 17th
Picon aperitif

3, boulevard Montmartre, 2nd
Cadum soap (restored)

rue de Charonne, 11th
intruder: Kub. In 1990, the libertarian artist
stian Zeimert revamped a period advertisement for
bouillion cubes. The work is called, "Kiss Me Kub."

23, boulevard des Batignolles, 8th
Crème Éclipse, a wax polish

20

Luck is innately mischievous and unpredictable. Its whims can transform the destiny of a store by forcing it into an elegant commercial about-turn. Here are some examples of these changes in use.

A new lease on life

Boutiques to benches

The Pont-Neuf was the first Parisian bridge to be built without houses on it. Instead, shops were set up on small semicircular balconies a few meters apart. When the bridge was renovated in 1854, the second-hand booksellers and trinket vendors who had set up there were sent packing for good. Half-moon-shaped benches were installed to replace the defunct stalls.

A café in a bordello

Quite a curiosity: the Delaville Café occupies the ground floor of a former house of ill-repute, one of the city's most mysterious brothels, in fact, since even police registers failed to mention it. The decor leaves no room for doubt, though: a double flight of stairs (so customers could avoid coming face to face with each other), corridors lined with mirrors that provide infinite reflections, and themed rooms—Moorish, Gothic, and so on. The monogram AYM, an invitation to pleasure, pronounced *aime*, features everywhere. The last-mentioned opulent extravagances are upstairs in what is now the studio of stylist Anne Valérie Hasch, not open to the public. However, visitors can admire the gilt mosaics on the ground floor (now the Delaville Café), along with the marble columns of the great stairway to heaven that once led up to the delights of the second floor.

34, boulevard de Bonne-Nouvelle, 10th

An apartment in a precinct house

119, rue Belliard, 18th

With no blue, white, and red flag flying above the door, this "precinct house of the Grandes-Carrières quarters —18th arrondissement" obviously no longer serves that purpose. The words "First aid for the injured—Nighttime medical emergencies" are still engraved in the wall, and bars remain across the windows with their cloudy panes. The same goes for the former police precinct house at La Plaine Monceau: a similar row of high, narrow windows, but with the bars removed. In rue Legendre, a sinister grille topped with spikes guards the entrance to the former imperial *gendarmerie*, now a condominium.

Also
132, boulevard Malesherbes, 17th
85, rue Legendre, 17th

Cool art

The former refrigerated warehouses of Paris-Ivry did business from 1921 to 1971. Over that half-century, trains filled with fresh produce (meat, fish, milk, butter, cheese, fruit, flowers, and more) rolled into the reinforced-concrete belly of the depot, which could hold up to 25 boxcars. Four goods elevators carried the produce up to the warehouses' five floors of cold storage rooms. Every day, more than 40 tons of ice were produced by ammonia compressors powered with electric motors.

In Hall B (at the end on the right): the vertiginous shaft of the former water tower.

The ice makers were fed by a water tower. The pipes (now gnawed away by rust) still run along the corridors. When the wholesale market Les Halles moved to Rungis in the Paris suburbs, the facility—known as Les Frigos (fridges)—was no longer needed. So in the 1980s, artists moved into the building, which is now a well-known melting pot of contemporary creativity.

Rue des Frigos, 13th

The artful dodger

Let's now turn our attention to some commercial establishments that might get the quick- witted out of trouble. At one time or another, we have all had the uneasy feeling of being followed. So whether or not our consciences are pure as the driven snow, it may be useful to know ways of losing a tail. Here is a selection of practical hints about public premises with more than one exit, which can serve to get rid of a stalker or simply pamper one's paranoia.

Leopold-approved

In 1943, the Bailly pharmacy was the scene of famous ploy used by Leopold Trepper, the head of the French Resistance intelligence network L'Orchestre Rouge, to baffle his Nazi nemesis. When arrested, Leopold managed to persuade his captor that he was urgently in need of medicine. Walking into the pharmacy's rue de Rome entrance, he then slipped out onto the rue du Rocher as his guard waited patiently at the other door. If he had been on the Left Bank, he might have employed the same ruse at the pharmacy that can be entered from either the boulevard du Montparnasse or the rue Notre-Dame-des-Champs. These thoroughfares form a hairpin corner, so locals use both the dual-entrance pharmacy and the bakery as shortcuts. There are a few steps to allow for the slight difference in level between the streets.

15, rue de Rome and rue du Rocher, 8th

Also
153, boulevard du Montparnasse and 112, rue Notre-Dame-des-Champs, 6th

I'll have a decamp, please

In much the same way, you can savor your espresso at the counter of 43, rue Beaubourg; wander off towards the bathroom; and slip through the

Le 43.
43, rue Beaubourg, 3rd

unobtrusive door that leads to the hall of a building on the rue du Grenier-Saint-Lazare. The people who work in the offices above enter the café directly without going out onto the street. The brasserie Les Associés, located on the corner of the rue de Lyon and the boulevard de la Bastille, is similar.

Also
Les Associés.
50, boulevard de la Bastille, 12th

A prayer answered

Churches are wonderful places to lose someone who's following you: they often have multiple entrances. One can enter Saint-Louis-d'Antin through the main doors at 63, rue de Caumartin and then make for the parish hall, which leads to the lobby of an office building at 4, rue du Havre. The reverse route is equally startling. Saint-Sulpice, Saint-Germain-des-Prés, and other churches also have built-in escape routes.

Église Saint-Louis-d'Antin

Église Saint-Louis-d'Antin. 63, rue de Caumartin and 4, rue du Havre, 9th

Église Saint-Germain-des-Prés. The exit on the left-hand side leads to 9, rue de l'Abbaye, 6th

Also

Église Saint-Sulpice. No fewer than three exits: two at the back on the rue Garancière and one at the side on the rue Palatine, 6th

Église Saint-Denys-de-la-Chapelle. 16, rue de la Chapelle: there is a second entrance in the place de Torcy, 18th

Église Saint-Germain-des-Prés

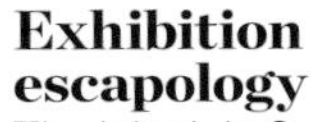

Exhibition escapology

The hôtel de Sully is the ideal place to lose a pursuer in Le Marais. It regularly hosts exhibitions, leaving passers-by free to enter through the front door (place des Vosges) and leave via the back one (rue Saint- Antoine), or vice versa.

Hôtel Sully. 62, rue Saint-Antoine and 7, place des Vosges, 4th

21 Au fur et à mesure

This expression, meaning "as and when" is a pleonasm that appeared in the century of the Enlightenment, when people were fond of linguistic redundancy ("safe and sound" is another example). It seems very suitable for this chapter, which is all about measures and estimates of every kind: flood gauges, boundary and leveling markers, barometers, and so on.

Bourse du commerce.
Rue de Viarmes, 1st
(see p. 184)

13, place Vêndôme, 1st (to the left of the Ministry of Justice)

36, rue de Vaugirard, 6th

The standard meter

Under the monarchic Ancien Régime, measurements were bewilderingly chaotic. Lengths could be given in inches, feet, miles, or leagues (for travel), ells (for fabrics), and so on. Liquids came in pints; grain in bushels; oats in pecks. Weight was calculated (by apothecaries) in scruples, ounces, marks, or quintals. To confuse things further, the values of all these measurements varied from one region to the next. In 1795, when equality was now the watchword, the Convention (France's Revolutionary National Assembly) stepped in and standardized the metric system at the request of traders in dire need of uniform weights and measures. To familiarize citizens with decimal measurements, standard meter rules were mounted on display in cities in 1796. Sixteen of them were in Paris. Today, only two are left. They are in the rue de Vaugirard and the place Vendôme (the second is no longer in its original location, it was moved in 1848). A short segment of these marble rules is marked in centimeters.

Kilometer zero

On the square in front of Notre-Dame, a bronze plaque set in the ground is engraved with a compass rose. It marks the starting point from which kilometers are counted on France's *routes Nationales* (the ones that run from Paris). The marker is the result of some extraordinary suggestions made by Abbé Teisserenc in 1754. The treatise the priest published in that year recommended "transferring the map of France onto a map of Paris of the same size and naming the streets for the towns that fall on them." (Géographie parisienne en forme de dictionnaire contenant l'explication de Paris mis en carte géographique du royaume de France [*Parisian Geography in Dictionary Form Containing the Explanation of Paris Mapped Geographically after the Kingdom of France*]). His (crazy?) ideas were never taken up —except for kilometer zero, marked by a post planted in the ground in front of Notre-Dame in 1769. In 1924, the municipal authorities gave their seal of approval to the landmark, installing the compass rose mentioned above.

Place du Parvis de Notre-Dame, 4th

10, place Dauphine, 1st

League stones

The roads of the Roman Empire were lined with military markers showing each mile (about 1,460 meters). In the provinces of Gaul, there were also league stones (a league was about 4 kilometers). Along the roads radiating out from Paris,

there were markers about every thousand *toises* (1,949 meters). The only one remaining is in the rue de Vaugirard. Its inscription (now worn away) showed it was half a league from point zero (*see p. 177*). In its oval cavity, there was once a royal fleur-de-lys, which was removed after the Revolution.

85, rue de Vaugirard, 6th

The navels of Paris

Where is the center of Paris? Not an easy question to answer: the city has more than one. First, there are both surface and perimeter-based centers. The data supplied by the IGN (National Geographic Institute) take into account the bois de Vincennes and the bois de Boulogne. The central point of all Paris is the barycenter of the surface of the entire city. It is in the place Dauphine (1st). The center of the contour of Paris (the point central to the boundaries of Paris) is in a rear yard on the rue Lacuée (12th). Finally, the center of the arrondissements (in other words, the starting point of their spiral) is in the middle of the pont Saint-Michel.

Also
In a rear yard at 9, rue Lacuée, 12th
Middle of the pont Saint-Michel

Kilometric markers

Kilometer markers are a common sight on country roads, but in Paris, they have become an uncommon breed or even an endangered species. The four cast-iron markers that remain today are rare signs of French national roads within the city's walls. Two are located on the former route d'Orléans (which is now the RN20 and starts at Montrouge beyond the beltway). Another marker is on the RN10 near the Maison de la Radio-France.

15 and 73, avenue du Général-Leclerc, 14th
219, rue de Vaugirard, 15th (behind glass)
Avenue du Président-Kennedy, 16th

A spurious boundary marker

Historians argue heatedly over a marker on the rue Berton. It is not one of the wheel guards designed to protect pedestrians from horse-drawn carriages in the days before sidewalks (which stand every 3 or 4 meters along the road), but the unevenly shaped stone near the green porch of Balzac's house. According to a plaque on the wall, the stone was placed there in 1731 to mark the boundaries of Auteuil and Passy. However, other ancient records contradict the claim, presenting powerful arguments that situate the border on the site of the Maison de Radio France. So this large stone may only have been placed here to warn carts not to enter the narrow passage.

Rue Berton, 16th

Crossing the line

Two plaques (one in the 8th arrondissement, the other in the 12th) bring smiles to the faces of passers-by: "1726. Boundary marker. In the reign of Louis XV. In the name of the King. It is expressly forbidden to build beyond these markers and limits until the next village, on pain of the penalties laid down by His Majesty's declarations of the years 1724 and 1726." The surrounding urban density shows that the royal orders were not exactly obeyed to the letter. In fact, not just Louis, but generations of sovereigns struggled with the thorny issue of Paris's city limits. On a number of occasions, for administrative and public-safety reasons, they forbade their subjects to build homes outside the boundaries of the capital. The first ban was announced in 1548 and renewed in 1627, 1633 and 1642. From that year, houses built beyond the markers were to be demolished unless their owners paid a tax. However, the law was continually flouted, the suburbs spread inexorably and the markers were moved a little further out each time. The process continued under Louis XV, who ordered the display of 294 markers divided into five categories. Only two are left. The one in the rue de Charenton regulated suburban housing on the rural side, banning the creation of streets and the construction of large buildings. Only small, one-story buildings with no coach gates would be allowed. The marker was originally placed at the corner of the rue de Picpus and the rue Lamblardie. In 1910, the historian Lucien Lambeau found it broken in two in the rear of a hardware store. Weary of the vicissitudes of its long existence, the plaque was fixed to the facade.

306-308, rue de Charenton, 12th

Also

4, rue de Laborde, 8th (in the courtyard)

Hommage à Arago

This is the official name of a monument dispersed throughout the city: a series of 135 saucer-sized bronze medallions sealed in asphalt. Engraved with François Arago's name and the letters N and S (for north and south), they pay tribute to the work of this scientist who helped to measure the Earth's meridian axis. The medallions follow the exact line of the Paris Meridian (the international standard before it was ousted by the Greenwich Meridian in 1884). The artist Jan Dibbets created the work (considered "Land Art") in 1994 to mark the bicentenary of Arago's birth.

Place de l'Île-de-Sein, 14th. The 135th and last medallion of the Arago monument is inset vertically on the pedestal of the former statue of François Arago (melted down during the German Occupation).

Clean doorsteps make good neighbors

Like the sweep of one of the buildings of this factory, the curve of the rue Berbier-du-Mets followed a meander of the River Bièvre that once ran at the foot of its wall. A stone engraved with the number 66 and the code 70 T 4 P (i.e. 70 *toises* and 4 feet) was a reminder of the company's duty to maintain the river and keep its banks clean and well-maintained along a 137-meter stretch (the length of the building). The street was laid over the river (now underground) in 1906.

8, rue Berbier-du-Mets, 13th

Flood measurement

Since time immemorial, Parisians have had to cope with rises in the level of the Seine. The 1910 flood remains in the city's collective memory for two reasons: it was unusually high (8.62 meters) and progress in photography by that time meant that pictures of it were seen all over the world. Yet there were many other floods before that one. From 1651, water levels had been recorded and the highest known was in 1658 (8.81 meters). The height of the Seine's waters was measured on a cross in the place de Grève (now the place de l'Hôtel-de-Ville). Today, underwater sensors provide the official measurements. The basic reference is the gauge by the pont d'Austerlitz, but Parisians traditionally refer to the Zouave statue at the pont de l'Alma. On an arch at the bassin de l'Arsenal near the outlet into the Seine, marks show the heights of famous floods. The firefighters of the La Monnaie barracks moored at the quai de Conti do the same on the side wall of the shelter on the quay. The 1910 mark touches the roof.

Left to right, top to bottom
Bassin de l'Arsenal, 4th
Pont-au-Change, 1st (near the tour de l'Horloge)
Opposite 11, quai de Conti, 6th
Pont de l'Alma, 16th

Water, water, everywhere

After major floods, commemorative plaques appeared on the bases of buildings and the parapets of quays. They were installed by the municipal authorities or individuals to remind everybody of the danger. On the place Maubert, a stone engraved with Gothic lettering is a memorial to the March 1711 flood (7.62 meters), but the yellowing Plexiglas that protects it makes the inscription illegible. To the left of the porch of the hôpital des Quinze-Vingt, passers-by can read that the peak of the river reached this stone. Commemorating the flood of 1740, the words were engraved by a Tomas Bouquet. There are many memorials to the 1910 flood: either enameled plaques with white letters on a green background (about 30 of them) or simply marks in stones that show the highest level. You can find these signs on certain bridges (on the upriver side) or along quays (about 30 of them, too).

There are a number of flood marks at the Pont-Neuf, on a pillar on the downriver side and one (from 1910) on the upriver side on the wall of the quay next to a grotesque mask.

Near 70, rue de Lille, 7th

Also
Corner of the place Maubert and the rue Maître-Albert, 5th

28, rue de Charenton, 12th. In front of l'hopital des Quinze-Vingt, a plaque certifies that during the flood of 1740, the water rose much higher than in 1910.

"You are invited to come and see the Earth turn"

It was with these words that Léon Foucault summoned the scientists of his day to an amazing demonstration at the Observatoire de Paris on February 3, 1851, where he showed them direct evidence of the Earth's rotation. One month later, crowds flocked to the Panthéon for a public repetition of the experiment, organized at the request of Louis-Napoléon Bonaparte, who was then President of the French Republic. According to Foucault, the principle was very simple: "While the plane of oscillation of the pendulum is fixed in relation to the ether, the rotation of the Earth relative to this same ether will be visible in the form of a rotation of the plane of oscillation of the pendulum." In the months that followed the demonstration, dozens of pendulums were set swinging all over the world and thousands observed "the Earth turning."

Panthéon, 5th

Leveling Markers

The Nivellement Général de la France (General Leveling of France - NGF) uses a network of height markers all over the country to conduct its surveys. Such markers were positioned throughout Paris in the mid-19th century, just before work began on water supply and sewer systems. Leveling was needed to plan the gradients that would allow the water to flow by gravity. According to an administrative order issued by the prefect of the Seine region in 1856, the leveling benchmark was point zero (average sea level on the coast of Marseille). Surveyors subsequently used the leveling markers set in the bases of building or quas for all kinds of purposes (and still do today). The oldest markers are rectangular cast-iron plates topped with a horizontal bar. Known as *repères console* (console markers), they are decorated with the coat of arms of the City of Paris and provide three height coordinates.

The first is based on zero level on the water gauge of the pont de la Tournelle (corresponding to the lowest water level of the River Seine: 26.25 meters above sea level in 1719). Its information was needed to plan the sewers, whose contents had to flow into the Seine by gravity. The second number shows the difference with the level of the water in the bassin de La Villette (51.49 meters) plus 50 meters (so 101.49 meters) and altitude above average sea level. That figure was used to manage the supply of drinking water (by gravity, too) sourced from the bassin de La Villette. Finally, the last coordinate is height in relation to sea level. In some places, there are also smaller cylindrical markers that only show that final figure.

4

6

7

9

8

10

5

1 Under the porch which links cour Carrée and rue de l'Amiral- Coligny, 1st

2 Corner of rue du Cherche-Midi and rue Jean-Ferrandi, 6th. A "small model"marker in excellent condition because it is sheltered from rain water and hidden from the eyes of the public (at ground level behind a potted plant).The tiniest details of the city's ship symbol are perfectly apparent.

3 Pont-Neuf.

4 Since point zero is at Marseille, Paris is at + 25.92 NGF on the reference marker at the pont d'Austerlitz. This explains the numbers 32, 33, 34, etc. on this staff gauge at thequai de Conti near Pont-Neuf, 6th, and the one at the Pont-au Change, 1st.

5 Between 8 and 10, rue des Grands-Augustins, 6th. This console marker is probably the best-preserved (and so the most legible).

6 Corner of the rue Charlot and rue de Turenne, 3rd. There is an anomaly on the Boucherat drinking fountain: when it was renovated, the marker was replaced too high up and and upside-down as well! There are two types of marker on the fountain: console and cylindrical.

7 The highest leveling marker in the public street network of Paris is on the rue du Télégraphe, 20th.

8 Corner of the rue des Archives and rue des Francs-Bourgeois, 4th. On the Chaume drinking fountain, apart from the marker, there is another cast-iron plate from the same period, also displaying an effigy of the ship of Paris.

9 Quai de l'Hôtel-de-Ville.

10 1, rue de Bièvre, 5th (at the corner of the quai de la Tournelle).

Barometers & thermometers

These instruments are to atmospheric pressure and temperature what clocks are to time, but much less common. In any case, Parisian barometers and thermometers can always take comfort in the knowledge that the city's inhabitants like nothing more than to talk about the sun and rain... whenever they stop looking at the time!

Weigh anchor!

The Brasserie Lipp's nautical barometer has observed generations of Saint-Germain society come and go since 1880. It is relatively small and set in a sea-anchor frame.

151, boulevard Saint-Germain, 6th

Under a glass roof

This barometer was installed when the passage du Bourg-l'Abbé was created in 1862. Together with the entire arcade (facades, floor, ceiling, and lights), it was restored in the 2000s.

Passage du Bourg-l'Abbé, 2nd

Heads and tails

The barometer under the dome of the Bourse du commerce (commodities exchange) is unusual: it can be read from either side (1889).

Rue de Viarmes, 1st

A rare circular thermometer

On the bell-tower of the église Saint-Germain-l'Auxerrois, two splendid blue and gold faces installed in 1862 and restored in 2004 delight the eye. One is a barometer, the other a rare dial thermometer. Temperatures to the right of zero degrees centigrade (*glace* or ice) are positive and those to the left, negative.

Place du Louvre, 1st

Société des Lunetiers

On the discreet rue Pastourelle, three dials are vertically aligned (a barometer, hygrometer, and thermometer). By chance or coincidence, just opposite at no. 6 was the headquarters of the Société des Lunetiers (Society of Eyeglass Makers), founded in 1849, which became the Essilor group in 1967. Its workers manufactured not only eyeglasses, but also magnifying glasses, thread counters, microscopes, models of camera obscura and lucida, stereoscopes, barometers, thermometers, hydrometers, hygrometers, and so on.

9, rue Pastourelle, 3rd

For the edification of the masses

An astounding dual display decorates the facade of an optician's store in the rue Duphot. At the top is a dial barometer; below, at window level, is a giant thermometer. Both are in terrible condition. The thermometer's gauge marks are labeled with all kinds of added educational information, explaining to nursemaids that the temperature of a baby's bath falls between the warmth of a swarm of bees and that of a silkworm incubation chamber.

2, rue Duphot, 1st

The Montsouris instrument collection

The first meteorological observatory in France was set up in the parc de Montsouris in 1872. It was housed in the palais du Bardo, a pavilion from the Universal Exposition of 1867. In 1972, the observatory was moved a few meters, but remained in the park. The meteorologists there partly base their work on data provided by automatic stations (temperature, atmospheric-pressure, rain, wind, sunlight and humidity sensors). These stations are located in five places in Paris and its immediate suburbs. Montsouris is the benchmark station. Its collection of instruments includes a set of thermometers placed 10 and 50 centimeters above and below ground, pluviometers (wind gauges), and a hygrometer (measuring humidity). There is also a gauge to measure snow depth. Perched on a tower are the wind meters, whose spinning cups measure speed and weather vane direction. A solarimeter observes overall radiance (daylight), while a heliogram records the duration of sunshine.

Parc de Montsouris, 14th

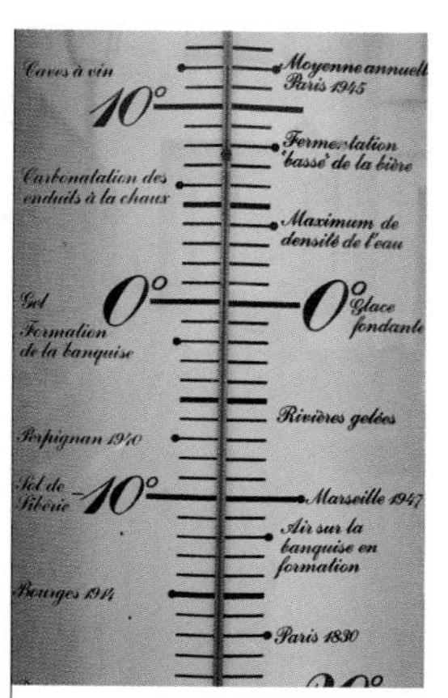

Record temperatures

Following the same principle as the antique educational thermometer on the rue Duphot, a modern example is installed in the quartier de l'Horloge. About two meters high, the different temperatures it shows range from the -70°C measured in the Lena Valley, Siberia, to the +70 °C needed to distil ethyl alcohol. They include the 8°C of the bottom fermentation of beer, the 12°C of wine cellars, the 17°C of equatorial oceanic water, the 22°C of a sick person's bedroom, the 30°C of an average summer in Paris, the 44°C melting point of phosphorus, and so on.

8, rue Brantôme, 1st

22 Egyptian Paris

In 1798, when Napoleon Bonaparte arrived in the land of the Pharaohs and declared, "Soldiers, from the heights of these pyramids, forty centuries look down upon us," a small group of scientists who had joined the expedition began to fill entire notebooks with their observations and sketches. When they returned to France, they published the results of their research. This led to a public fascination with Egypt's ancient, deliciously exotic landscapes and customs, and a growing wave of Egyptomania. Pharaonic fashions swept across Paris and a new *retour d'Egypte* (Return from Egypt) architecture brightened facades and left its lasting heritage on the city's stone walls.

Avenue du Général-Lemonnier, on the Seine side, 1st *(see p. 192)*

The rue du Caire was opened up through the Filles-Dieu convent, which had been demolished in 1798.

Cairo Fair

In 1806, a themed district dubbed "Foire du Caire" was built on the site of the former cour des Miracles, which had been "cleared" by Nicolas de La Reynie. The facade that surrounds the entrance to the passage at 2, place du Caire is to Egyptian architecture what Hollywood epics are to history: a strange, anachronistic fantasy. The Venetian neo-Gothic-style windows are framed by pillars with lotus-shaped capitals, fanciful hieroglyphs and a triple cloned face—that of the Egyptian goddess Hathor, recognizable from her cow ears. Originally, the ambience in the passage du Caire was supposed to suggest the Cairo bazaar, but things did not work out that way. Instead, it was occupied by traders of store-display supplies (mannequins, ribbons, and hangers), whose shops were eventually replaced by ready-to-wear businesses.

Rue, place and passage du Caire, rue d'Aboukir, rue de Damiette, rue du Nil, 2nd

Exotic toponomy

Eight Parisian street names refer to Egypt: the rues d'Aboukir, d'Alexandrie, d'Héliopolis and des Pyramides (all celebrating victories of Bonaparte or his generals), du Caire, de Damiette, du Nil, and de Suez (an allusion to the digging of the canal under the supervision of Frenchman Ferdinand de Lesseps). Obviously, many are in the quartier de la Foire du Caire, named following Bonaparte's entry into Cairo on July 23, 1798, an event that dazzled and inspired Parisians.

The oldest monument in Paris

The obelisk in the place de la Concorde dates back 33 centuries, no less! Its story began in Thebes in 1250 BCE, when it and its twin were raised in the temple of Ramses II. In 1830, during the reign of Charles X, Pasha Muhammad Ali, viceroy of Egypt, gave the two obelisks of Thebes to France. Different explanations were given. According to some, it was a compulsory gift insisted on by the general consul of France in Egypt; according to others, it was a spontaneous gift to thank France for Champollion's deciphering of hieroglyphs in 1822. In any case, it was decided that the smaller of the two monoliths (weighing 230 tons) would be shipped to France. To transport it, an eight-hulled vessel named Le Luxor had to be specially built. The colossal obelisk's voyage via Gibraltar, Le Havre and finally up the River Seine lasted 18 months. Quite an odyssey! The engineer responsible for the convoy had had enough: "Anybody who wants to can bring back the second one, but it won't be me!" In any case, the other half of the gift is no longer an issue: in 1994, President François Mitterrand symbolically returned the second obelisk "belonging" to France to Egyptian ownership.

Place de la Concorde, 8th

Pyramids of glass and stone

Designed by the architect I. M. Pei, the glass pyramid of the Louvre was constructed in 1989. It became the new starting point of Paris's Grand Axe—a series of landmarks that provide a continuous line of perspective across the city. They include the arc de triomphe du Carrousel, the obelisk, the arc de triomphe de l'Étoile, and the Grande Arche de la Défense. Now that the political and aesthetic controversy has died down, the pyramid has become as famous as its ancient cousins in Giza. Another pyramid stands in the parc Monceau, but it is made of stone and much older. It was one of the *fabriques*, or installations, built to decorate the park when it was the property of the Duke of Chartres in the 18th century. Originally, it held a statue of the goddess Isis (*also see p. 143*). Finally, a stained-glass transom on the rue Ballu features three pyramids and a palm tree. The design was the discreet insignia of a bordello called Les Pyramides.

Also
Parc Monceau, 8th
32, rue Ballu, 9th

Cour Napoléon, 1st

Pharaonic mausoleums

From the 19th century on, Parisians were fascinated by the Ancient Egyptians' exotic ideas about death (mummification, rites of passage to the afterlife, reincarnation, eternal life, and so on) and chose pyramid models for their tombs. The height of luxury was a pyramidal chapel of rest decorated with a sphinx, crowned with an obelisk and decked with bouquets of papyrus. There are 15 or so tombs of Egyptian inspiration in Père-Lachaise Cemetery.

Cimetière du Père-Lachaise, 20th.
The Egyptian-style tomb of a Scottish gentleman named Craufurd, who died in Paris in 1819.

Egypt at the Louvre

The Louvre's Egyptian collection—one of the finest in the world—was built in three stages. The department was created in 1826 on the suggestion of Champollion, who persuaded Charles X to acquire the private collections of Western diplomats in Egypt. From the 19th century on, the collection grew as the Egyptian authorities approved new archaeological digs. However, after the discovery of Tutankhamen's tomb in 1922, the Egyptian government canceled the agreement. In the 20th century, legacies, donations and sites excavated by the Louvre Museum or the French Institute of Archaeology added to the collection. The museum's Egyptian works (5,000 in all) cover 4,120 square meters. There are two options for visitors eager to explore the banks of the Pharaonic Nile: a chronological tour (from the earliest times to Cleopatra's day) or a thematic visit throwing light on the various aspects of Ancient Egyptian civilization.

Musée du Louvre, 1st

Mummies under Bastille

Napoleon Bonaparte brought back a collection of mummies from his Egyptian campaign and had them sent to the Louvre. Among them were the remains of princes and generals who had been dead for centuries, an unknown Pharaoh, and the High Priest Pentamenou, a contemporary of Senusret I. The mummies were displayed in granite sarcophagi in the Louvre. However, in Paris's rather damper climate, they began to rot, so it was decided to dispose of them. They were buried in the gardens of the Louvre. Three years later, during the July revolution, patriots died by the hundreds in the fighting of the Trois Glorieuses (Three Glorious Days). Because of the heat, they were hastily buried close to where they fell —32 of them a few meters from the mummies in the jardin de l'Infante. Once order was restored, the new king, Louis-Philippe, wished to honor the memory of the heroes of July. To provide them with a suitable tomb, he decided to have a monument erected in the square where the Bastille had formerly stood. On the day when the bodies were transferred to the July Column (July 27, 1840), the gravediggers accidentally took two mummies that were close to the other corpses. It was only in around 1940 when the vaults were repaired that the mistake was officially realized: there were two more bodies than there were names of combatants engraved on the bronze rolls.

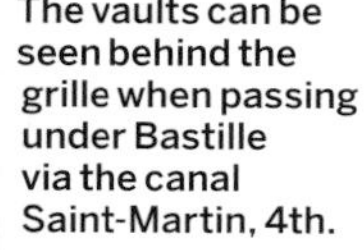

The vaults can be seen behind the grille when passing under Bastille via the canal Saint-Martin, 4th.

Crowning error

The fontaine du Fellah installed in 1809 shows an Egyptian farm worker (fellah) standing at the door of an Egyptian temple and carrying two jars. From them pour water from the Gros-Caillou pump. The farm worker is wearing a crossed loincloth, but his headgear is all wrong: it is a nemes, the emblematic headdress of the pharaohs. However, this detail does not seem to bother anybody.

42, rue de Sèvres, 7th

A sliding fountain with a palm-tree bole

The fontaine du Palmier was erected in 1808 to commemorate Napoleonic victories. It did not look quite as it does today—it was lower and completely sphinx-free. When the square was renovated after the opening of the boulevard de Sébastopol in 1858, the fountain was off center and its basin a meter underground, so it had to be moved. The operation—which involved putting the fountain on rails and sliding it 12 meters towards the Seine—took no more than 10 minutes. For good measure, it was raised onto a double base decorated by four sphinxes with water pouring from their mouths.

Place du Châtelet, 4th

The Nubian child

In the same style as the fontaine du Fellah, a Nubian child stands with his hips angled in front of an elegant double flight of steps in the courtyard of a former town house.

22, rue Dussoubs, 2nd

The Louxor-Barbes

Built in 1921, the Louxor-Palais du Cinéma was a temple to Egyptian epic movies until it closed in the 1980s. Renovation work ordered by the City of Paris finally returned the luster to its blue and gold mosaics with their scarab, cobra, and winged-disk patterns. It reopened as a cinema a few years ago.

Corner of boulevard de La Chapelle and boulevard Magenta, 10th

Champollion's house

Who would pass up a pilgrimage to the rue Mazarine and the house where Jean-François Champollion discovered the key to the Ancient Egyptian hieroglyph alphabet in October 1822? Champollion worked with a replica of the Rosetta Stone (which was inscribed with the same decree written in hieroglyphs, demotic script, and Ancient Greek). As the story goes, he was so shocked by his discovery that he fainted and only woke up five days later. The fact that the brilliant code-breaker had never set foot in Egypt and that many scientists before him had failed to solve the puzzle made his achievement all the more impressive.

28, rue Mazarine, 6th

The Nile in the Tuileries

In classical statuary, the River Nile is often represented as a recumbent bearded man holding a horn of plenty and leaning on a sphinx. The allegorical group in the jardin des Tuileries follows this rule. It is a marble copy unveiled in 1720. The original, created by Lorenzo Ottone in 1692, is in the Vatican. Every last trait that symbolizes the river is included, right down to the crocodiles.

Jardin des Tuileries, 1st (to the right of the octagonal basin when facing the Louvre)

Trains come and go… and fashions, too

The shape of the pillars supporting the Daumesnil viaduct where it passes over streets is unusual. They look like (stylized) palm tree trunks and their capitals spread like lotus flowers. That would be quite understandable if the viaduct had been built at the very start of the 19th century when Egyptomania was at its height, but it was actually constructed in 1859 to carry the Vincennes rail line, at a time when tastes had turned to Haussmannian classicism.

Viaduc Daumesnil, over avenue Ledru-Rollin and boulevard Diderot, 12th

Woman and the ankh

The Temple du Droit humain (Temple of Human Law) is home to the Grande Loge symbolique écossaise mixte de France (Grand Mixed Symbolic Scottish Lodge of France), which—as its name suggests—accepts female members. It was founded in 1893 by Maria Deraisme, a pioneer of feminism in France. Its facade features many references to Ancient Egypt: lotus-shaped capitals, a solar-disc cornice, ankhs that form a balustrade on the balcony, and so on. This was a way of reminding the public that Ancient Egypt was ahead of its time in terms of women's rights. Women were not excluded from initiation ceremonies and no basic spiritual distinction was made between men and women, who could both join the priesthood.

5, rue Jules-Breton, 13th

Sphinxes & sphinges

In the 18th century, it was the height of fashion to decorate the steps of one's town house with sphinxes. Such fabulous human-lion hybrids still guard the entrances to the hôtels Salé, Fieubet, and Gouthière. The ruling class was flattered by the creature's symbolism, a combination of strength and intelligence. Today, Paris has around a hundred stone sphinxes—some male, some female. No two are alike: paws crossed or flat on the ground, abdomens winged or not, a welcoming, threatening, or priestly expression, and so on.

1 Place du Châtelet, 1st. Water pours from the mouths of the fontaine du Palmier's sphinxes, which face the four points of the compass *(see p. 190)*.

2 Péristyle de Chartres, 1st. At Palais-Royal, a female sphinx watches over the entrance to the Constitutional Court, where the Court of Accounts sat from 1871 to 1912.

3 Avenue du Général-Lemonnier on the Seine side, 1st. This female sphinx has made her home on the Bord-de-l'Eau terrace and has her gaze firmly set on the Louvre.

4

5

8

6

9

7

10

4 2 bis, quai des Célestins, 4th. The sculpted stone female sphinxes of the hotel Fieub look particularly serene.

5 62, rue Saint-Antoine, 4th. The white marble ones at the hôtel de Sully seem remarkably distressed.

6 Rue de Thorigny, 4th. Good as gold, the female sphinxes with crossed paws in the courtyard of the hôtel Salé watch over the musée Picasso.

7 Quai Anatole-France, 7th. A sphinx stares fixedly at the Seine behind the hotel de Salm, now the musée de la Légion d'honneur.

8 93-95, rue de Montreuil, 11th. One curious multi-colored ceramic panel shows a torch and the words "Fiat Lux;" its counterpart features two sphinxes facing each other across a kind of wineskin. The combination is repeated 12 times over the entire facade of a building that housed workers'accommodations. It might just be a message of hope for the proletariat.

9 6, rue Férou, 6th. On either side of the gates of the hotel de la Trémoille, two sphinxes stare stonily at each other.

10 4, rue Jasmin, 16th. Across the entire width of the building, each third-floor balcony is decorated with a pair of female sphinxes.
11 88, rue Blanche, 9th.

23

Métro memorabilia

The signposts and accessories of Métro entrances all serve the same purpose, but differ in many ways—even when they initially appear to be the same. The Guimard entrances have many variations, depending on whether they are main or secondary and according to their construction date. The aim of this section is not to provide a complete typology of all the various types of Métro entrance, but to underline a few special features.

Station Madeleine

Guimard entrances

Guimard designed several standard models (pavilions, shelters, surrounding balustrades, signs, and candelabras) that could be mass-produced by manufacturing standardized parts and using cast iron. Nearly 150 Guimard entrances were built at the start of the 20th century. Only 86 are left, all protected as historic monuments.

A is for Abbesses

This entrance (*left*) initially provided access to the Hôtel-de-Ville station, but was moved here in 1974. It is the only survivor of nine Model-A type constructions—the kind consisting of four pillars and a glass shelter with a V-shaped roof.

Station Abbesses (line 12)

B is for Dragonfly

The Porte-Dauphine entrance (right) is a Model B: it has three pillars and a V-shaped roof with a rounded end, and is enclosed by enameled lava-stone panels. This type is called a *libellule* (dragonfly) because of the shape of its glass roof, which suggests the silhouette of the insect as it takes flight. It is the only example that has not been moved since 1902.

Station Porte-Dauphine (line 2)

Eccentric entrances

Sprays of lily of the valley

The Metropolitain sign is supported by a crossbeam between two long stems that are tipped with leaves and red spherical lights.

Station Château-d'Eau (line 4)

By analogy, the stems are known as *brins de muguet* (although the bells of that flower are white).

Station Gambetta (line 3)

A disappearing signature

The enameled plaques over Guimard entrances carry the word "Metro" or "Metropolitain." Their now-characteristic font was designed by Georges Auriol. The signs that were installed before 1904 are marked "Hector Guimard, architecte." After that date, the architect was no longer credited because of a rapid decline in his popularity.

The sign of Porte-Dauphine station (line 2) features the name of the architect, who was still appreciated in 1902.

North-South

Line 12 is different than the others. When it opened in 1905, it belonged to a licensee corporation, La Compagnie de chemin de fer électrique Nord-Sud (the North-South Electric Railway Company), competing with the CMP (Compagnie du métro parisien). The smaller business made every effort to stand out: more sophisticated wrought-iron balustrades, a stairway with ceramic facings and a painted frieze on the walls surrounding it, a "stencil" sign cut in a red panel, and so on. So the Nord-Sud network is genuinely different, both inside and out. It beveled white tiles are decorated with blue, green, or brown wave-patterned friezes and its NS monogram features on billboard frames. The two competing companies merged on January 1, 1930, but the subtle distinctions remained.

A "stencil" type sign at Lamarck-Caulaincourt station (line 12).

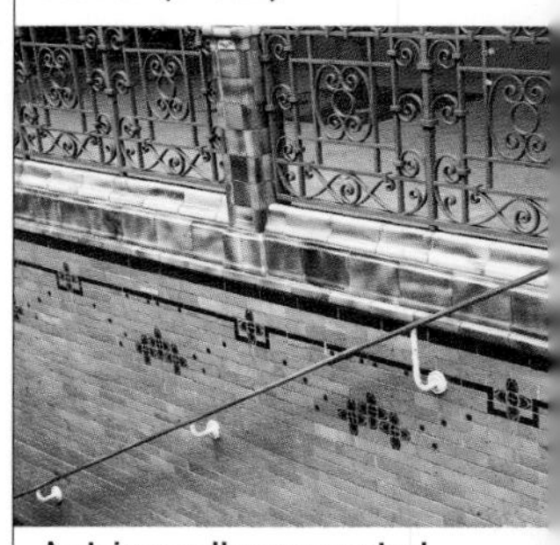

A string wall ornamented with a multicolored frieze at Solférino (line 12).

Ornate wrought-iron balustrades at Place-de-Clichy station (line 2, formerly Nord-Sud).

Sobriety and discretion

There is generally freestone facing around Métro entrances in major squares and plazas (Étoile, Nation, Opéra, République, etc.), and on the Champs-Élysées. This is for aesthetic reasons, so they do not clash with the setting.

Station Franklin-D.-Roosevelt (lines 1 and 9)

Kiosque des noctambules

A worthy successor to Hector Guimard's daring, imaginative entrances, the one designed by the artist Jean-Michel Othoniel has stood in the center of the place Colette since the year 2000. Named Kiosque des noctambules (*Nighthawks' Pavilion*), it consists of an aluminum framework on which giant Murano beads are "strung."

Station Palais-Royal-Musée-du-Louvre (lines 1 and 7)

Store subways

The vicissitudes of urban planning (for instance, lack of space on the sidewalk) led to the installation of unusual Métro entrances, such as Sentier, Riquet, Buzenval, or Pernety (opened in the ground floors of buildings), Place-Monge, Vaneau (in special small edifices), Volontaires (whose entrance is said to be *en boutique*) or Lamarck-Caulaincourt (under the rue Caulaincourt).

Opposite
Sentier station
Below
Station Monge

The concrete entrance to Vaneau station (line 10) was constructed in 1923 on a lot belonging to the hôpital Laennec, in line with the rue de Sèvres. It has two lit signs.

-MÉTRO-

Station Sentier

Unusually, the Val-d'Osne candelabra in the place Saint-Michel (line 4) is placed in the middle of the steps.

Sign supports

The Val-d'Osne candelabra (in very intricate wrought iron) was designed in around 1910 and was succeeded by the Dervaux candelabra, which became the standard model in the 1930s. The Dervaux was more somber, but topped by the same white lighting globe. The red M surrounded by a blue circle dates back to the end of the 1940s; the target sign with its blue and white panel to the 1960s; the yellow M to the 1970s. The Méteor line introduced a new rectangular glass sign in 1998.

Station Bibliothèque-François-Mitterrand

To mark the entrance to Lamarck-Caulaincourt station (line 12), which is set back from the rue Lamarck, the sign was placed well in front of it on the sidewalk.

Station Alésia

METRO

Station Franklin-D.-Roosevelt

Other Métro themes

The station-master's office

Once, every station-master had a small booth on the platform equipped with multiple telephone lines that connected it to the line's termini and neighboring stations, and the duty officers of the operations department. In the 1960s, stationmasters moved to station offices behind ticket desks.

Station Liège (line 13)

Pili

This acronym for *plan indicateur lumineux d'itinéraire* (lit route-indicator plan) was a kind of baby-boomer predecessor of the computer. Passengers delighted in pressing the button corresponding to their station and immediately seeing the route appear on the plan in the form of a string of lights. The first Pili displays were installed in 1937 to help guide them through the Métro maze. By 1981, there were 184 Pilis. Today, around a hundred are left, but they are not all in working order.

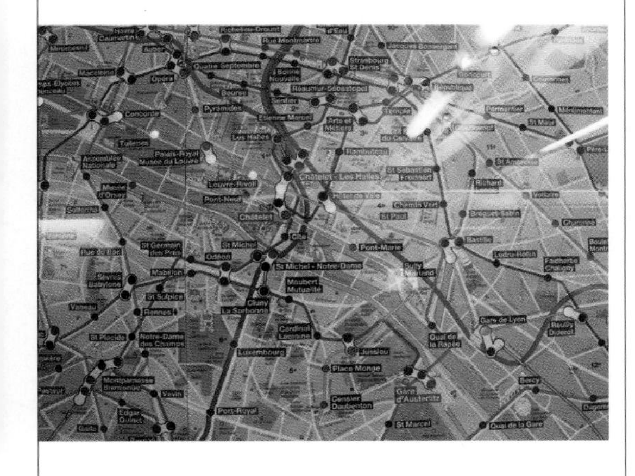

Cream or white beveled tiles

The tiling used when the Métropolitain was opened in 1900 consisted of off-white varnished bricks. These can still be seen today on the vaults that rise from the platforms of Porte-de-Vincennes and Porte-Dauphine stations. The prototype tiling provided a flat surface that could easily be disinfected—a definite advantage at a time when society lived in fear of epidemics. Even so, from 1902, it was replaced by beveled white tiles that diffracted light and made it easier to see in the subway. We should remember that, in those days, light bulbs emitted only 5 lux compared to 250 today.

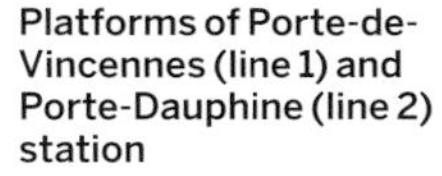

Platforms of Porte-de-Vincennes (line 1) and Porte-Dauphine (line 2) station

"Treasure" hunt

The idea is to search each renovated station to find the single tile where the dates of refurbishment are recorded. The name of the station, the words "Renouveau du Métro" and the date when work was completed are handwritten on it. A hint: these tiles are relatively close to the ticket desk in the entrances.

24 Hotels of legend

Tourist brochures delight in singing the praises of Paris's 1,470 or so hotels, describing a number of them as "legendary." For tour operators, a simple celebrity stopover is enough to justify the use of the word. Of course, tourists take the bait, flattered that they can shave in a mirror that has reflected a star's features or sit in a chair where some tormented poet once toyed with his or her grim thoughts. Others are excited by the idea of enjoying a brief encounter on the very mattress where... Blues or bawdiness: to each their own. However, the hotels (past and present) listed below are truly 24-carat legends.

Beat Hôtel
(see p. 203)

Hôtel du Nord. 102, quai de Jemmapes, 10th

Eugène and Marcel

The Hôtel du Nord became a part of popular culture thanks to the classic Arletty movie. But who still remembers Eugène Dabit? He was the author of a collection of short stories entitled L'Hôtel du Nord, published in 1929. A couple, the Lecouvreurs, inherit a modest sum that enables them to buy a hotel. Its guests are the main characters in a series of stories that are probably based on Dabit's own experiences. Even though the plotlines are as thin as an alley cat, in 1938, the great filmmaker Marcel Carné turned them into a stormy, engaging movie that became far more famous than the book. He shot the scenes on mocked-up sets in the studio. The hotel stopped taking guests a long time ago, but its legend continues to attract curious visitors in search of atmospheric sensations on the banks of the canal Saint-Martin.

Opposite **The stairway** *Below* **The replica of Oscar Wilde's room.**

© L'HÔTEL

Oscar's abode

L'Hôtel (with no other name) is an iconic destination. Among a thousand others, its guests included the French actress and singer Mistinguett and Oscar Wilde. The star-crossed writer stayed there in 1898, when it was called the hôtel d'Alsace. Under the name of Mr. Sebastian, he took two rooms on the second floor: 6 and 7 (today, his bedroom is replicated in no. 16). His literary income was significant, but not enough to fund his lifestyle, and was supplemented by the generosity of a female neighbor. He wrote *An Ideal Husband* and *The Importance of Being Earnest* at the hotel before his death from meningitis on November 30, 1900 at the age of 46. Many more personalities have followed in the footsteps of the Irish writer and wit on the hotel's amazing spiral stairs: Jorge Luis Borges, Robert De Niro and many others who appreciate the establishment's cozy ambience.

L'Hôtel. 13, rue des Beaux-Arts, 6th

A select rendezvous

The Istria, a modest hotel in Montparnasse, saw all the great names of arts and letters pass through its doors between the wars. Pass very discreetly, because those current or future luminaries were generally meeting their lovers secretly. Setting aside the gangster Pierrot-le-Fou, they included the artist Man Ray, the writers Elsa Triolet and Louis Aragon, the painter and poet Francis Picabia, the artists Marcel Duchamp and Moïse Kisling, the model Kiki de Montparnasse, the composer Érik Satie, the poet and novelist Rainer Maria Rilke, the poet Tristan Tzara, and the author Raymond Radiguet (who came to the Istria to cheat on writer, artist, and filmmaker Jean Cocteau with a woman). So did these legendary figures ever meet in the hall?

29, rue Campagne-Première, 14th

La Lousiane. 60, rue de Seine, 6th

The Louisiane

How did this unpretentious little hotel manage to attract so many artists? It was not entirely due to its location in the heart of Saint-Germain-des-Prés. After the Liberation, American jazzmen visiting Paris chose to stay there: Miles Davis, John Coltrane, Chet Baker, Charlie Parker, and others. The aristocracy of rock followed —Jim Morrison and Pink Floyd among them. Juliette Gréco, the muse of Saint-Germain, shared a room in the hotel with fellow singers Annabelle Buffet and Anne-Marie Casalis, and the musicians Mouloudji and Boris Vian met there. Many writers became long-term residents: Albert Cossery (for nearly 60 years!), Ernest Hemingway, Antoine de Saint-Exupéry, Henry Miller, and especially the founding couple of existentialism, Jean-Paul Sartre and Simone de Beauvoir. From the 1950s, filmmakers were among the guests: Louis Malle, Bertrand Tavernier (who set his movie *Round Midnight in the Louisiane*), Leos Carax, Quentin Tarantino, and others. Not to mention the painters: Bernard Buffet, Alberto Giacometti, Salvador Dali (who met with singer, actress and model Amanda Lear there), and so on. A hotel with a rich past of old-fashioned charm.

Beat Hotel

Before it was dubbed the Beat Hotel, the Hôtel du Vieux Paris had no name, just a street number, and was known as "The Nameless Hotel." Between the end of the 1950s and the start of the 1960s, it was home to a handful of penniless American artists, including Ian Sommerville, Brion Gysin, William Burroughs, and Harold Norse. Norse wrote: "This sleeping-bag haven will be dissected by art historians." He was right. Back then, it was not the comfortable hotel that it is today, but a shabby guest house with hole-in-the-floor lavatories in the halls and pot smoke on every floor. Something was going on in each room: resident beatniks were writing, painting, fiddling with their tape recorders, or discussing the issues of the day while their protector, Madame Rachou, kept an eye on her flock from behind her desk in the lobby.

Hôtel du Vieux Paris. 9, rue Gît-le-Cœur, 6th

A picture sent by Allen Ginsberg as a memento of his long stay at The Nameless Hotel.

25
Whispering walls

Old stones have many stories to tell to those who are ready to hear them. Many years ago, people shared their sorrows and joys on walls or used them as indelible notebooks. Graffiti is hardly the right word for such lapidary inscriptions; we might use the rather more delicate term "spontaneous expression in stone" to refer to these sources of glyptological fascination. So this chapter is a compendium of heartfelt cries, official notices, and contemporary artistic statements.

la musique adoucit les murs

Butte-aux-Cailles
(see p. 209)

Antique engravings

11, place des Vosges, 4th

Rue des Jardins-Saint-Paul, 4th

Stonecutter's signatures

Centuries ago, stonecutters were pieceworkers, paid for each job. In other words, the more they produced, the more money they made. They had to mark the stones they cut to enable them to be counted up at the end of the week and the right wage handed over. So every stonecutter had to choose a "signature"—a geometric sign, letter, or monogram (intertwined initials). Their marks can be found on the walls of medieval cathedrals, châteaux, fortresses, and fortifications such as Philippe Auguste's city walls, built on the Right Bank in around 1200. On the Montgomery tower and its 60-meter-long parapet, there are many different stonecutters' signs at eye level: crosses, arrows, Zs, inverted Ns, and so on, each one a touching allusion to the labor of a long-departed artisan.

Griffon news updates

Nicolas Restif de la Bretonne was both a writer and a great Parisian hiker. An insomniac, he spent his nights walking the streets of the Marais and the île Saint-Louis. His minor obsession was to scratch inscriptions (they were not yet called graffiti, a word that only gained currency in the 19th century) into walls with a key or piece of iron: a date, a name, and a few abbreviations, often in Latin, describing memorable events in his everyday life. Because of his hobby, he became known as *griffon* (scratcher), "the man who scratches stones with an awl." When he returned home, Nicolas meticulously recorded his words in a notebook, which was published after his death as Mes Inscripcions (from 1779 to 1785). All his street engravings seem to have been lost over time, except maybe the words: "1764 Nicolas," which can be seen on the pillar of an arcade in the place des Vosges.

Left to right
89, rue de l'Hôtel-de-Ville, 4th
Corner of rue Villehardouin and rue de Turenne, 3rd

Administrative census

We know little about this fine uppercase D engraved in stone on the rue Villehardouin or this B on the rue de l'Hôtel-de-Ville. They were probably administrative markers cut by the authorities during a census, features on an 18th-century plan of Paris.

Manor markers

In 1779, the archbishopric of Paris brought nine fiefs (domains belonging to lords or religious communities) into its fold and marks were made on stones to show the confines of each one. In the Marais, the inscription "FCSG," the initials of Fief des Coutures-Saint-Gervais (*coutures* meant crops) can still be seen. It was the fief of the Hospitaller nuns of Saint-Gervais, which explains the cross. Another mark has survived on the Left Bank: "FDT" for Fief des Tombes, so called because it was home to the largest Gallo-Roman cemetery in Lutetia, on the site of today's rue Pierre-Nicole. These engravings in stone were called *marques de censive* (the *cens* was the annual tax owed to the local lord).

Also
Corner of rue du Faubourg-Saint-Antoine and rue de Charonne, 11th

Top to bottom
Corner of rue Saint-Jacques and rue des Fossés-Saint-Jacques, 5th
Corner of rue de Thorigny and rue des Coutures-Saint- Gervais, 3rd
Corner of rue de Thorigny and rue Debelleyme, 3rd

Stucco stratification

At the two ends of the galerie Vivienne (at eye level and up on a cornice), a little scraping produced a fascinating color chart. Curious restaurant owners removed the arcade's coats of paint over small surfaces to reveal the different layers of stucco applied over its history. The colors of the nine layers range from brown, ochre, and brick-red to green, as can be seen in this "window," which shows the successive appearances of the arcade from its opening in 1826 until the present day. Various antique inscriptions have similarly been revealed in different places in the arcade.

Galerie Vivienne, 2nd

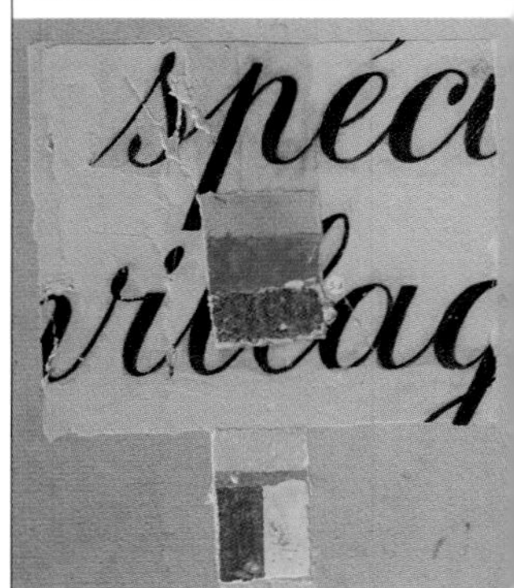

Embassy of Texas

It takes a keen eye to notice the sign of the "Embassy of Texas" on the facade of the hôtel Vendôme. There was a Republic of Texas? Yes, for a short time, from 1836 to 1845—just long enough for it to open a few embassies around the world, especially in France, the first nation to recognize Texan sovereignty. After gaining independence from Mexico in 1836 (the siege of Fort Alamo was more than just a movie script), Texas remained an independent republic until 1845, when it became part of the United States of America. The building that housed the embassy was turned into a hotel in 1858.

1, place Vendôme, 1st

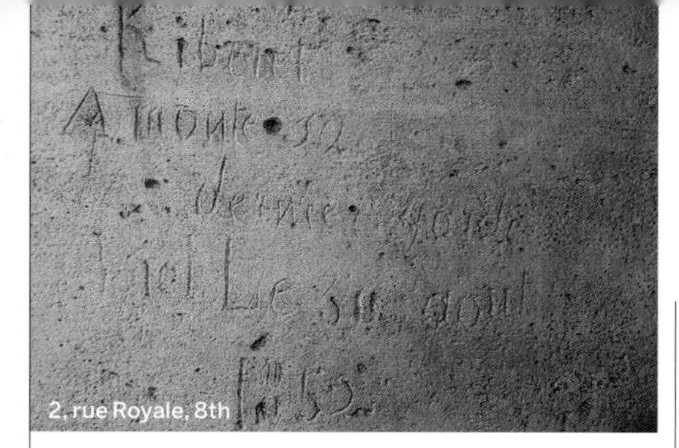
2, rue Royale, 8th

A farewell to arms

Was this soldier named Riberel relieved or nostalgic when he recorded the date of his final tour of guard duty on the stone wall of the Naval Ministry? The words "Riberel stood his last guard here on August 30, 1852" are almost invisible, since they are engraved in the recess (on the left-hand side) of the first window to the right of the entrance of the Ministry (viewed from outside).

Louis, Gustave, and the rest

It is amusing to hunt for antique graffiti on monuments recommended by the Baedeker guide (the ancestor of today's travel guides and Europe's standard tourist manual in the 19th century and the first half of the 20th). The Baedeker was popular with both provincials and foreign tourists, who liked to leave a memento of their stay in the capital even back in those days. On the pillars of the gazebo in the Jardin des plantes are overlapping signatures in neat joined-up handwriting or trim capitals: "Louis Ouinel 1840," "A. Schubs 1899," "Gustave 1896," "Danninger September 1823," and so on. The same goes for the facade of the hôtel Crillon near the rue Royale, where an empty niche is ornamented with graffiti dating back to 1810 and 1828. There are almost certainly many other inscriptions just waiting to be deciphered.

Top to bottom

Jardin des plantes, 5th
6, place de la Concorde, 8th

Diamond or bauble?

The private rooms of the restaurant Lapérouse are justly notorious. In the 19th century, they hosted the furtive dalliances of some great names in the worlds of literature, politics, and law, who came here to discreetly make love to their paramours. And for a very good reason: according to an article of French law (still valid today), no evidence of adultery obtained in a public place was admissible in court. Inconstant and infamous writers such as Charles Baudelaire, Gérard de Nerval, Gustave Flaubert, and Guy de Maupassant had their personal napkin rings here. The most romantic private rooms are the Quai des Fleurs and the salon des Anges (35 and 36 for those in the know). Their soft lighting adjusted to perfection, they are furnished with a small table and garnet-colored velvet sofa. The bidets that once lurked beneath the banquettes are now just a memory. However, the mercury mirrors on the walls are still covered with initials, first names, and dates. They were scratched by the belles of the Belle Époque to test the authenticity of the diamonds their lovers gave them, so making sure they were not selling their virtue short. The names changed according to the fashions of the times: Berthes and Renées were gradually superseded by Sonias and Laetitias.

©LAPÉROUSE

Scratches are visible on the mirror to the left.

51, quai des Grands-Augustins, 6th

Street Art

Mercifully, what we know as "street art" is not limited to the dubious graffiti sprayed here and there by street kids keen to mark their territory. Spontaneous contemporary expression is infinite in its variety: collages, stencils, mosaics, frescos... It is the work of underground artists, poets, and activists; women and men who walk in the shadows and cultivate an air of mystery. Occasionally, one or another steps out into the broad daylight of official recognition. As they migrate from the guerilla to the collector art world, their standing rises. Nemo, Jérôme Mesnager, Miss. Tic, and the creator of the Invaders are just some of the street artists whose work now embellishes galleries more than alleys.

68, rue de Ménilmontant, 20th

The man in the raincoat

If you see street art featuring an umbrella, suitcase, butterflies, or a red balloon, you are looking at a Nemo. The artist's polished, masterly compositions are mainly to be found in the 20th arrondissement. Poetical, oneiric, and airy, they shine with subtlety and lightness of touch. They may suggest *Plume* by Henri Michaux, Calder's mobiles, or the Surrealists—Magritte chief among them.

38, rue de Ménilmontant, 20th

The white body

The first *corps blanc* by Jérôme Mesnager appeared in 1983. Since then, its clones have been climbing the world's walls by the hundreds, from the Great Wall of China to the facades of Red Square or the chambers of the Paris Catacombs. In his creator's mind, the muscular figure symbolizes light, strength, and peace.

Passerelle de la Grange-aux-Belles, 10th
A personal take on Géricault's *The Raft of the Medusa* by Jérôme Mesnager.

Opposite
Place Stravinsky, 4th
Jef Aérosol is now a recognized artist, as shown by this fresco created in partnership with the Pompidou Center in 2011.

Below
A Mesnager "white body" and a Jef Aérosol dancer in the Mouffetard district, 5th

Jungle animals

Giraffes, zebras, tigers, and other fauna decorate the Paris jungle—thanks to Mosko et associés. Behind the name Mosko are two old pals with a mutual interest in stencils: Michel Allemand and Gérard Laux from the capital's Moskova district (18th). The *associés* are a number of other artists who work hand in hand with the duo. These include Jérôme Mesnager, Nemo, and Hondo.
29, rue de Bièvre, 5th

The little black dress

It is impossible to ignore these femmes fatales and their associated aphorisms: they confront, unsettle, challenge, and plunge their stiletto heels into objectified female stereotypes. Behind the pseudonym Miss.Tic is Radhia de Ruiter, a plastic artist who describes herself as an urban-art poet and who actually physically resembles her creations. Her plays on words remain firmly in the memories of passers-by. One is "*Tes faims de moi sont difficiles*." When *faims* is pronounced, it can be understood as "hungers" or "ends," and *mois* as "me" or "month," so the spoken sentence means both "Your hungering after me is hard" and "Your ends of month [when you run low on money before you get paid] are hard."

The red arrow

This is the trademark sign—almost the second signature, in fact—of Jef Aérosol (aka Jean-François Perroy), who paints portraits of famous figures (including Presley, Gandhi, Lennon, Hendrix, and Basquiat), but devotes much of his work to nameless people met in the street: musicians, passers-by, panhandlers, and so on.

On the corner of rue des Cascades and rue de Savies, 20th
Strange, isolated, and a little disturbing, these deeply etched graffiti portray tormented Edvard Munch-style faces.

Invaders

These little pixelated guerrilla mosaics all over the city appear overnight and can vanish just as quickly. There are around a thousand such perpetually mobile, morphing works based on the Space Invaders videogame released in Japan for the Atari 2600 console in 1973. So which artists create them? Do they work alone or as a group? What is their strategy? Do they employ lookouts or have assistants to hold their ladder? They are fiercely protective of their artistic secrets, but do follow one self-imposed rule: to total as many points as possible. A score table gives the number of each Invader in order, its production date, the number of the arrondissement and its score (10, 20, 30, or 50 points, depending on its difficulty). Each unique Invader with its own alias is photographed and positioned on a giant plan of Paris. The invasion particularly targets the northeast of the capital. The Invaders' commanding officer (single or plural) has a good, subtle sense of humor. Some of the works are direct allusions to a street name—French flags in the rue Française, full moons in the rue de la Lune, and so on—or a famous local feature—an amphora near the Montmartre vineyard or a Gitanes smoker on Serge Gainsbourg's house (*see p. 132*).

1 2 3 4 5 6 7 8 9

Rue du Morvan, 11th
Le Cyklop worked with children from the neighboring school to turn the hundred posts in this street into friendly cyclopean monsters.

Cyklops

These anti-parking posts topped with eyeballs are the work of Cyklop, aka Olivier d'Hondt. He specializes in turning dreary street furniture into fun, colorful "NACs" (Nouveaux Animaux de Compagnie —New Pets).

Also
"Mixed couple" facing 9, passage Dubail, 10th

6, cité de l'Ameublement, 11th

Composite mosaics

These discreet, eye-level, poetic works combining mosaic shards, paste, and pieces of mirror are meticulously composed by plastic-arts teacher Jérôme Gulon. The finest of them feature portraits with a clue (often a book title) to the identity of the figure depicted, who always has a connection with the location: a portrait of Giacometti on the site of his studio in the rue d'Alésia (14th); a tribute to Modigliani on the walls of La Ruche (14th); another to Jean-Baptiste Clément, (author of the revolutionary song Le Temps des Cerises [*The Cherry Season*] at the Butte-aux-Cailles (13th); rails above the Petite Ceinture beltline in Ménilmontant (20th); and so on.

Rue du Cloître-Saint-Merri, 4th
Among this series of faces is a portrait of the poet Robert Desnos, who grew up in the Les Halles neighborhood. He mentions this street in some of his verses.

1 A camouflaged Invader on the base of the fontaine du Palmier. Place du Châtelet, 1st

2 An amphora. Rue Saint-Vincent, 18th

3 A giant mosaic. 22,rue de Poitou, 3rd

4 A bonus on a sanitation building Passerelle de la Grange-aux-Belles, 10th

5 Rubik's cubism. Corner of rue Saint-Victor and rue de Poissy, 5th

6 Rue Paul-Escudier, 9th

7 Rue de la Huchette, 5th

8 Maison de Gainsbourg. 5 bis, rue de Verneuil, 7th

9 Rue de la Lune, 2nd

10 This Invader at the foot of the Montmartre funicular railway appears as an unintentional, anachronistic extra in the movie Le Petit Nicolas. Place Suzanne-Valadon, 18th

11 17, rue Étienne-Marcel, 2nd.

Place Stravinsky, 4th

14, rue Bonaparte, 6th

A yellow tom

Monsieur Chat is the name of this big yellow feline with his Cheshire-cat grin. Portraits of him are painted high above the ground on facades or blind side walls in places you would swear were completely inaccessible. His owner was called Thoma Vuille and in the 2000s, the cat's stomping ground ran along the route from the porte de Clignancourt to the porte d'Orléans. The past tense is in order: the master moved house and his tomcat left with him.

Hotspots

Ménilmontant, Belleville, Montmartre, the area surrounding the canal Saint-Martin, and the Butte-aux-Cailles (where the collective Les Lézards de la Bièvre operates) are the favorite canvases of stencil painters and other street artists, who sometimes leave lasting marks in the center of Paris, too—for instance, here at 59, rue de Rivoli, a former squat that is now the official residence of 30 or so artists of every kind. Attracting nearly 80,000 visitors a year, it has become a temple of contemporary art.

Also
Rue Dénoyez, 20th

Chez Robert. 59, rue de Rivoli, 1st

60, rue des Francs-Bourgiois, 3rd, behind the wall, l'hôtel de Soubise (the museum of the history of France). On the wall, a reversed stencil makes the words "Histoire de Paris" appear on the stone as if it had been washed by a super-powerful jet.

Gregos

A 3-D mask poking out its tongue? It must be a self-portrait by Gregos, a highly polyvalent artist who has mastered molding and acrylic painting among other skills. Depending on his mood, he may be smiling or glum, but usually looks mischievous with that protruding tongue. He makes masks of his face, paints them, and then puts them up in his neighborhood (Montmartre) or elsewhere. To date, more than 250 of these faces have been installed, but sadly, given their popularity, they are soon purloined.

Place du Calvaire, 18th

Class of 1995

Class of 1998

Subterranean yearbooks

Until the 1850s, underground quarries were the perfect place for students from the École nationale supérieure des Mines de Paris to practice their skills. They regularly went down with their teachers to carry out topographical exercises. Such official descents are a thing of the past, but the students still visit the tunnels and chambers in secret. In the 1960s, they launched a long-term artistic project, taking over a remote tunnel (in the southern sector of the Saint-Jacques gallery) and turning it into a sort of hidden temple to cave art. Each year, the students produce a fresco that is unveiled on the evening of December 4, the feast of Sainte-Barbe (the patron saint of miners), in the presence of a media celebrity—always a woman—who "sponsors" their class. Initially, the idea was simply to display the year, their sponsor's name, and their ENSMP school logo (a lamp, a sledgehammer, and a mallet), but from 1988 on, these inscriptions became splendid frescos. The actor Nathalie Baye (1989) and the singer Catherine Ringer (1994) are among the sponsors. The Class of '95 fresco—a watercolor-style view of the roofs of Paris—is one of the finest exhibits. It was painted by Gilles Cyprès. And the sponsor? The words are now illegible. It was actually Ségolène Royal, the future presidential runner-up. In 1998, she sponsored an anti-hazing law... and the young graduates immediately erased her name!

Class of 2001

Class of 2002

Class of 2006

26

The last of the Mohicans

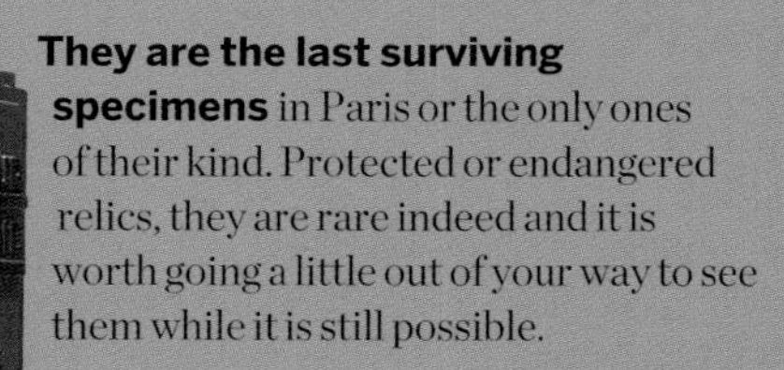

They are the last surviving specimens in Paris or the only ones of their kind. Protected or endangered relics, they are rare indeed and it is worth going a little out of your way to see them while it is still possible.

9, rue de Sévigné
(see p. 216)

Église Saint-Étienne-du-Mont.
Place Sainte-Geneviève, 5th

Jube, Domine, benedicere

The église Saint-Étienne-du-Mont has one of the last remaining rood lofts in France (there are only nine left in all and just one of them is in Paris). A rood loft is a transversal gallery above the nave of a church from which the priest read holy scriptures. The French name, *jubé*, comes from the Latin prayer *Jube, Domine, benedicere*... (Pray, Lord, a blessing). Almost all rood lofts have been replaced by pulpits. Sculpted in 1545, this splendid example has a spiral stairway on each side decorated with superb stone "lacework."

Blessed relief

Say "Arago" to a male taxi driver and he will think affectionately of the good old urinal in the boulevard of that name, where he has answered so many calls of nature. Police officers on the beat around the prison de la Santé are equally beholden to this *vespasienne*, also familiar to professional drivers, since they can make a lightning rest stop there, almost with one hand on the wheel. "I have to go see Ginette!" is the expression employed by regular users. This model of circular urinal for two men that was introduced in around 1877 is the last of its kind in Paris. The others vanished from the city streets at the end of the 1970s, replaced by unisex automated restroom cabins.

In front of 86, boulevard Arago, 13th

Scales

Until the mid-20th century, this type of scales was a common sight in public places: on Métro platforms, in front of drugstores, in the gardens of squares, and so on. Not every family had bathroom scales at the time and checking ones weight was a Sunday ritual. During their walk in the park, people took the opportunity to slip a coin into the slot and watch the spring-loaded pointer turn. Children enjoyed the novelty and their mother could see whether she needed to cut down on the calories. Only a few of these scales have survived. Nobody uses them today for one very good reason: they only take francs.

Jardin du Luxembourg, 6th
Two specimens stand guard by the porte Saint-Michel and there is another near the tennis courts.

Also
Place du Parvis du Sacré-Cœur, 18th

A manpowered carousel

Morning and night, it looks like an enormous iron spider, but late in the afternoon, the slumbering arachnid comes to life. The wooden horses are unpacked from their crates and attached to its legs, and the spider becomes a carousel —but one with no motor, power supply, or automation. Since 1870, its driving force has been the biceps of a carousel turner.

Square du Ranelagh. Rue Mallet-Stevens, 16th

Fire alarms

The first public fire alarms in the City of Paris were introduced in 1886. The perfectly maintained fire-engine-red model in front of the fire station on the rue de Sévigné is the last of these street alarms. It was manufactured in 1947 by the Association des ouvriers en instruments de précision in partnership with the technical department of the Sapeurs-Pompiers de Paris (military firefighters). In the 1970s, the rise of private telephones and phone booths spelled the end for these *avertos*, which were mainly giving false alarms by then. Only a very few specimens remain in some Parisian fire stations (for purely decorative purposes).

Also see Morris columns: temples of gas culture (p. 32).

9, rue de Sévigné, 4th

Say cheese!

The good old film photo booths of the 70s and 80s have steadily been replaced by digital versions that reel out four monotonously identical pictures. Even so, a few vintage photo booths have bucked the trend with the help of La Joyeuse de Photographie, a group founded in 2008 to seek out these antiques, restore them, and reopen them in the capital—usually in the hip neighborhoods of contemporary art. They can be recognized by their sign reading Foto Automat and the fact that for €2 (compared to €4 in the modern booths), they supply a vertical strip of small, film-camera portraits in four different poses.

Palais de Tokyo. 13, avenue du Président-Wilson, 16th

Also

Maison Rouge. 10, boulevard de la Bastille, 12th

Cinémathèque française. 51, rue de Bercy, 12th

See www.fotoautomat.fr for the locations of mobile booths.

Caution: one Métro train may conceal another

Closing a street to let a subway train pass is a rare event in Paris, seen only in the rue de Lagny. Métro traffic is rather light there and the crossing gates are not lowered every day. However, from time to time, the crossing closes when Line 1 or 2 trains are sent for maintenance or parked in the workshops of the RATP Paris transport authority, which were originally constructed in 1900 by the CMP Métro corporation beside the belt rail line near the Porte-de-Vincennes terminus. Because the tracks crossed at street level, a grade crossing had to be created.

In front of 10 bis, quai Henri-IV, 4th

City stop signs

It is often said that there are no stop signs in Paris, but that is an urban myth—as the Prefecture of Police confirms. "Given the density of traffic in the capital, AB4-type signs [aka stop signs] are not generally installed on public thoroughfares so as not to cause jams in those streets where they might be installed. Certain private thoroughfares or parking-lot exits are equipped with AB4-type signs, but they are not installed on public streets." However, there are two exceptions to this rule.

Quai Henri-IV, 4th
Quai Saint-Exupéry, 16th

Corner of rue and passage de Lagny, 20th

Bronze colleagues

That was the nickname given to the communication terminals introduced in 1928, together with the Police-Secours emergency service. At the time, not enough radio resources were available and so the terminals were installed 500 meters apart on the sidewalks of Paris. Police officers had a key to open them and could use them to call the duty officer at the precinct station if necessary, while the general public had to break the glass to use one. Despite the introduction of an emergency phone number (17) in 1930, the terminals remained in service until the 1970s. Two police terminals dating back to the 1950s have survived. The one that is just a nightstick's throw from the place Beauvau (the address of the Ministère de l'Intérieur) is in poorer condition: with its missing front, it has no glass to break, no call button, and no speaker.

100, rue du Faubourg-Saint-Honoré, 8th
114, boulevard Macdonald, 19th

Wooden pavements

In the 1880s, the streets of Paris were surfaced with a "revolutionary" new material that provided a smooth, relatively quiet ride, muffling the sounds of hooves and reducing jolting to a minimum. These paving slabs made of wood (that was the innovation) were pine rectangles about 8 centimeters wide, 12 centimeters high, and 22 centimeters long. They were laid in strips perpendicular to the street and grouted with bitumen and mortar. A groove was cut in them every 40 centimeters to prevent horses from slipping. The system does not seem to have worked very well, though: when it rained, the surface was as slippery as an ice rink. What is more, as the wooden slabs rotted, they smelled terrible and became breeding grounds for germs. So eventually, no more were laid and they were steadily replaced until all were gone in 1938. Only a few square meters of wooden pavement remain in places with very little traffic.

At the entrance to the passage Saint-Maur (at 81, rue Saint-Maur), 11th

38, rue Notre-Dame-de-Nazareth (at the entrance to the building), 3rd

Chopping stone

Some yards in the older parts of Paris, especially the Marais district, still have a chopping stone—a sandstone slab larger and more evenly shaped than the others. Residents propped a block against the stone and used it to chop wooden firewood, the only fuel used in many homes until the neighborhood was supplied with gas. In those days, all courtyards and lean-tos had such a chopping stone. Stonecutters would split large paving stones in two to make them.

28, rue Charlot, 3rd.

Sandboxes

These metal cases 1.5 to 1.7 meters high are sandboxes installed between 1901 and 1919. When ice or snow made a street slippery, the municipal street cleaners opened the hatch at the base of the casing and used the sand to grit the surrounding area. The sand was also used to soak up horse urine before a thoroughfare was swept (manure never remained on the pavement for long: it was prized as a fertilizer for yard, garden, or balcony plants). Only five remaining sidewalk sandboxes have survived since those long-gone days. Most have now been converted into ventilation shafts for underground facilities used by City of Paris sanitary workers. This ingenious piece of recycling has preserved the antiques for posterity.

1

2

1 22, avenue de Saxe, 16th
The highest is 1.7 meters high.

2 39, avenue Trudaine, 9th

3 Place Georges-Guillaumin, 8th

Also
41, avenue Gabriel, 8th
2, place de la Reine-Astrid, 8th

3

27 So what's that for?

Impasse de Conti, 6th

Many of the curious objects described in the previous chapters could just as well have been listed here in this catch-all for the weirdest, most baffling items whose purpose is not immediately apparent. This final inventory includes quite a few pieces of rusty iron embedded in walls and miraculously untouched by successive renovations. Naturally, this platoon of decrepit heritage would be delighted to welcome any new recruits you may be able to identify in the future.

131, boulevard de Sébastopol, 2nd (courtyard)

Top to bottom
118, rue Monge, 5th
67, rue des Meuniers, 12th

Boot scrapers

Boot scrapers were widely used in the days before sidewalks became common and the streets cleaner. When city lanes were open sewers overflowing with detritus and filth, pedestrians about to enter a house would scrape their soles on an iron blade provided for the purpose. These scrapers were to be found about 15 centimeters above the ground to the left or right of entrances (or even on both sides). Visitors used them to remove not only the dirt from their shoes, but also any little pebbles embedded in their soles that might scratch their host's parquet flooring. Boot scrapers were also a universal fixture next to church and hospital doors—for reasons of both decency and hygiene. There are scrapers on both sides of the doors of the église Saint-Roch; the one on the left has a grip above it for the user's convenience. In the rue des Meuniers, two are set in recesses at the foot of a building built in 1913. Note: the horizontal position of the door-code keypad is unusual, too.

Also
Église Saint-Sulpice, 6th
Église Saint-Roch. 296, rue Saint-Honoré, 1st
Rue Bichat, 10th (in front of the entrance to the hôpital Saint-Louis)
133, boulevard du Montparnasse, 6th
140, boulevard Saint-Germain, 6th

1 bis, rue Chapon, 3rd

Cellar hooks

Cellar hooks owe their nickname, *queue de cochon* (pig-tails), to their corkscrew shape. Ropes were hung from them and used to lower or hoist heavy loads between street and cellar level (sacks of coal, barrels, casks, et cetera). They basically served the same purpose as pulleys but were easier to use. Looking at this setup in the rue de Bièvre (the hook fixed in the wall above the cellar hatch), it is easy to visualize the process.

Also
Impasse Saint-Denis, 1st
Impasse de Lévis, 17th

1, rue de Bièvre, 5th

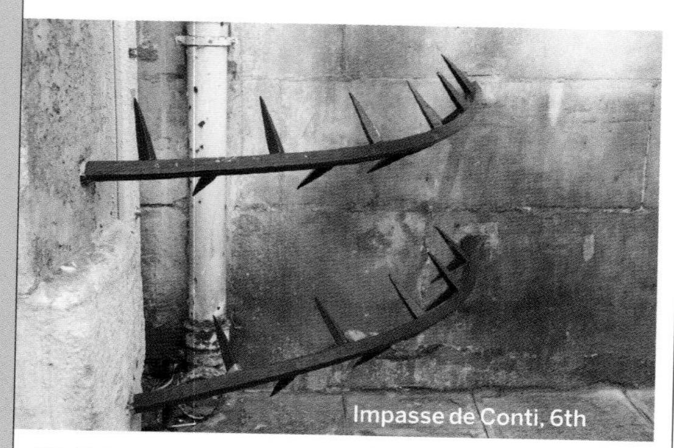
Impasse de Conti, 6th

Hold your water!

Empêche-pipi (pee-preventer) is the common name for anti-urination systems to be found throughout the city. The term won out over other handles such as *pisse-pala* (no-pee-here), *borne sanitaire* (sanitary post), *casse-pipi* (pee-break), *casse-brayette* (fly-break), and *éclabousseur de chaussettes* (sock-splasher). It is common knowledge that some people are singularly lacking in restraint when they urgently need to answer a call of nature and they turn to the nearest discreet corner for relief. The inconsiderate perpetrator then strolls away whistling, leaving behind an odiferous puddle. Showered with complaints, in 1850, a prefect of police ordered designated corners to be equipped with metal fixtures (some bristling with spikes) or conical constructions to prevent any close approach. The sloping mounds were very dissuasive: they caused the offender to soak his own feet and pants, however strong his stream. Really? You already knew?

Boulevard de l'Hôpital under the Métro viaduct (13th), an impressively tall, sculpted model.

Salutary stone shields

Until the end of the 18th century, streets had a central gutter to channel rainwater. On either side, the ground sloped down towards it, so people on foot who were not keen on wading through mud up to their knees had to stick closely to the walls on either side (the origin of the French expression *tenir le haut du pavé* meaning "to be on top"—literally "to occupy the high pavement"). This was in the days before sidewalks, so when a horse-drawn carriage passed, pedestrians could only avoid having their toes crushed by throwing themselves against the nearest wall. To protect them, large stone guards were installed, preventing coaches from passing too close to the houses. In case of danger, amblers merely had to shelter behind one of them.

Also
Rue Berton, 16th
Rue de Savies, 20th

Impasse du Marché-aux-Chevaux, 5th

Halt, no entry!

This bar bristling with spikes once held a portcullis that closed off the passage, which was then a dead end. Next to it was a cemetery supposed to have been a burial ground for victims of plague and cholera, and very much a no-go area. To keep out unwanted visitors, the religious orders that owned the buildings on either side of the dead-end street built a barred gate at its entrance. All that remains of that barrier is this rake-like crossbar.

Corner of rue Rataud and rue Lhomond, 5th

Water, gas and réfrigérette on every floor

Before refrigerators became a common household appliance in the 1950s, food was either kept in cellars or in ventilated larders—small closets under kitchen windows that stood out slightly from external walls. They were generally above the backyard, but this seems to have been impossible in one building on the rue de Poissy, whose street-side facade features elegant, sculpted-stone *réfrigérettes* in an Arab moucharaby style on three floors. There are now lavatories behind their gratings—not a convenience provided when the building was constructed.

1, rue de Poissy, 5th

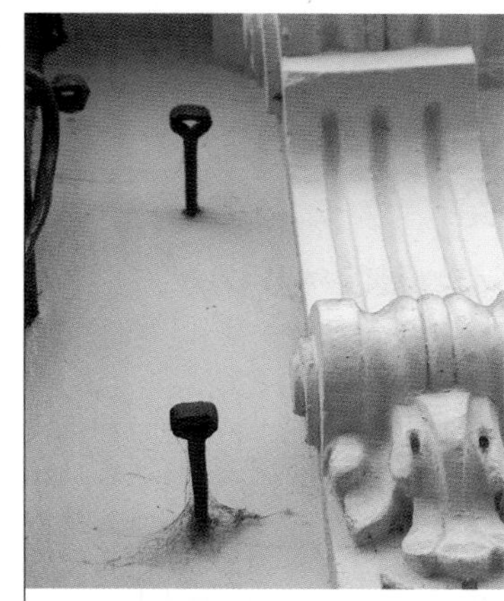

Opposite
4, rue Flatters, 5th
Below
103, rue Bobillot, 13th. A rare intact sign holder

Phantom sign holders

Have you ever noticed two small metal pegs some way up the wall near the entrance of a building? Tipped with a squared ring, they were used to put up temporary signs to advertise rooms, apartments, or commercial premises to let. The janitor had a selection of enameled sheet-metal signs and, whenever necessary, they would hoist one or another up onto the facade, slipping a pin or padlock into a hole to prevent it from being stolen. There are still many of these sign holders, although since few people know what they were for, they tend to be removed when buildings are renovated. They cannot be mistaken for store-sign holders: they are found on purely rental buildings with no shop at street level.

Also
24, rue Vieille-du-Temple, 4th
32, rue Lamarck, 18th. An arabesque specimen.

Corner of rue Saint-Blaise and rue Riblette, 20th

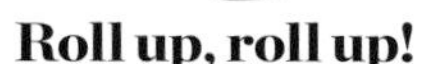

Roll up, roll up!

Before store shutters were equipped with electric motors, a strong arm was needed to turn the crank handle that raised and lowered them. That kind of mechanism can still be seen in some places. The toothed wheels are either visible or housed in a casing, and some have external shafts running from them.

94, rue du Bac, 7th

Utilitarian medallions

What was the point of these metal fixtures at second-floor level on certain facades, some shaped like lion's heads? They were used to attach the metal rods holding awnings over café terraces or the external stalls of stores. In some places, they are still in use. The most remarkable ones are those that equip the Bon Marché department store, shaped like lion's heads holding rings in their jaws. They are used to attach the cables that support the awning that surrounds the entire store. They should not be confused with the ends of tie rods: metal cables that hold together two supporting walls to stabilize a building, which are usually anchored by circular metal plates.

Rue Paul-Bert, 11th

Rue de Charonne, 11th

Hôpital de la Salpêtrière.
4 allée des Étoffes, 13th
(behind pavillon Paul-Castaigne)

A shameful "freak show"

Tiny semicircular seats are lined up on the front of a small building with miniature doors and windows. A dolls' house? If so, one accommodating some very unfortunate "dolls." At the end of the 18th century, women who were (or were judged to be) "lunatics" were locked up in tiny cells in this building. When the weather was fine, their orderlies allowed them out for some fresh air, sitting them on these seats where they were chained to rings set in the wall (the marks are still there in the stone). On Sundays, Parisians brought their children to see the women, just as they might take them for an afternoon at the zoo.

Sinister slabs

Passers-by pay little attention to these five rectangular granite slabs set into the asphalt. Part of the pavement, they extend under the crosswalk and have a very murky utilitarian past. They were laid to support the scaffold set up here on days of public executions between 1851 and 1899 and actually gave the guillotine one of its nicknames: *abbaye des cinq pierres* (five-stone abbey). The condemned were brought from the prison de la Petite-Roquette opposite (today, all that remains of the jail is the porch with its two guardrooms, now the entrance to the square). The executions were carried out at night and always attracted a crowd of gawkers. Once the executioner had performed his grisly task, the guillotine was returned to its depot at 60, rue de la Folie-Regnault. More than 200 people were beheaded here, including the anarchists Auguste Vaillant and Émile Henry.

Also see p. 107.

Top to bottom

16, rue de la Croix-Faubin and 164, rue de la Roquette, 11th

9, rue Royer-Collard, 5th

1 bis, passage des Patriarches, 5th

A garret and pulley

The pulley is to the attic what the pig-tail (*see p. 221*) is to the cellar. It is used to hoist loads that are too heavy or bulky to be carried up often-narrow stairs leading to upper floors. Some garrets still have a pulley, while others are equipped only with a metal bracket.

Also
26, rue Charlot, 4th
7, rue Christine, 6th
16, rue Séguier, 6th

Jamming with the DGSE

Why is there always radio interference on the beltway between the porte des Lilas and the porte de Bagnolet? It is a security measure taken by the DGSE (Direction générale de la sécurité extérieure), the French equivalent of the CIA, whose headquarters are on the boulevard Mortier. Behind the high walls topped with barbwire and lined by CCTV cameras is a massive building known as La Boîte (The Firm) to its staff and La Piscine (The Swimming Pool) to Parisians because of its proximity to the Les Tourelles aquatic center.

141, boulevard Mortier, 20th

IDC covers

This cast-iron disk looks just like a sewer manhole cover, but it is not. The shaft beneath it leads down to the quarries, as the initials IDC—standing for Inspection des carrières (Quarry Inspectorate)—indicate. IDC covers are generally fixed in place to prevent any unauthorized incursion.

Rue du Faubourg-Saint-Jacques, 5th

Bi-bops

In these days of smartphones, who still remembers the bi-bop, the precursor of the cell phone and the must-have gadget for 90s geeks? It was a sort of limited-mobility phone booth: users could make and receive calls as long as they stayed near a relay station. Paris, a pioneer in the technology, was well equipped: you were never more than five minutes' walk from the nearest station. Call zones were identified by blue, white, and red tricolor stickers on lampposts or drainpipes. Whenever they saw one, users could "pick up the line," but had to remain reasonably close to the relay.

Notausgang
II M
METRO
ÉCLAIRAGE
EDISON
Impot territorial
ROUTE
DE. PARIS
À CHARENTON
CÔTÉ. DU
LEVANT
COMEDIE
ENVOUTEMENT
DOMINANTE
4e ARR
RUE

Index by street

1st arrondissement

2nd arrondissement

3rd arrondissement

4th arrondissement

5th arrondissement

6th arrondissement

7th arrondissement

8th arrondissement

9th arrondissement

10th arrondissement

11th arrondissement

12th arrondissement

13th arrondissement

14th arrondissement

15th arrondissement

16th arrondissement

17th arrondissement

18th arrondissement

19th arrondissement

20th arrondissement

Originally published as *Curiositiés de Paris, Inventaire insolite des trésors minuscules*
© 2014 Dominique Lesbros
© 2016 Parigramme/Compagnie parisienne du Livre (Paris)
All photographs © Dominique Lesbros unless otherwise noted

Editors Francois Besse & Mathilde Kressmann
Copyediting and index Lucie Fontaine
Artistic director Isabelle Chemin
Layout Anne Delbende
Maps Julie Hiet (base map © Intercarto)

English Edition
© 2017 The Little Bookroom
Translation © 2016 Simon Beaver
Production Adam Hess

A catalog record for this book is available from The Library of Congress.

Printed in the United States of America

ISBN 978-1-68137-110-8

10 9 8 7 6 5 4 3 2 1

Published by The Little Bookroom
435 Hudson Street, Suite 300, New York NY 10014
(212) 757-8070
www.littlebookroom.com
editorial@littlebookroom.com